MAKING IT BIG

LESSONS FROM A LIFE IN BUSINESS

FEMI OTEDOLA

FO BOOKS

ADVANCE PRAISE

"In this book, readers have a rare front-row seat adventure into Femi's compelling and transformative entrepreneurial journey. As someone who came from an entrepreneurial family myself, venturing into business early by selling sweets in primary school, going on to become a trader and now an industrialist, I vividly relate with this enriching account, that effectively unpacks useful insights for surmounting business hurdles, as well as connecting many corporate dots for budding entrepreneurs. This is a highly recommended read for anyone who aspires to be successful in a challenging environment."

Aliko Dangote, GCON
President/CE, Dangote Group

"When a very successful person openly tells you their weaknesses, you know you are reading an honest account. Femi tells us a frank story of how he stopped being chief executive and transitioned to being an entrepreneur to save his business empire. This book contains a lot of hard truths we all know, but are hardly discussed in public, such as the delicate relationship between business and politics. This is one of the most important books you will ever read on entrepreneurship in a developing country."

Arunma Oteh
Chair, Royal African Society

"Success is celebrated, but rarely do we get to see what goes on in the background, in the literal sand-filling of swampy fields wherein the foundations of success are laid. Rarely do we get to hear honestly and transparently, with a lot of humility, from successful people about their ups and downs, their challenges and how they overcame them. In reality, most of the time the success we see is built on failures, inner fears, anxieties, and discouragements enough to sink any dream.

This book by Mr Femi Otedola is not written to celebrate his successes, but to demystify success, and lay bare the foundations of vision, resilience, courage and determination to overcome and excel, against all the odds.

Mr Otedola has shown us through his life that failure should not discourage, but inspire those determined to remain tenacious even in the face of storms of adversity and business uncertainties. He explains how he lost his fortune, never gave up on himself, re-engineered his business model, held on to his faith in God and re-emerged stronger, more successful, and richer than ever before. Today, his riches are not merely in money, but in character, one that has been tried, having passed through the fire and the crucible of business challenges.

The book is a must-read for all business leaders, policy makers and young people venturing into the world of entrepreneurship and business. It should be a recommended text in all leading business schools."

Dr. Akinwumi A. Adesina
President, African Development Bank Group

"I have known Femi since his childhood. In this book, he passed on his experience in attaining success in business and building wealth, which I view as an accurate guide to establishing a successful business and life in general. The book confirms Femi's resilience. Like the eagle, Femi braced through the storms of life and remained focused, committed and hardworking, despite going through difficult and trying times. He never gave up.

He was decisive in taking business decisions, but still had the fear of God Almighty and forgave where appropriate. I highly recommend this book to every person who intends to succeed in business. Family, integrity and hard work are some of the important values I hold dear. Femi has mirrored these values and made them a mantra in his day-to-day life. He has mastered the art of persistence and never giving up.

It's no wonder that with God on his side, he has been singled out as one of the most successful businessmen of his time. I wish him even more success and hope that the Lord continues to bless the works of his hand."

Prince (Dr) Samuel Adedoyin (FNSE, OFR)
Chairman, Doyin Investments Nigeria Ltd

ISBN: 978-978-69774-8-5 (Paperback)
978-978-69774-9-2 (Hardcover)

Published in 2025 by FO Books
13, Walter Carrington Crescent, Victoria Island, Lagos.
info@makingitbigbook.com
To find out more visit www.makingitbigbook.com

A catalogue record for this book is available from
the National Library of Nigeria.

CONTENTS

FOREWORD

NGOZI OKONJO-IWEALA

DIRECTOR GENERAL,
WORLD TRADE ORGANIZATION

Africa is often perceived globally as a continent that needs help and support, a continent of aid not investment, a continent of poverty and hunger not of entrepreneurship. Yet, one of Africa's best kept secrets is its wealth of entrepreneurial talent, abundant in the women and men struggling to run their micro, medium and small enterprises, often in the informal sector, as well as in the established; businessmen and women successfully running multi-million and billion-dollar enterprises.

So, when Femi Otedola, one of Nigeria's and Africa's most successful entrepreneurs decides to capture his experiences in the form of this book, it is important! As the author himself notes, there are very few books by successful African business leaders documenting their journey and sharing lessons learned for posterity, but in particular for a younger generation.

Femi Otedola is an energetic and versatile businessman whose candid portrayal of his entrepreneurial and personal journey is fascinating. We learn how business is done; the good, the bad, the ugly of it. And we live with Femi through the rough and tumble of 'making it big.'

At each stage of this journey there are important and enriching lessons learned that are pertinent not just to the Nigerian and African business environment but to the global environment. *Making It Big* is a tour de force that I commend to everyone's attention – young and aspiring entrepreneurs and policymakers alike.

INTRODUCTION

SETTING OFF INTO ENTREPRENEURSHIP

On 18 December 1958, in north London's St Pancras borough, a modest wedding ceremony took place between two unlikely lovebirds. One was an introvert, the other an extrovert. One a journalist, the other a caterer. The wedding between Michael Agbolade Otedola and Christiana Adedoja Onakomaiya was attended by just a few family members and followed by a modest reception and lunch.

My parents had studied at London's Regent Street Polytechnic.[1] My dad read journalism, while my mum studied catering. They'd met a couple of years earlier in the city of Ijebu-Ode, in what was then the western region of the British colony of Nigeria. Their romance was put on hold when they both travelled abroad to continue their education. However, they ended up at the same school, rekindled their love and decided to tie the knot. My elder brother, Ayo, was born in London in 1959, a year before Nigeria's independence from British colonial rule. My dad—who had joined the western region public service as an information officer in 1953, later working with the sage of Nigerian politics, Chief Obafemi Awolowo,[2] as press secretary—returned to Nigeria that year to continue his career in the city of Ibadan. He edited the *Western Nigeria Illustrated* before joining the Western Nigeria Broadcasting Corporation (WNBC), the first television station in tropical Africa, as its PR manager.

Mum wanted to further her studies but sacrificed that for the family. They returned to Nigeria on 15 August 1959—Assumption Day, a major feast in the Roman Catholic Church. By this time, Mum had converted to Catholicism.

I was born on 4 November 1962, in a maternity home in the Jericho neighbourhood of Ibadan, capital of the western region in those days. My mum teases me to this day that I am an 'amala boy,' because I was born in the city that's home to the popular Yoruba staple of smooth yam flour paste. We moved from the Bodija housing estate to Lagos, the capital of the newly independent country, two years later. The Bodija housing estate was the first housing estate in Nigeria, built in 1959, when the regional government decided to increase the number of modern houses available in the city. It was built on 400 acres of land in the area known as Bodija.

Mum got a job as catering manager at the University of Lagos, which had been recently founded in Akoka, a neighbourhood in the Yaba suburb (often regarded as the 'Heartbeat of Lagos Mainland' Yaba is one of the most popular suburbs located in the Lagos Mainland Local Government Area). The students loved Mum. They called her 'Madam Efficiency' because of the quality of her service and her warm relationship with them. My parents enrolled me at the University of Lagos Staff School in 1968, at the age of six. Kola Abiola—the first son of Chief Moshood Abiola, the future business magnate and presidential candidate who was at the time an accountant—sat beside me in class. But there was something about academia and me; we were not compatible. I finished primary school in 1974 because I repeated a class. Even when I was allowed to pass, I consistently anchored the bottom rungs of our end-of-term examination results. My interests were definitely not in academia.

I proceeded to Methodist Boys' High School, on Broad Street, Lagos, for my secondary education. The school had been founded almost a hundred years earlier, in 1878. Alumni include grand names in Nigerian history: Benjamin Nnamdi Azikiwe, Mobolaji Johnson, Ola Rotimi, Fola Adeola, Olusegun Osoba and Hezekiah Oladipo Davies. When I joined the student body in 1974, the principal was D. A. Famoroti, who'd taken up the post in 1963 and would leave in 1980. I started Form 1 at age 12 and was there for three years.

In 1977, I was packed off to finish my secondary education at Olivet Baptist High School, a boarding school founded by Southern Baptist missionaries in 1945. Its four houses—Atanda, Odetayo, Locket and Pinnock—were named for Baptist preachers. During the time I was there, my principals were Chief S. O. Omitade and Chief J. I. Popoola. My parents' thinking was that all my siblings were boarders, and they seemed to be doing well. They thought this change would help turn around my attitude towards academia, but nothing changed.

I started in Form 3 at Olivet, and as I rounded off the first year of my A Levels, my father was establishing his printing company, Impact Press, in Surulere, a residential and commercial district in Lagos State. I grew fascinated with the machines and told myself that my future would be inextricably tied to them. I managed to remain in school until the Lower Sixth examination was over. And then, I was finished. I never returned for my Upper Sixth.

All I wanted to do was get involved in business. My father kept watch over me and drew me close. My sister taught me shorthand. I knew how to type and began typing letters for my dad. I prepared all his business correspondence. I was fascinated by the way printing machines treat paper. The white paper is placed on one end, the ink and plates are fixed, and printed material comes out of the other end. It was captivating.

Despite the protests and tears of my mother, who could not accept that I wouldn't be returning to school, I started working fulltime for my father's printing operation at that point. I became the managing director there in 1987, around the time I turned 25.

However, I soon became restless. I had immersed myself in all aspects of the business and learned the ropes at my dad's right hand. I certainly enjoyed the job more than grappling with the Pythagoras theorem and struggling through homework at Olivet. As time went by, though, I also thought it was time for a measure of independence from my dad. I still wanted to work for him—I really enjoyed hearing the rumbling of machines and savouring the smell of freshly printed material—but I also wanted to do things differently. I told him I wanted to become a sales consultant for the press, and he agreed. He said he would pay me a commission of 10-15% on any work I brought in. That was a significant break for me. I invested my money in buying cars for sales and marketing outreach and moved on to the next phase in my nascent professional life.

I was bringing in jobs from big companies and almost all the big advertising agencies, as well as calendars and diaries. We could hardly keep up with the demand. Our unique selling point was quality, thanks to the state-of-the-art machines we owned. We were also always on time with job delivery. We were engaged in healthy competition with Academy Press, a company located in the Ilupeju area of Lagos.

I served as my dad's sales exec up until 1991, when he started his Lagos State gubernatorial campaign. It was a run for office—ultimately successful—that I had initiated.

In November of 1993, my dad became former governor, as the military took the reins of power in an ongoing political crisis following the annulment of June presidential elections won by my former classmate's father, Chief Abiola.

After things calmed down, I set up my own business in 1994, with working capital of ₦10 million. Named Centre Force Ltd, my company gave out short-term loans to small businesses and individuals. It was a loosely run, makeshift operation, to be sure, but it earned me my first million naira as an entrepreneur. Centre Force was also an investment company—people would bring in ideas, we'd look at them and we would then agree to invest in some. It was not too big, but things were clicking. I had a lot of money in the bank and was living off the interest. On top of that, I am naturally a very contented person, so all was right in my world.

I indulged in clubbing at night and sleeping during the day. I went out partying one Friday night in 1997 and came back at 5 am. My wife, Nana, was upset. I'd just bought a new Mercedes-Benz, and could not resist going out again on Saturday to show off the car. I came back on Sunday. Nana was furious, but her anger was by no means unproductive. It was the spark that created another entrepreneur in the family.

When she asked for money to get her hair done on Monday, she complained that she needed to make her own money instead of bombarding me with petty-cash requests. She wanted to be gainfully employed and decided to create a dry-cleaning business. I gave her a start-up loan of ₦40 million, and in 1999 she opened Garment Care on Isaac John Street in Ikeja, the central business district of Lagos. It did well, and she established three additional branches in Lagos—two on Victoria Island and one in the wealthy Lekki neighbourhood. The start-up loan was dutifully repaid.

At the time of our wedding, seven years earlier, Nana and I did not know we would both end up entrepreneurs. I was my dad's personal assistant, and she was the assistant's wife, but we both longed for something more, and we had the drive and determination to make it so.

Even though I was making money from Centre Force, I did not find it challenging, and was soon looking for something else to do. That was how I came up with the idea for Zenon Petroleum and Gas, which was registered on 10 March 1999, and was where I made my first million dollars the following year. It was also where I made my first billion dollars, four years later. In 2009, *Forbes* valued the company at US$1.2 billion, and it was valued at US$1.8 billion in 2016. I would also buy African Petroleum, the successor company to the Nigerian branch of British Petroleum. BP's downstream assets in Nigeria had been consolidated and renamed in 1979, as part of the country's Nigerianization policy.[3] I rebranded it Forte Oil. I would eventually sell my stake for a handsome sum years later. I also went into the power sector by buying Geregu Power PLC, an electricity generation company.

It has been quite a journey for me, from my little adventure as a kid, charging my parents' guests to cut their nails, to leaving school, becoming an apprentice in my father's print shop, and ultimately setting up the businesses that have made me a multibillionaire.

My children, Tolani (born 21 April 1986), 'DJ Cuppy' Ifeoluwa (11 November 1992), Temi (20 March 1996) and Fewa (2 June 2000), have all followed their own paths. I have always encouraged them to pursue what will give them fulfilment in life. They're free to express themselves, to be whatever they want to be. Society typically builds a mould that it expects people to fit into. Only God knows how many people would have been happier and felt more whole in life if they had been allowed to follow their hearts and minds.

Whatever I have been and whatever I may become, I look back and say, "Thank God I did not fit into the mould. Thank God I chose my path and, with encouragement from my dad, I stayed the course." This is the story of my life.

SECTION ONE

IN THE BEGINNING

CUTTING MY TEETH, FINDING MY FEET, PUTTING MY BEST FOOT FORWARD

LESSON ONE

START SMALL, KEEP DREAMING

One weekend in 1973, my father's boss strolled into our living room on Victoria Island's Festival Road, in Lagos. John George Luttrell, a big, blond-haired American, was Managing Director of Mobil Oil Nigeria, and my father, Michael Otedola, was its Corporate Affairs Manager. As Luttrell came in, shook hands with my dad and took his seat, something else was playing on my mind: I wanted to cut his fingernails, and charge a modest fee for the service.

I had been cleaning and trimming nails for my parents' visitors since I was seven years old, but today was going to be different: this was a big fish, as they say. My memory of the event is fuzzy, but I imagine that the huge Missourian spoke with a travel-tempered midwestern accent. He hosted Christmas and Boxing Day parties for the company's employees at his home in the opulent Ikoyi neighbourhood of Lagos. He would go on to become Mobil's youngest MD, and run the company's operations in places as varied as Libya, Nigeria and the UK, retiring as Vice President of Worldwide Exploration and Production. And here I was, an 11-year-old who wanted to give his dad's boss a manicure and pedicure. I was prepared; I had a nice set of clippers and an invoice/receipt book that I'd started using with my bemused 'customers.'

I was shy but confident—self-assured enough to sell my services to anyone who entered my turf, but reserved enough to know the line that separated cute from intrusive. I did not hesitate to ask my father's big boss if I could cut his nails for a modest fee. Perhaps he was just being kind to me, or maybe he genuinely wanted to have his nails cut that weekend. I would never know.

He stretched out his hands, and I started the job. He then stretched out his legs, and I completed the job. I cleaned things up, got paid and pulled out my booklet, with its carbon-paper copy pages, to write him a receipt. I cannot remember the exact sum, but I think it was 20 kobo (about 13 cents).

That was the beginning of my entrepreneurial voyage. Many business names ended with 'co,' so I named my venture Femco, a play on my first name that I thought sounded legitimately businesslike. I enjoyed trimming nails. It was fun, and as icing on the cake, I was getting paid for it.

In this chapter, the lesson I intend to provide is how to use little things to hone your skills for the bigger challenges. Cutting nails in your parents' living room is not the surest path to becoming a billionaire. It's certainly not the most exciting business choice if you want to rule the world. But, something that simple can help you along as you take those first little steps. It taught me things like having a nose for opportunity; creating value and getting rewarded; summoning the courage to pitch for a job; nurturing your commercial sense; getting yourself organized; and having fun while pursuing your passion. And, do not forget that stooping to conquer is a time-tested principle. I bent down to cut nails, but I did not stand up empty-handed.

What did my nail-trimming business as an adolescent teach me about entrepreneurship?

(1) Start as early as you can, even if they pay you a pittance. There were things I learned from this venture that would later help me in the big adventures of life. For one, I could smell an opportunity. People need a trim because nails inevitably grow. There was a ready market for me. Also, I rode on the back of my parents, whose visitors I cultivated as my customers. Having an advantage is invaluable to success in business. I couldn't go to the living rooms of other people to conduct this business.

At the same time, if I were cutting nails for other kids my age, they surely would not pay me. There was no advantage to targeting them in that line of business. What's more, I began to understand that business processes help you become, and stay, organized, so I got the receipt book to keep records.

(2) Do not wait for the 'perfect' time or until you need money; create value now. I have to say that I was not in a dire situation. I was a primary school pupil. I did not need to fend for myself. My parents were comfortable, so there was no pressure to earn my pocket money. However, I possessed an instinct for commerce that would not be tamed or clouded by any sense of comfort or feeling of youthfulness. My parents were receiving visitors, and I was not going to let them come and go just like that. I saw the value in cutting their nails and making their fingers look good. One of the fundamental drivers of business is the creation of value. The moment you have something to offer, no matter how seemingly little it is, you can use it to activate your business sense.

(3) Identify, encourage and nurture business acumen wherever you find it. My parents knew all along that I was business-minded. My father in particular identified that trait in me very early in my life, and did not make any attempt to dissuade me. He didn't deter me from marketing my nail-cutting venture to his guests. I had many customers, and all of them were his friends, mostly from Mobil. I saved my coins in a *kolo*—a piggy bank—that I bought with my income. I kept the money there until I opened an account with Federal Savings Bank, which catered to low-income earners and students.

With my savings growing, I began to think big. The more I cut nails, the more I grew in confidence. I was the managing director and chief financial officer of my own business. I was making money in my little way, saving it when my mates would rather spend theirs, and still getting my regular pocket money from my parents. What else could a little boy ask for?

In no time, I started carrying a briefcase.

My friends and classmates at the University of Lagos Staff School would laugh at the sight of this kid with a briefcase. I had asked my father to give me one of his old ones, which he did so with no questions asked. I wanted to look like a big man, a businessman, like the entrepreneurs and senior officials in the private and public sectors who all carried briefcases. That was the profile of a successful executive. I cannot remember how long I carried the briefcase, but I stopped trimming nails when I got into Methodist Boys' High School in 1974.

TAPPING INTO A HUGE OPPORTUNITY

I zeroed in on another opportunity in the early 1990s, and it led to the birth of my first real business.

Many pseudo-financial institutions were cropping up in my country in the late 1980s and early 1990s, promising their depositors unimaginable returns of up to 100% a month. Some of these—which were nicknamed 'wonder banks' because they promised mythical returns—were paying depositors 50% interest up front. It was all the rage, driven by the harsh economic realities of the day in Nigeria. People needed to make money, and this was all too easy. No hard work, no stress. Just give your money to a wonder bank, and you'd be pocketing ridiculously high interest. It was too good to be true, but too tempting to resist.

In Port Harcourt, capital of the country's oil-rich Rivers State, there was a wonder bank on Aggrey Road named Resources Managers Ltd. Nicknamed 'Umana Bank,' it was owned by businessman Umana Umana, and was paying 100% monthly interest on deposits. This attracted thousands of customers, who kept spreading the news about the wonders of Umana. In Lagos, there were more than a dozen wonder banks, the most prominent being Forum Mortgage Finance Ltd, set up by Duro Owolabi, an accountant. The wonder bankers seemed to have the world at their feet. They rented big offices; their employees drove flashy cars and dressed ultra-stylishly. They made conventional bankers envious.

Traditional banks lost customers in droves and saw their fortunes plummet, as all roads led to the wonder banks. But the bubble soon burst as the world discovered it was all a Ponzi scheme,[4] using new depositors' cash to pay existing customers, and recycling deposits again and again, until the market was saturated and everything crashed.

It's a deviously simple trick: if you collect ₦10,000 from someone, and pay him ₦5,000 in interest up front, he will become what Stalin called a useful idiot. He'll become a free advertiser, as he deposits more money and boasts of his success, enthralling others with his overnight wealth. If you add an incentive, like a bonus for every new customer he brings in, he will even market the dubious scheme to his closest friends and family. But the interest rate is unsustainable, and the Ponzi scheme will inevitably come crashing down.

There will be a diminishing rate of new depositors, and a resulting shortfall of funds to pay the interest promised to the old investors. The customer will eventually lose the other half of their deposits. Paying 100% monthly interest will attract depositors, but they'll certainly lose all their money down the line. There are those who suggest getting in on a Ponzi scheme early, and cashing out early, before everyone catches on. I say to them that by the time you hear of a Ponzi scheme, it's already too late. It is a sure-fire losing proposition.

The wonder bank phenomenon set me thinking, and I concluded that since people always needed money to finance businesses and a desired lifestyle, I could offer them credit for a little monthly interest.

These were the factors that led to setting up Centre Force, and the vital business lessons I learned along the way:

(1) Take advantage of a poorly executed model and clean it up. As the fly-by-night finance houses crumbled like biscuits, tales of woe by customers who'd lost their life savings dominated the news. As I read these stories, it dawned on me that people genuinely needed fast cash for personal needs but were finding it hard to secure from reliable sources. Regular banks wouldn't give them loans, and the lending rate was sky-high for those who were lucky enough to get one. Some needed funds to do quick business—such as financing LPOs[5]—but the banks were unfriendly. That was why it was so easy for wonder banks to con the public with their promises of quick returns.

(2) Mark time; do not despair at unexpected changes in circumstances. In January of 1994, I finally decided to provide a service that would give people fast cash that was repayable on a short-term basis. My father was no longer governor. I needed to start something on my own, having served more or less as his assistant from his campaign period to when General Sani Abacha, a Nigerian military officer, overthrew the democratic government in November 1993.

In a sense, it took the coup for me to start thinking of a line of business that would be entirely my own, not connected to my father or the family in any way. The collapse of the finance houses provided the opportunity for me to put my brains and talent to use.

I wasn't interested in running a finance house, and definitely not the way the wonder banks did it. I was not going to get involved in collecting deposits and promising big returns. I obtained a licence from the local government to set up a money-lending business. That was how Centre Force—a much bigger proposition than nail trimming—was born. The concept was similar to, but different in many ways, from what is today called micro-financing.

(3) Meticulously execute your idea, and never fail to ask for help. Centre Force was a small setup that I started with only two employees, Bola and Idowu. They were responsible for sales and marketing. They put the word out, bringing people in to apply for loans. Our office was a bungalow in the Victoria Island extension business district of Lagos. I had limited capital, and as demand grew, we soon ran out of funds. I'd underestimated what I was getting into, and it became clear that I needed help. I had borrowed once before, but it was a personal bank loan for just ₦1 million. Now, I needed as much as ₦30 million to sustain and expand my new business.

With a stiff dose of courage, I approached the Sociéte Génerale Bank of Nigeria (SGBN) for the loan. It was certainly a steeper step than asking to cut the fingernails of a family friend. But SGBN looked at our business case, saw the value we were creating, and lent me the ₦30 million, with an interest rate of 15% per annum. This was a huge help. I was lending at 10%

per month, and I was making money. It was profitable, because it did not cost me too much to set up; I had the start-up cash and got a boost from the loan. As word spread, people flocked to us for fast cash.

(4) Grow gradually and steadily, and master how to plug leakages and halt abuses. Centre Force quickly grew its customer base and workforce. From just two employees, we soon had 20. Within two years, the working capital of ₦10 million grew to more than ₦100 million. Surprisingly, loan repayment was about 90%, which was very, very good for business. Even those who defaulted did not get away with it, because we sold their collateral to cover the loans.

They couldn't complain; we treated everyone fairly and gave them enough room to repay.

Both we and our customers were making money, so it was a win-win situation. My best customer was Alhaji Abubakar Aliyu, head of the petroleum company AA Oil Ltd. He was taking loans regularly—₦3 million, ₦4 million, sometimes up to ₦6 million—and repaying at an interest rate of 12.8% a month. We were happy to do business with one another. Another sizeable client was a company doing printing and packaging, producing diaries, calendars and record sleeves. We did good business together too.

(5) Don't start a business because you want an empire. Centre Force started small, but soon surpassed my expectations. Why, I wondered, did I not dream big and start big in the first place? The reality is that the idea for a business doesn't always come from wanting a world-dominating empire. It more likely comes from needing to do something to fend for yourself and your family, and it grows from there. To the guy who sets up that little business, it is the equivalent of a 9-5 job with a salary. It is for sustenance, and you take it from there. If God blesses it, it grows. For the lucky few, you end up with a large business that succeeds beyond your wildest dreams.

(6) Do not shun multiple streams of income. Centre Force was a modest dream that grew big. It gave me a platform to meet with some big guys in society. I became friends with the military brass in General Abacha's government. They included Lt General Ishaya Bamaiyi, who was Lagos Garrison Commander; Brigadier Patrick Aziza, who had been a military governor, garrison commander and Minister of Communications; Colonel Olagunsoye Oyinlola, then military administrator of Lagos; and General Bashir Magashi, the military administrator of Sokoto State, who was garrison commander and would go on to serve in the government of President Muhammadu Buhari as Minister of Defence. That presented another opportunity. I started executing contracts with military figures, the most significant of which were to supply cars. It appeared that once the military brass made some money, the first thing they wanted to do was buy cars. Jumping at the opportunity, I was always there to source vehicles and make money. I supplied them with more than 40 cars during that period. It was part of the purview of Centre Force.

HOW TO LISTEN TO THAT INNER VOICE AND TAKE NUDGES SERIOUSLY

By 1997, I was already losing interest in finance. Doing the same thing all the time just wasn't for me. I felt a need to be challenged, and knew it was time to move on to something else, but I had no clue what it would be.

There is a little secret I have to share here. My daughter, Ifeoluwa, inadvertently played a significant role in my next move, which would catapult me to new heights in business and national life. She was just five at the time. A teacher at Grange School asked her, "What is your father's occupation?" She innocently replied, "Sleeping."

Admittedly, I used to be a late riser. Since I was always in bed when she set out for school, and she wasn't getting a good morning hug from dad, she had every reason to believe my occupation was *sleeping*. I was coming across as a jobless dad. It jolted me.

My wife, Nana, would get up at 6:30 am and head to work at 7. I usually left home around 11. I finally told myself, "Pull it together, man. Get serious and set up a proper business." I had to rise from my slumber to get something else going.

I was making good money from the car supply contracts, but nothing was demanding or challenging about providing army generals with cars. I was partying in nightclubs through the night and sleeping half the time. I had to do something more concrete and satisfying.

That was when I conceived Zenon Petroleum and Gas Ltd. And here's what I learned in the process:

(1) Providence plays a significant role in our lives. Again, there is a backstory, which I can only attribute to God's providence. I had wanted to do something else, but had no clear idea what it might be. Sometime in 1998, a major failure at the Maryland Power Substation plunged the city of Ikeja into weeks of darkness. I used to get diesel to power generators in our home from my friends in the military, when Aziza and then Magashi were Lagos garrison commanders. But I was out of luck this time. Out of the darkness, a ray of light lit my path and pointed me to my next line of business: selling diesel.

I got home from work one day and realized there was not a drop of diesel in the house. I was living on Sir Michael Otedola Crescent, named for my dad, in the Ikeja Government Reserved Area, a highend housing development. With the entire property in darkness, I moved my family to Sheraton Hotels & Towers, while I scouted for diesel. I called a friend, Tayo Ayeni, the founder of Skymit Motors—one of the retailers I knew from my car-supply business—to ask about his diesel suppliers. He mentioned Flame Petroleum, owned by one Dr Ibe Kachikwu. A man of many talents, Kachikwu was a lawyer who also ran a popular magazine called *Hints*. He had worked in Mobil for many years, becoming general counsel for the Nigerian operation, and he'd go on to serve as Minister of State for Petroleum Resources between 2015 and 2019. I asked my office to contact his company and learned that they had diesel at ₦14 a litre. We paid for 2,000 litres to have my home's reservoir filled.

The fuel did not show up as scheduled, even though I had paid in full. The following day, still no diesel. Day three, the same. On the fourth day, I was driving home from my office in Victoria Island and saw a broken-down truck with a Flame Petroleum logo on the Third Mainland Bridge.[6] I parked and approached the driver. "You were supposed to bring me diesel days ago," I said. The guy checked his chart, located my name and replied, "Tomorrow. We'll come tomorrow at 11 am."

This time, they came as promised. My house was new, and the way I had designed it, I had a clear view of the outside through an all-glass wall. I saw an ancient, dirty truck drive into my compound, leaking engine oil and diesel. This really irritated me, and I rushed downstairs like a man possessed. "Move this truck out of here!" I shouted. They pushed it out, and we spread newspapers and rags on the ground, to protect it during a second attempt.

As the truck moved back in and discharged the diesel, still leaking here and there, I stood and watched intently. I knew instinctively that I could do this better. I told myself the business was not well managed or presented. I could clean it up and give it a good image. I had trimmed and cleaned fingernails before. In a sense, another such opportunity was staring me in the face.

After the truck left, I sent for the manager of Flame Petroleum and he came to see me in the office. Straight away, I said, "I want to set up a diesel business. Will you work for me?" He declined the offer.

Much later, he approached me for a job when he realized my outfit was first class, and I employed him.

(2) Do your research and think about your business name. As soon as I made up my mind to go into the diesel trade, I started to research every aspect of it. "You can clean up this business," kept ringing in my head. I had value to add. I mentioned it to my friend, Tunde Folawiyo, managing director of the Yinka Folawiyo Group, which has interests in energy, shipping and real estate. Tunde introduced me to Victor Enelamah, who worked at Nigeria's Department of Petroleum Resources (DPR). The agency had undergone myriad transformations as the country's oil industry grew and evolved. It began as a section under the Ministry of Lagos Affairs in the colonial government, went on to become the Ministry of Petroleum Affairs, and merged with the old Nigerian National Oil Corporation in the 1970s. It then became a department of the subsequent Nigerian National Petroleum Corporation, absorbing the Petroleum Inspectorate. Victor filled me in on the requirements for breaking into the sector, one of which was to get a licence from the DPR, the industry regulator.

So where did the name 'Zenon' come from? As soon as I'd decided to go into the business, I started thinking about a compelling name for my company. I discussed this with my friend Tunde. As we tossed around possible names, it occurred to me that when I'd ordered cars from Mercedes-Benz, they asked if I wanted xenon lights. Mercedes had just developed the technology, which generated a bright, fluorescent-like glow. It struck me like a lightning bolt: 'Xenon.' I loved the notion of illumination. Diesel. Lights. Bright lights. I would call the company Xenon.

I called a graphic artist who used to work at Insight Communications, a big Nigerian advertising agency, and asked him to design a logo. However, I didn't want the name to be confused with Xerox. I asked the designer to try changing the X to Z, and put a flame where the O was. Perhaps we could make the word blue and the flame yellow, orange and red? Thus, the Zenon brand was born.

(3) Start where you are, with what you have. I started Zenon with ₦15 million in capital, but did not take a loan. Every cent was from my savings. We used my Centre Force office for some months, worked through the start-up phase, and got the business established. We then moved to another rented office on Tiamiyu Savage, a highend residential and commercial street on Victoria Island. And from there, I proceeded to expand the business. I bought a second-hand Toyota van and employed a driver, Samson Okpali. Initially, it was just the two of us in the van, with drums of diesel in the back.

My mind went back to that encounter with the rundown, leaky truck, the delay in supplying my house during a sustained blackout, the diesel stains on my front yard, and the cleanup afterwards. I was certainly not going to serve prospective clients in beat-up old vehicles. I hired Gibraltar Construction to fabricate two fuel storage tanks, but they weren't delivered on time. I complained and was told again and again that they were on their way. The tanks were ultimately delivered six months behind schedule. The business was growing, we needed to scale up our facilities and capacity, and the delay in getting the storage tanks installed was a real setback.

There were already some influential players in the industry. One was Jean-Claude Meyer, a Frenchman who owned Marca International Ltd, who was on top of the industry. The others were Tony Onoh of Eurafric, and Oba Obateru Akinruntan, founder of Obat Petroleum and Oil Ltd, who would go on to become the traditional ruler of his people, the Ugbo Kingdom in Ilaje, in Nigeria's Ondo State. These three were the most prominent people I met in the business.

I would go to Meyer's place to buy truckloads of diesel, which I would pump into drums and drive to customers' locations for delivery. In addition to the initial van, I also rented various trucks before eventually purchasing a new fleet of vehicles.

(4) To prosper, accept that nothing is beneath you. In the beginning, I went around pushing diesel, riding in the van beside Samson, the driver. I always wore jeans and a polo shirt as we went from door to door, to market or deliver the product. When we met at nightclubs on weekends, my friends would tease me with questions like, "Where's your truck?" They'd laugh when I walked in, and ask, "Are you here to sell diesel?" I took the wisecracks in stride. I didn't feel that selling diesel was beneath me. I had my wife and children to look after; there were school fees to pay. I had to survive and face up to my responsibilities.

(5) Maximize opportunities and expand to meet demand. After I'd started this small-scale selling, I came to realize that the entire country was running on diesel—homes, offices, factories, trucks and trawlers. The energy situation was dire, with constant blackouts and shortages, and the demand for diesel was enormous. The opportunity was certainly there; we had to rise to the occasion. I got to work on an ambitious marketing strategy. I employed 14 sales executives, all young, brilliant and driven women, and gave them new cars. In my experience, female salespeople were more effective in convincing prospective clients, perhaps because of their commitment, ability to charm and reluctance to take no for an answer.

It also helped that the new trucks I'd ordered from the Turkish manufacturer BMC had arrived, which we started using for home delivery. With the marketing team out on an aggressive sales drive, the orders came rushing in. I had given them a list of big companies—Nestlé, Coca-Cola, Flour Mills of Nigeria, the Dangote Group—and they closed one deal after another. I would pay Marca or Eurafric for supplies, they would send trucks loaded with diesel, and I'd add my margin, which came to about ₦8 per litre.

(6) Ask for help when you need it. When I realized in late 1999 that I needed trucks to meet the insatiable demand for diesel, I asked my dad for a loan.

He gave me £250,000 at 1% interest, with a five-year note. You might expect that he would provide me with an interest-free loan, but he was a shrewd businessman and wanted me to learn the ropes properly. In the real world, nothing is free. I would have paid double-digit interest if I'd gone to a bank, and the terms would likely have been less than five years. I jumped at my dad's generous offer.

I started buying diesel in bulk and renting storage tanks. It was a significant leap for me. I still needed to buy more trucks, as we kept expanding. I decided I was not borrowing any more, so I sold my house for ₦40 million, intending to use the proceeds to grow the business. I'd built it for less than ₦11 million in 1996, but I'd had to get a loan when I ran out of cash, and I still had ₦2 million debt left to pay in 2000. So, that was not bad in the scheme of things. We moved from the beautiful mansion in Ikeja to a rented four-bedroom house on Victoria Island, just behind the Mega Plaza shopping mall.

I rented from Chief Bode Akindele, Ibadan's Parakoyi—a class of traditional Yoruba chiefs responsible for administering trade and commerce. Among other interests, he owned Fairgate Group Ltd, a real estate development and management company based in the UK. Whether I owned or rented, the most important thing for me was to have a roof over my head. The lesson here is that if you have a big dream, support it with all the resources available to you.

(7) Place yourself close to those with influence and capital. If I was going to make this venture truly successful, I needed more capital. As was the case at Centre Force, demand was growing astronomically—the market was consuming diesel at a voracious clip. Having sold my house, mobilized all my savings and taken a massive loan from my dad, I still needed more cash to meet the demand and grow bigger. I might have started small, but I would never stop dreaming. That was the fun of it: planting a little seed, nurturing it and making it grow apace. Despite my earlier vow not to borrow from banks, I needed extra liquidity, and it had to come from the big, traditional lenders.

Many Nigerian banks had their head offices on Victoria Island, where their managing directors lived. Moving there and living close to banking executives would help. No banker would approve a ₦1 billion loan for your business without knowing your house. No banker would come and meet me in my old Ikeja neighbourhood. Location is critical in corporate 'packaging.'

I remember a party I'd had at my Ikeja house. It was attended by the up-and-coming young businesspeople of the era. They included Bukola Saraki of Société Générale, Nigeria (and future Governor of Kwara State, and eventually Senate President of the National Assembly); Segun Agbaje of Guaranty Trust Bank; and Tayo Amusan, the property developer who was chairman of the retail and real estate giant Persianas Nigeria Ltd. They left my place at around 5 am to return home to Victoria Island. These guys liked me, I realized. That's why they drove all the way to my part of town for the get-together. But I needed to move, if only to be close to the banking chiefs, who didn't yet know or like me. I had to be strategic. Anything could go wrong with this calculated risk I was taking, but you must take risks at some point in life, especially when you're younger and can recover quicker if things go wrong.

Relocating to Victoria Island was also for personal convenience. I used to leave my Ikeja home at 5 am and get to the office on Victoria Island at 6 am. I'd work there until 9 pm. I would then drive to the fuel depot near the seaport in Apapa to supervise operations until 1 am. I was sleeping just a couple of hours a night. For somebody whose primary activity had until recently been 'sleeping,' as my daughter had observed, that was a radical change. But things were booming, and I loved it. Moving to Victoria Island made sense on many levels. In any case, I had lived there before. When my dad worked at Mobil, we lived on Festival Road, from 1972-1977. That was in fact where I'd started cutting nails and writing invoices.

In a sense, I was returning to my roots, to the former HQ of Femco. This time, though, it was with a heavier briefcase and a much bigger ledger.

(8) Keep an eye on your debtors and don't be afraid to demand repayment. We faced many challenges in those early days, but we reasoned through them, solved the problems and continued to build capacity. Although we were getting orders, some of our customers were not paying, and that tied up capital. At the start, when the sales team brought in purchase orders, I would say without hesitation, "Supply them." But time and again, they failed to pay. Meanwhile, I owed the banks. Interest was piling up.

Exasperated, I went early one morning to the office of the MD of a major civil engineering and construction company. When I arrived, I saw 50 people—poor people, poor women—asking for their payments, for work they had done. It was heartbreaking. I was yet another service provider that this company had failed to pay. We'd been told that the government owed them for some big contracts, and that they in turn could not pay others until they'd recouped those revenues. I saw that the director had arrived; I could see his car inside the compound. I blocked the gate with my car. I promised myself that I was not leaving, and would not let him leave, without my money. The gloves were off. I would not allow anyone to ruin my growing business with their irresponsibility. I got their attention and was invited inside. I met the MD, a German, and told him off.

"Look at the poor people you owe," I shouted at him. "You're a big company. You collect money from the government, take it abroad and leave these people high and dry." I told him that if they didn't pay me, there and then, I was not leaving. "And you are not leaving, either," I threatened. They called in the police to remove my car and escort me off the premises. The police arrived, and I shouted them down, telling them I was being robbed by this foreign company. I shouted that I was owed ₦7.4 million, a vast sum. They had been ordering and ordering, without any plans to pay.

The police quietly left.

My next collection call was to a big electronics importer and exporter, and after that I visited a subsidiary of theirs. Both had been taking my diesel but failing to pay.

I was ultimately able to collect what I was owed from the three companies, and promptly blacklisted them. With such customers, your business will die. I did not need them to survive. Many responsible, upstanding customers were courting me because diesel was in such high demand. Industry CEOs were beating a path to my door. The country ran on diesel, and I was there to provide that vital lifeblood.

(9) Identify opportunities and take over areas of interest. I also faced challenges with transportation, as I had no real control over it. And so, I concluded that I had to go into the transport business. My friend Biola Akinola accompanied me to Holland in 2002 to buy lightly used trucks, and made them look beautiful. I first bought 12, then another eight, and another 20. In 2004, I had enough financial muscle to order 100 new trucks from DAF, the Dutch manufacturer. I was accompanied to Holland for that purchase by a DAF representative from Nigeria. I now had control over the transport aspect of the operation. Step by step, we were inching towards controlling the entire chain, putting every piece of the business in our own hands. Still, we faced even more challenges. One evening, I received a purchase order from West Africa Portland Cement Company (now Lafarge Africa PLC) for 20 truckloads of diesel. I called one of my old suppliers for help filling the order. I could not provide immediate payment because the banks had closed for the day, but told the fuel company's owner I would send a cheque. He would have none of it: "No bank draft, no product." I was furious. How could he do this to me? I had never owed him, and had done at least ₦600 million in business with him. I now had a situation, and had called upon someone I considered a trusted supplier. I couldn't believe it. I didn't have 20 truckloads of diesel to deliver, and lost the contract. It was painful.

That day opened my eyes to another reality. I told myself things had to change. I could not be beholden to these unreliable distributors. Where were these guys getting the diesel from? I assumed it had to be from NNPC, the Nigerian national oil company. I vowed that one day, I would no longer be reliant on them. I took my loss and began casting a wider net for crucial diesel supplies. I met Chief Henry Omorodion of the oil and gas company Hensmor Nigeria Ltd, who agreed to sell to me in bulk. He was getting his allocation directly from NNPC. I also bought from businesswoman Nike Adebayo, who got her product from Obat Oil and Petroleum Ltd, which, like Hensmor, got it directly from NNPC.

I established good working relationships with them and others, and broadened my supply base, allowing me to reliably execute more orders. I also started renting storage tanks so we wouldn't have to be running around like crazy, trying to fulfil surprise orders.

(10) Be available to your customers 24/7, and service their needs ASAP. One advantage I enjoyed was that even if a company's CEO called me at 2 am, in need of diesel, my drivers were on standby around the clock, ready to load and deliver. It was a big plus for us, and we developed a reputation for being super reliable. Unfortunately, I learned that the drivers were stealing diesel. I dealt with them appropriately: anyone caught in the act was immediately sacked and handed over to the police. This served as a deterrent. The crime carried a punishment, and we enforced the penalty. Meanwhile, I also made sure to befriend the leaders of the tanker drivers' union. In return, they were supportive of Zenon.

(11) Reinvest, consolidate and shun extravagance. One thing I also did was tell myself not to live extravagantly. I would plough everything I made back into the business. This formula worked well, as Zenon grew in capacity and efficiency. Before I knew it, I was in control of diesel supplies to all the big companies. At that point, I decided it was time to stop renting storage tanks and build our own. The tank owners were known for taking money from customers and disappointing them. It made sense to not be at the mercy of these guys.

I went to my old friend Tunde, whose family had a cement factory. They had surplus space, and I asked if I could lease it. Tunde asked his dad, Chief Wahab Folawiyo, who agreed and invited me to his Ikoyi home.

"*E ma j'a fira*," he encouraged. Don't foot-drag! He wanted the project to take off immediately, and he gave me his blessing.

Tunde later handed me a monthly bill of ₦30 million. I almost fainted. If I had to pay ₦30 million for rent alone, the business would die.

Tunde then cautioned: "What if the refinery starts working?"

I did not respond, but clearly understood the implications. If the refinery started working, there would be no need for middlemen. I needed to build my own tanks. I decided to go to Oskar Ibru,[7] scion of a family of businessmen that had large landholdings close to the port in Lagos. He only had space for a single million-litre tank, as the plot behind Ibru's was set aside for a shipping container business. However, he suggested I approach the container business owner and see if he would do a deal with me. The plot was next to space leased by Marca, where Jean-Claude Meyer had just completed his ₦300 million state-of-the-art fuel storage facility.

I approached the container company, and to my delight they gave up the land. And so, in 2000 I built my first, second and third storage tanks. My total investment was ₦100 million that year. But that was just a start; I continued building tanks. I had also expanded enough to start renting ships. Zenon had blossomed into a major bulk buyer of diesel. The people I bought from shipped product down to my jetty to discharge. But still, I was at the mercy of suppliers. If only I could bypass them and get the product directly from NNPC, the sky would be my limit.

(12) Fairness and willingness to give more can get you a bigger chunk of a market. How did I break into NNPC? In a country where connections seem to count more than competence, I knew I could not just knock on the door of the national oil company and boast, "See how far I have gone. See how big I have become. See how many big companies I'm supplying. See how efficient I am. If you are using capacity and competence as criteria to allocate diesel, Zenon Petroleum and Gas should be number one on your list!" Things didn't work like that in Nigeria, or in other developing economies. You always needed a push from a well placed 'someone.' Most of those getting allocations did not even own a truck or a tank.

I learned that the man in charge of diesel allocation at NNPC, Odekhoa Akhume Okaisabor, was the person to lobby. I didn't know him, but was chatting one day with Dapo Abiodun, who would go on to found Heyden Petroleum Ltd, and brought up the matter. I was delighted to learn that he knew Okaisabor. Dapo arranged a call, made the introduction.

My son Fewa was born on 2 June 2000, in a hospital in the UK. On 9 June, I travelled for his naming ceremony in London, planning to return to Lagos the following day. Several of my friends attended—Tunde Folawiyo; Dele Momodu of *Ovation*, the society magazine; Demola Adekogbe; Toyin Saraki, Bukola Saraki's wife and former first lady of Kwara State; the lawyer Toyin Pinheiro; and a few others—but duty called back in Nigeria. The day after the ceremony, I grabbed my bag and told my wife I was on my way. She was angry.

"You just came, and now you are leaving," Nana half-shouted.

She asked me to stay longer, to be around the new baby and keep her company. I said that I could not, as I had a business to run. I left for Victoria Station and caught a train to Gatwick Airport. I felt guilty leaving my wife and newborn, but they were in good hands and work beckoned. I was at the airport with my friend, Toyin Pinheiro, when I saw a guy approach us. He said hello to Toyin and completely ignored me.

As he walked away, Toyin said, "Doesn't your company, Zenon, sell diesel?"

"I do. That's all I do."

Looking stunned, he said, "Are you on bad terms with that guy?" "Who?" I asked.

Then he dropped the bomb. "That is Ode. Ode Okaisabor." The man responsible for all of Nigeria's diesel allocation!

I ran after him. "Excuse me, Sir," I said respectfully. "I spoke with you on the phone recently." My words came out in a semi-coherent stutter. I could not care less. As Pentecostal Christians would say, my miracle was on the way.

"Wait," he said, as he checked in. I realized we'd be on the same flight.

I patiently waited until he finished and walked back up to him.

"Sir," I said, "I'm Femi Otedola. I spoke to you recently, along with our mutual acquaintance Dapo Abiodun. Regarding diesel allocations for my company, Zenon."

He remembered, or at least seemed to recognize my name. "Yes, yes," he said, nodding his head.

I stayed with him and chatted until we boarded. He was in business class, and I was in first class. When the plane took off and had reached cruising altitude, I went and sat beside him. I needed to position my agenda with him, front and centre. In a country where you have to befriend people in authority to be able to do big business, you can't afford to miss a golden opportunity like this. Okaisabor was a quietly reserved man, and he listened to me thoughtfully. I explained my situation and told him of my diesel needs. He was so impressed with my presentation and proposal that he said I was going to become the 'King of Diesel.'

Soon enough, I started getting the allocation I needed directly from NNPC, instead of through Dapo. Although my margin was not as significant as I was expecting, because of the associated costs, it was still better than buying from intermediaries. But the retail business thrives on volume, and I started getting huge quantities of fuel from NNPC, which made all the difference. Okaisabor was so impressed with me that he even began advising others to do business with Zenon. From someone who had initially ignored me, and I almost missed the chance to speak with, this was nothing short of a miracle.

(13) Always be prepared to take advantage of breakthroughs. Things would only get better when Nigerian President Olusegun Obasanjo deregulated the diesel market in 2004. NNPC would no longer be the nation's sole importer. That was my most significant breakthrough in this business. With the enormous stores of fuel Zenon had stockpiled over four years—building immense storage capacity, renting ships and amassing prominent clientele—we were in the best position to control the market. There were no anti-trust laws, so a winner-takes-all instinct rose up in me. Indeed, it took Zenon just a few years to take full control of the country's diesel market.

This was how things stood:

- We'd gone from selling small quantities of diesel out of drums in 1999 to greater than 90% market share.
- I'd gone from driving around in jeans, in a second-hand van next to Samson, to employing more than 500 workers.
- I'd gone from begging Marca in vain to supply me with 20 trucks to building and running depots that could supply 2,000 trucks a day.
- I'd gone from literally running after the man in charge of allocation at NNPC to importing diesel inside our own ships.
- I remembered a line in a TV commercial for a popular drink in the 1990s, and recited it back to my once-sceptical friends: "Great things start from small beginnings." Of course, everything starts small. It all begins as an idea. You start small and then grow. And we grew and grew and grew.

TAKEAWAYS

- The first step to awaken your inner entrepreneur is to recognize an opportunity when you see it
- It's good to start small so you can learn, grow and scale up in a controlled, orderly fashion as your market expands
- Create value to make your product or service attractive, and utilize any advantage you have
- Be courageous in making business decisions, and don't be afraid to keep dreaming

LESSON TWO

LEAD FROM THE FRONT, AND THEN TAKE A BACK SEAT

My alarm goes off at 5 am. I've slept barely two and a half hours. No matter how tired I am, I have to get up, shower, dress quickly and jump into my car. It doesn't matter that I went to bed at 2 am. That was yesterday; today is a new day. There are new things to do and new challenges to tackle.

Because my house is in Ikeja and the office is on Victoria Island, 30km south-east of home, I always have to set forth before 5.30. The journey encompasses two bridges and if I left it any later, I would get stuck in the early morning traffic on Third Mainland Bridge. It still takes me at least an hour on average, but that's better than the two or three hours I'd be facing if I ignored the alarm.

My typical morning didn't involve an alarm going off, or much else, before I started Zenon Petroleum and Gas Ltd. Those were the days when my daughter had embarrassingly described my occupation as 'sleeping.' I ran Centre Force, dispensing short-term loans, but it needed little attention from me. I could even decide not to be in the office for a few days at a time. As long as my staff ticked all the relevant boxes in processing loan applications, they could bring the documents to me at home to approve, or I could provide provisional approval on the phone before getting to the office at 11 am. Sometimes, I wouldn't show up until midday.

I treated Centre Force as something to do with my time; it was a way to make a living. I started getting juicy car supply contracts, and was making money, but the desire to push the company higher, to really excel, was not there. I did not set a good example for the staff. It was a case of 'do as I say' rather than 'do as I do.' Centre Force was always going to die a natural death.

But, I had to change my ways with Zenon. With this exciting new enterprise, I needed to up my game.

Consider a footballer in a Nigerian club with no desire to play abroad. Now, compare him with one who wants to play for the biggest clubs in Europe, and does everything possible to get there. His commitment, passion and discipline will be dramatically different. The former was me at Centre Force. The latter, yours truly at Zenon.

It's no exaggeration to say that I was *a new me* at Zenon. I wanted to supply diesel to end-users, where and when they needed it, dirtcheap and with unerring efficiency. I identified a big hole in the supply chain that I could fill, and I did so. I envisioned endless possibilities, as if I were sitting with the pilot in the cockpit of a jet, surveying the expansive landscape below. I felt newly energized. Zenon needed to be on sound footing, doing business differently. I had to be in front, truly leading, steering things in the right direction. I was not going to become the 'King of Diesel' by spending most of my time at nightclubs and sleeping until lunchtime.

My intentions were clear from the beginning. Samson, the driver, was the pilot of the plane (the second-hand van I bought to distribute drums of diesel). I always sat beside him, in our cockpit, as we made our rounds, reaching out to clients and delivering the product. From my vantage point, I could see the proverbial landscape of promise and potential rolling out in all directions. I saw a country gripped by an erratic power supply, and I saw homes darkened. I saw factory engines silenced. Above all, I saw a golden opportunity—the chance to solve a problem, meet people's needs and make good money doing it.

They say that problems and opportunities are the same thing, and I came to see the wisdom in that. I would have been stupid to stay asleep.

I was now a textbook no-nonsense boss. I arrived at the office at 6.30 every morning, although the starting time was 8.00. Employees had to be punctual; I would not tolerate truancy or lateness. I stayed later than anyone else, generally until 7 pm but often as late as 9. As mentioned earlier, I'd then head to the ports and terminals west of Lagos Island, to oversee operations at the Apapa depot. That daily visit was primarily to supervise the loading of the product by my trucks. I'd be there until 2 am, sometimes 3, before heading home.

(1) There's a lot of hard work and sacrifice behind any worthwhile achievement. Not many know this behind-the-scenes origin story of Zenon, and how we came to dominate the market. Some seem to think we came out of nowhere, and were handed a monopoly on a silver platter. In fact, there is a story behind every success. Dr Sam Adeyemi, the pastor and leadership consultant, once said, "Don't envy my harvest. You were not there when I was planting my seed." It took blood, sweat and tears for me to build Zenon from the ground up, but many only got to know about us after we'd made it big. They thought we just sauntered up to the podium to receive the trophy.

If Nigeria had been working well, I would have no business controlling the diesel market. There was no good reason for diesel to be scarce in an oil-producing country. But scarce it was. I simply saw a gap and capitalized on the inefficiency in the system. If the power sector had worked as it should have, diesel would only be for trucks and ships. It wouldn't have been necessary for homes, offices and factories. The demand was huge due to millions of people needing this resource to survive, because there was no reliable electricity. Still, dominating the market required hard work, manoeuvring and investment.

(2) Give your business the attention, time and energy it requires. Your goal should be to take it to the next level. My midnight adventures were no overkill; they were a necessity. Seeing me work until late at night, every night, M. T. Onukogu, the NNPC operations manager, became quite supportive of me. At times, he would even call in the wee hours to inform me that it was time to pick up the product. I was always by my phone, waiting for the golden call. "Get ready to receive," he would say, or, "The weather is calm; pull your ship alongside." He would be there to help when it was time to load.

As a result, I could not afford to sleep. I had to be in constant communication with my ship's captain, to pass this information on to him.

Before deregulation, NNPC was the alpha and the omega of diesel. There was no other source. It was the agency's inefficiency that made scarcity inevitable. For instance, if total demand was 200,000 metric tonnes per month, NNPC would import only 80,000—less than 50% of what was needed. Because the country's four NNPC-owned and operated refineries were out of commission, they were not producing petrol, much less diesel. Nigerians were in perpetually short supply.

To beat your competitor at the monopoly's Atlas Cove jetties, you needed to be awake, alert and ready to move. At any given time, there were 40 ships lined up and waiting to load. By midnight, when everybody else would be sound asleep, I was on standby, awaiting the call from Onukogu, so our ship could position itself at the front of the queue. I could have designated an employee to oversee those midnight operations, but I couldn't guarantee that they too would not be sleeping.

This delivered numerous benefits, in addition to being first in line.

(3) More luck comes the way of the prepared. Late one night, when I was overseeing a fuel transfer at the depot, I saw another vessel out at sea, manoeuvring to come in. It was the Ocean Challenger, owned by Wale Tinubu, CEO of Oando PLC. The ship was going to supply diesel to someone, but I had other ideas for it.

Around 1 am, I called Oando's operations guy and asked him to sell the load to me. He told me that wouldn't be possible, as it was earmarked for one of their customers.

I would not take no for an answer. I immediately called Wale and threw him a juicy proposal.

"That cargo, how much do you plan to sell it for? I'll pay an extra ₦6 per litre," I told him.

Without hesitation, he asked them to discharge it into my tank. Like Don Corleone's famous line from *The Godfather*, I'd made him an offer he could not refuse.

(4) Conquer your fears and always look for better options. One major problem I encountered with NNPC was my location. I was living in Lagos, while Ode Okaisabor, the man in charge of diesel allocation, was in the nation's capital, Abuja, where the national oil company was headquartered. After I started getting a direct supply from NNPC, I needed to develop a smooth working relationship with him. There were always meetings and events in Abuja that he wanted me to attend. But I was afraid to take local flights, which weren't exactly known for their safety. Interestingly, I hadn't been frightened of such things before. It only took hold when I started making money. At this point, I was worth about US$100 million, and out of an inflated sense of self-importance, I suppose, I developed an acute fear of dying. Yet, I knew it would be advantageous to be closer to the decisionmakers in Abuja. Okaisabor used to call me *alaye*, Yoruba slang for 'chairman' or 'strongman,' so I knew I was on his radar and he took me seriously.

"Come on, *alaye*," he'd say. "What's a 45-minute flight? Come on."

One day, when he was in Lagos, he called me and said, "We're going to Abuja on Chanchangi Airlines'[8] first flight out in the morning."

It was not a suggestion; I took it as a command. I could not sleep that night. I drank until 6 am, showered and got to the airport in the hope that I had drowned my fear of flying.

As we walked towards the plane, I could feel my legs shaking. The liquid courage was failing me. I could not climb the gangway. I slumped to the side, a total wreck. It was very embarrassing.

"*Alaye*," Okaisabor barked. "Let's go!"

I just could not muster the will to climb. He boarded in anger, and the plane left.

I told my guys, "Let's go to Abuja by road."

We left around 9 am. When we got to Ibadan, a city located about a quarter of the way into our drive, I called Okaisabor on my mobile phone, but he didn't answer. We reached Abuja in the evening and went straight to see him. To my great relief, the incident on the runway was seemingly forgotten, and we got back down to business.

Ironically, and quite sadly, Okaisabor died several years later, aboard a Bellview Airlines flight that crashed in October 2005.

Anytime he requested a meeting after the Chanchangi fiasco, I would go to Abuja by road, setting out at 8 am and arriving at 4 pm. I'd stay at the Transcorp Hilton in Maitama, a leafy, upscale district of the capital dotted with embassies. I soon realized this wouldn't work—government officials would not come to business meetings in a hotel. And so, I decided to buy a property from Alhaji Aliyu Abubakar, the man behind AA Oil. The house on Aso Drive cost me US$2 million, which the company paid for. This proved to be advantageous, as I could stay in Abuja for longer periods, receive distinguished visitors in style, and dedicate more time and attention to lucrative business deals.

I used to stay for a month at a stretch. Being in Abuja gave me a strategic advantage over my key competitors—Obat and Ascon—as they were not in the capital that frequently. They would fly in, leave the following day, and not return for another month. Like me, they were rightfully scared of domestic air travel in our country.

Zenon was now growing in stature and making US$5-6 million every month. At the time, the exchange rate was ₦112/US$1. That came to more than ₦600 million a month. For a company that was making just ₦100 million a few years earlier, that was something.

THE LIMITATIONS OF LEADING FROM THE FRONT

As heady as things seemed, leading from the front has its limits. I started getting many things wrong, and spectacularly so. These would later combine to bring Zenon from its multibillion-dollar heights to complete ruin.

In retrospect, I made three significant mistakes with the business. Here's what I learned from these missteps:

(1) Formal company structure is critical. Zenon was a topheavy enterprise, without much structure or delegation. You might have noticed that I've interchangeably referred to 'I' and 'Zenon' in this narrative. I rarely say 'we.' I was Zenon, and Zenon was me. I practically ran it like a one-person business, and this held us back.

(2) Relying too heavily on one person is not ideal, even if that person is you. While I adhered to complying with the minimum of board meetings required, I know I could have done things better. I should have had more structure, and invested in bringing in the right experts and talent to give the organization direction.

(3) When hierarchy isn't respected, tensions can build up. I would give people assignments without informing their direct superiors. Managers would hear about the new roles and activities from their subordinates. I would issue directives that were driven more by my youthful hunger for success than any management science. I didn't have the patience for meetings, and wasn't prepared to listen to other people's ideas. I wielded my undisputed authority, and that was the final word.

This worked for a while, but there's a limit to how far you can get doing things this way. When you're just starting out, and still trying to find your feet, you can be everywhere, holding the reins, burning the midnight oil, calling the ship's captain to move into position at the jetty, even sitting down to interview and recruit the office cleaners. But at some point, you need to step back. You have to put an appropriate administrative structure in place, give a degree of power to your managers and interfere less in the day-to-day operations of what you have created.

I didn't appreciate these principles until the Zenon empire came crashing down. The fall of the 'King of Diesel' was dramatic, and I hit the lowest point of my life. I had operated my business based on ambition, raw talent and instinct. I looked up to nobody, and had no mentors or advisers. In the end, your natural talent and intuition can only take you some distance, especially when you find yourself running a huge enterprise.

I'd never studied anybody's model to try and understand what they did right, and what they did wrong. I didn't bother to find out how other Nigerian business leaders had built their empires. At times, I look back and wonder if things might have turned out differently for Zenon if I'd just taken time to study the success of others and learn from their experiences.

There's no question that I would have been better off if I had done the research, studied the principles of delegation and management, and grown the business in a more conventional manner. For one, Zenon would have been better structured, and probably wouldn't have collapsed as it did. I was the chairman, CEO, CFO, Company Secretary, Operations Manager, Admin Manager, and everything in between. Literally everything revolved around me. My 'yes' was the law and my 'no' was a decree. I sacked people without any disciplinary process. I'd shout, "You are fired!" at the drop of a hat, with no discussion, recourse or appeal.

A NEW LEADERSHIP APPROACH AS WE REBRANDED

My style had to change when I bought the majority stake in African Petroleum in 2007. AP, a retail and wholesale entity, was the downstream arm of British Petroleum before reorganizing into a separate firm in 1977, in response to the Nigerianization decree for foreign companies operating in our country.

It was a different model altogether. As Chairman and CEO, I realized I was now playing in a different league, organized and buttoned down in every sense. This footballer was no longer playing in the local league. For starters, there was a definitive management team and a board of directors. There would be no more calling up ship captains and interviewing cleaning crews.

AP was listed as a publicly traded stock. The stringent reporting and transparency requirements of the Nigerian Stock Exchange would not allow it to be run as a one-man operation. AP was a traditional institution with well-defined processes, a situation that even I, as an investor and ostensibly the owner, could learn from. I wasn't starting from scratch and making it up along the way, as I had done with Femco, Centre Force and Zenon. We're talking about a big business that would be raising billions from public offerings, which was all about regulatory oversight and public trust.

Still, I can recall some reluctance on my part to let go. It was when we rebranded AP as Forte Oil in 2010 that I can confidently say I had a properly structured business for the first time in my entrepreneurial career. I took the position of Non-Executive Chairman and appointed an experienced CEO. We developed a strategic vision, created appropriate institutional processes, and I removed myself from day-to-day operations. If I'd died in the Forte Oil days, the business would have continued to run without any hiccups. There were succession plans in place. That we were always the first to submit financial reports to the stock exchange spoke volumes.

Given all that, it began to dawn on me that I have always been more of an entrepreneur than a manager. I had a lot to learn, and certainly had to fine-tune my style, following the Zenon experience.

Leading from the front doesn't mean you have to recruit the receptionist. Leadership does not always entail reporting to the office at 6 am. That would be good for a small business, just starting out, but Forte Oil was bigger than me. I needed to adopt a fundamentally different mentality and assume an entirely different role.

The entrepreneur can be Executive Chairman if he so chooses. However, he needs a competent and robust CEO as his deputy, someone who will oversee the day-to-day management of his company. Before the Forte Oil experience, I found it difficult to recruit a good CEO that I could trust to do the job. As a result, there was a high turnover, until I found the right person. It took me nearly a decade to find the ideal CEO for Zenon.

FIND AN EXCELLENT CEO, TAKE A BACK SEAT

In Akin Akinfemiwa, I finally found the perfect fit, which made my transition from entrepreneur to leader much easier. He was someone I could sit and have a discussion with. He would give me blunt advice, even when he knew I might not be predisposed to it. He was not a sycophant—nothing he said was meant to simply please me or massage my ego. I finally had someone I could trust to put me in check and run the business honestly, professionally and competently. I took the back seat without any fears.

Akin previously worked as a business process analyst at FSB International Bank. From there, he moved to the oil and gas sector, where he earned his stripes as an international oil trader with Oando PLC. He was executive assistant to Deputy MD Mofe Boyo, before being moved to

Oando Supply and Trading Ltd, a sister company, where he trained as a products and derivatives officer. He was the first true derivatives trader in Nigeria. That gave him a platform to develop into a key personality in oil trading and supplies beyond the shores of Nigeria. It was from that position that I poached him.

I needed an experienced hand, someone familiar with the biggest oil traders, to run Fineshade Energy Limited, my energy-trading company in London. Akin joined Fineshade in November of 2006, moving to Zenon as CEO in late 2009, and came to Forte Oil in December 2011. He is now the CEO of Geregu Power PLC, the gas-powered electricity generating company in the city of Ajaokuta, on whose board I sit, following my divestment from Forte Oil in 2019. My trust in him is complete and unwavering.

TAKEAWAYS

- I still lead but have learned to lead differently—as an entrepreneur. Being an entrepreneur does not mean you will be removed entirely from the business once it matures. That would be like jumping from one extreme to the other
- Your managers need supervision and direction. Despite any urge to have your company operate at your whim, you need to draw the line and formalize some structure and discipline
- The role of the entrepreneur is markedly different. They are the ones with the resources and, sometimes, the ideas, but they must engage managers to run the show. They don't have to deal with the nuts and bolts, or the bricks and mortar. I am not cut out to be a manager. I am an entrepreneur, although I discovered this quite late. Fortunately, it was not too late

LESSON THREE

SELF-BELIEF IS NON-NEGOTIABLE

What is self-belief? Remember the incident at my house on Sir Michael Otedola Crescent, when the rickety Flame Petroleum truck spilled diesel in my yard? I realized that I could do better at this business, by cleaning it up and delivering more value for the money. And I did.

That was self-belief. And it reflected my instinct and capacity to follow through. It propelled me to set up my first real business. I didn't know where it would lead. I certainly hadn't envisioned owning depots and ships and controlling up to 93% of the market. I didn't know I was going to buy African Petroleum PLC. I surely had no inkling that I'd buy a private jet. I just grew and grew, from selling a few 200-litre drums of diesel to becoming a multibillionaire. But it all started with self-belief, propelled by instincts.

Self-belief is having an idea and pursuing it, convinced that you will make a success of it. Believing you can do this better than others is taking self-belief to the next level. Staying the course amid doubt and difficulties propels you to yet another level of self-belief. The moment you get mired in doubt and fear, the instant you give in to those trying to discourage you and pull you down, your self-confidence erodes, and you shy away from steps that can carry you to success. The journey is not plain sailing. My core piece of advice to the aspiring entrepreneur is to believe in yourself. And keep believing in yourself. You cannot begin to think of starting a business without a healthy and enduring sense of self-belief.

No successful entrepreneur can honestly tell you that they knew for sure that they'd become rich when they started their business. You think you have the talent to create a business and make some money. You start small; everything starts somewhere. Sometimes, before you know it, things click and money starts flowing in, perhaps beyond your projections.

Now, a warning: this is where many people lose it. They were not expecting this wealth, and didn't plan for it, so they spend it recklessly. Many people make that mistake at some point in their life.

As the money rolls in, and you can afford what you could not before, you realize you are now rich. Many will fall prey to selfishness and greed—you want to make more money and begin to think about controlling the market. You've made your first million bucks, and you want another million. Soon you want 10 million, and then 100 million. And then you won't be satisfied until it's a billion. You want to be valued in dollars; that becomes how you self-identify. You did not set out to become a billionaire—it's just that you now see that you can do it. That is a product of self-belief.

These are simple truths to help you with self-belief, learned from an extraordinary journey:

(1) You don't have to see the full picture right away—just begin. When an entrepreneur starts out, it's difficult to see the bigger picture at first. They get to work, hoping to make enough to pay the rent and put food on the table. Later, the entrepreneur who's on a roll may think themselves a genius. Ingenuity is critical to entrepreneurship, sure, but not everyone with a good idea ends up successful. Things will happen along the way that may supercharge your success, but do not let them turn your self-belief into self-delusion.

(2) Talent counts: nurture and hone it via an engaging endeavour. Behind self-belief, there must be talent. If you have the ability, self-belief is critical in putting it to use. If you know you're talented, have the confidence to explore this talent and develop it for maximum impact. I knew I had business acumen. I knew I could set up an operation, put in the hours and make something of it.

(3) Identify that killer instinct and be willing to risk more. When my dad established his printing press, and I decided to quit school and join him, I knew I had that spark of ambition that would bring me success. I knew I had the shrewdness and savvy to make a living as an entrepreneur; I was only looking for the right opportunities to pull it all together. Intuition is a critical springboard to taking risks, like leaving paid employment and starting blind. That self-belief is the real driving spirit of entrepreneurship. You tell yourself, "I can start my own company." You may fear leaving the safety net that conventional employment provides. You may be frightened about not being able to take care of your needs and sustain your family, but you still take a leap. You want to seize an opportunity, and if you don't jump in with both feet, you'll never know.

The entrepreneurial spirit is something you can see and feel, even in young people. Some are fortunate enough to have others who support their dreams early in life, so they begin to make use of their inherent entrepreneurial skills. Femco, the youthful manicure venture, was entirely my idea. Although I was an adolescent, it was evident that I was entrepreneurial. I felt I could provide a service, and nobody discouraged me. In the long run, neither of my parents was surprised that I ended up in business, although my quitting school really hurt my mum.

(4) Entrepreneurship is purposeful, committed and goal oriented. Some are called entrepreneurs but are mere opportunists. Yes, entrepreneurs do go for opportunities—they see an opening, seize the chance and try to make the best of it. But when you see a so-called entrepreneur jump from one business to the other, just because they want to be everywhere, and compete with those they consider rivals, you have to question their sense of purpose. An entrepreneur must be committed and goal oriented. That means their energies will be focused and well directed, and they can measure their progress against their goals. They're not doing things just to compete with, or copy, others. They are purpose-driven.

(5) Entrepreneurs are visionaries, even when they seem crazy. It is tough to be an entrepreneur, and I'm not just talking about my field. Often, it's not until you are successful that people begin to respect the path you've chosen. At first, you began seeing things nobody else seemed to notice. You may have tried to discuss your ideas, and people stared at you as if you were about to jump off a cliff. But to see what nobody else sees is an entrepreneurial gift.

My decision to go into the energy sector was fuelled by things I noticed, and propelled by self-belief, despite the harsh realities spread out before me. The industry was in a bad state, in need of billions of dollars to get it functioning properly. The government was in control, partly because of the enormous capital that largescale power generation required. But I realized that the government would take its hands off at some point, and the field would open up to those ready to invest. The sector had to be fixed to facilitate the economic development of Nigeria. I thought deeply about it—the problems and the prospects—and concluded that if I didn't get in, it would be tougher, if not impossible, in the future. I took the plunge.

It is not like the tank-farm business, which was an all-comers affair. I had invested in storage tank facilities when I set up Zenon, and suddenly 150 people followed in my footsteps. The price of entry was more or less zero, and banks were essentially giving away money. For the power generation business, though, you needed more than US$500 million just to open the door. I could see a massive opportunity in front of me and was ready to go for it.

In 2013, I decided to buy into Geregu Power PLC. The vehicle I used was Amperion Power Distribution Company Ltd, a subsidiary of Forte Oil. I somehow saw into the future; this was my destiny.

Aliko Dangote, the richest person in Africa, according to *Forbes's* 2022 ranking, is a textbook example of an entrepreneur who can see into the future. When he was paying ₦20 billion to acquire land for his refinery and petrochemical complex, he was driven by self-belief and a vision others didn't possess. Many thought him crazy, but he had a clear picture in his head. In many cases, it takes a 'crazy' mind to conceive such an idea. In two years, he completed construction of 160 kilometres of road. In 20 years of democracy, the government of Nigeria has not delivered 80 kilometres of new roads.

HOW TO BUILD SELF-CONFIDENCE

(1) Others can help you boost your self-confidence. Can self-confidence be built? Yes, but it's infinitely easier if there are people who can help your dream along. In charting your entrepreneurial path, you will encounter people who are waiting like angels to open the door, and others intent on slamming it shut in your face. They are inevitable players in your story. The good ones—the benevolent helpers—will surface at the right place and time. Akin Akinfemiwa and Chris Adeyemi did so for me. Knowing that someone has your back can enhance your self-belief and push you on to bigger and better things. Hone your ability to identify how each person you meet could affect your journey and try to surround yourself with those who will support you.

(2) Integrity strengthens self-confidence. Building personal integrity can enhance your self-belief. When you deal with people fairly and genuinely, they'll come away with a good impression of you. This will spread by word of mouth, enhance your reputation, and boost your confidence when approaching people for business, or for any other purpose in life. When you embody integrity, honesty and a fear of God, you will know within yourself if you're walking the right path. In turn, this will embolden you to confidently walk through any door. It may take time—it could take 20 years in the trenches—but you *will* get there.

HOW TO NURTURE YOUR INSTINCTS

(1) Take time off to reflect and meditate. Self-assurance requires trusting your instincts. You can nurture your inner compass if you are a deep thinker, and someone who meditates. Intuition resides deep inside of you. It drives you, like an inner spirit—you are not completely in control. With confidence, you will act on that inner voice when it tells you that if you embark on that project, you will succeed.

Unfortunately, some people take things for granted. Maybe they have been fortunate all their lives and expect their good fortune to continue. But what happens longer term—how everything sorts out years down the road—is what really matters. Ending well is as important as starting well.

(2) Train yourself to be fair and generous. At times, it's difficult to explain what is driving you. You cannot point to a particular thing. But it helps to try and gain an understanding of your needs, wants and motivation. When you reach an important decision, ask yourself what you were thinking when you made your move. I like to close deals quickly. So, when I negotiate, I am not greedy. I don't seek to keep all the benefits to myself. I have done business deals in which I gave 75% of the upside to the other party. I give and I take. My instincts just tell me to do a particular deal that way. My gut tells me that I won't regret it. In most cases, things turn out fine for me, even though it may have looked questionable at first.

WHAT HAPPENED WHEN I IGNORED MY INNER VOICE

A friend once asked if my instincts told me Zenon was going to be in trouble. I must confess that my inner voice failed me in that instance. It happened overnight—oil prices collapsed and ruined me. I was monitoring the market on my computer and saw oil at US$147 per barrel. I had already ordered diesel worth US$500 million. Then, just like that, it began to go down. It dropped to US$110. I thought it wouldn't possibly dip below that. I calculated the odds and felt I would still be OK, but right before my eyes, it crashed to US$37.

The diesel I'd ordered when the price was astronomically higher was already on the high seas, heading for Nigeria. Now, it was worth a fraction of my purchase price. I said to myself, "I'm finished."

I'd fallen into suffocating debt in mere seconds. What could I do? Still, I remained confident, certain that a solution would arise from somewhere. To make a dire situation even worse, the oil price crash also meant foreign currency flow into Nigeria nosedived. The Central Bank decided to devalue the naira. And with that, my debt load skyrocketed. The loans I took when the exchange rate was ₦117/ US$1 would now have to be paid back at ₦165/ US$1. That was a massive blow. ₦60 billion was evaporating before my eyes, and I was saddled with ₦40 billion in interest.

I resisted the impulse to sell my bank shares, which would later be one of my greatest regrets. I'd have made huge profits if I had done so. I had bought into Zenith Bank at ₦12 per share and would have made ₦110 billion if I had exited when the price rose to ₦60. I owned 2.3 billion shares, which represented an 8% ownership stake in Zenith. I had 6% of the United Bank for Africa, and I would have cashed out with ₦81 billion. In total, I would have reaped a ₦191 billion windfall. But that was not to be.

My total debt from the oil crash catastrophe was ₦220 billion. The stock market crashed because of the oil price crash, and those shares were worth next to nothing. Such things are always clearer in the rear-view mirror, but if only I'd followed my instincts.

On the other hand, when the opportunity presented itself to pay off the debts by giving up my properties to AMCON[9]—a lifeboat in the Nigerian economic crisis—I disregarded those who advised against doing so and jumped at the opportunity. The time comes when you have to concede that if you sink, you sink, and if you grab onto a life preserver, you'll stay afloat. On this occasion, I was ready for it. I gave up extensive property holdings in exchange for debt relief and set out to rebuild my life.

I relinquished ownership of truck parks and land in Lagos, buildings and estates in Lagos, Abuja and Port Harcourt, filling stations all over the country, a Bombardier private jet, stock in various banks and oil companies, and fuel storage tank farms near Apapa. I gave it all up to start anew.

The experience showed me that there is no absolute certainty in life. If God wants to take anything from you, it will not take him one minute. Look at me: my financial life was upended in the span of one week. Great wealth can be wiped from the books in the blink of an eye.

I look back and conclude that I had to experience what I did to be able to move to the next phase of my life. I was now free of debt and more introspective about entrepreneurship. I suppose it had to happen at one point or another in my life. If it did not happen then, it would later. Let us assume that oil prices had not collapsed. I would have gone upstream. I would have continued taking on more debt, pursuing more high-flying opportunities. One day, at some point down the road, oil prices would eventually crash, because the market is cyclical, and I would have found myself in even greater debt and bigger trouble.

I suffered to learn and am better off than I was before the Zenon crisis.

SOMETIMES, YOU NEED TO FOCUS ON BEING PRAGMATIC

While I am a believer in following my instincts, I can be flexible in that regard. I look at the bigger picture and choose rigid pragmatism at times. But being too stiff can also be a problem. Ignoring your intuition can be harmful, while relying solely on it can be counterproductive. Life experience will teach you who and what to trust, and when. By and large, I follow my instincts. I am pleased with many decisions that were based on my visceral sense of what to do, such as settling my debts with my properties. That's the best decision of my life. Separating family from my business was another excellent decision. Handing over management to a new team of professionals was also the right way to go. I followed my instincts, and I am the better for it.

TAKEAWAYS

- If you are to realize your potential as an entrepreneur, you must believe in your abilities
- This self-confidence is critical, allowing you to follow your instincts and take the plunge into the unknown
- Many people have shied away from doing big business because they focus more on the limitations than the opportunities. Be better than that
- Self-belief is the antidote to doubt and indecision

LESSON FOUR

HIRE WITH CAUTION, FIRE WITHOUT REGRETS

It took me nearly ten years to find the right CEO for my business empire. I expect that puts me in a good position to talk authoritatively about hiring and firing. Yes, I mis-hired several times, until I finally got it right. I never gave up. And when I got it right, the system began to run smoothly, independently of me. I had peace of mind. Knowing that the right person is at the wheel is one of the most satisfying experiences an entrepreneur can have.

There are three feasible ways to recruit:

(1) Advertising. You can take a transparent, formal approach by advertising openings and giving everybody a chance to compete. You can then pick the best person to fill the position. Or you can engage a professional agency to recruit for you. This will come at a cost, but you can expect a good field of candidates. Either way, be wary of people who talk a good game during an interview but fail to deliver once they're on board. They may be great interviewees, but they won't be good employees.

(2) Referrals. There's no shortage of recommendations and referrals circulating in business circles, chiefly by word of mouth. While this is cost-effective, and probably saves time compared to the open system, there is no guarantee that a professional referral will prove to be the best choice. People may make recommendations for all the right reasons, but they could also be driven by wanting to do a favour for someone. It may even be you doing someone a favour, trying to establish or consolidate commercial, social or political relationships. You may end up with a poor fit, or an influence peddler who will be out of control because they know a key client.

(3) Headhunting. You can decide to headhunt. You, your staff, friends or associates can identify a particular individual and go all out to convince them to join your company. Targeted recruitment could originate with a recommendation, but merit—the candidate's proven skills, attributes and track record—should be an overriding consideration. Headhunting is usually focused on your competitors' employees; in which case the candidate will already have a good knowledge of the sector. The target may not be actively seeking to move to another job, so you could have your work cut out for you in trying to lure them to your corner. You should be ready to pay a premium; you can't expect to attract top talent away from their job just like that. Headhunting does not always yield the desired result. It's a gamble, but when things work out it can pay off in a big way.

My experience with recruiting, hiring and firing has quite a lot to teach anyone interested in looking at it closely.

HOW I POACHED AKIN AKINFEMIWA FROM OANDO

My best recruitment ever: Akin Akinfemiwa, the CEO who helped turn Forte Oil into a world-class company. I paid a premium to poach him from Oando PLC after a colleague had recommended him.

It involved a combination of two recruitment options: word-of-mouth recommendation and headhunting. I had a short phone conversation with Akin after we were introduced. A year later, he started working for me. That was in 2006. I put him in charge of Fineshade Energy Limited, my energy trading company in London. His performance blew my mind.

I moved him back to Nigeria in 2009 and appointed him Group Chief Operating Officer of Zenon. He became the CEO of Forte Oil at the end of December 2011.

Before finding Akin, I had recruited a woman from Habib Bank, based on recommendations. She clearly could not do the job. I then decided to get a trader from BP, but she proved too frustrating to work with. Neither of them provided any direction. That all changed the day Akin came on board.

I learned several lessons from recruiting this powerhouse leader:

(1) Do due diligence before hiring. I learned early on that it pays to really research the candidate before hiring. I go the extra mile to root out as much as I can about an individual. These days, with a rich array of digital resources at your disposal, you can quickly get information on anybody. You first assess the vacancy, work up a job description and hiring timeline, schedule an interview and work through a short list of candidates who would be a good fit. Once you zero in on a likely target, you initiate intelligence gathering. What sort of person is he or she? Is there something about their record that doesn't sit well with you? After giving them the job, put them on probation for a few months. That gives you the opportunity to observe their performance, read their character and further assess their suitability. Therefore, my recruitment process doesn't end when the engagement letter is issued.

I monitor the new employee. I keep an ear close to the ground. I ask people around them to give me a reading on their conduct and character. I don't like working with people who are too laid back or too forward, those who lack focus, or don't take their career too seriously, or individuals who are just plain arrogant. I don't want employees who are busybodies. I don't want those who try to brag that they are close to the boss. All these are deal breakers for me.

The mistakes I made in the past taught me several lessons. I learned how *not* to do things. The experience was not a waste, in any sense. I have no regrets, because working through all of this helped me identify what works for me and my interests.

(2) Recruiting by referrals is a disservice to the business. Truth be told, recruitment is one of the most challenging aspects of running a company, especially the way I used to go about it. To get the right resources to help you implement your vision, you need efficient processes, no matter your recruitment style. I never had a proper human resources structure until I bought African Petroleum PLC, which I later rebranded to Forte Oil PLC. The organization did professional recruitment, and I was not central to it. Earlier, at Centre Force and Zenon, I employed people mostly based on referrals and did not follow the tried-and-true rules of recruitment.

At Zenon, my initial strategy was to get people knowledgeable in the business of selling petroleum products. I could not force myself to go through the tedious process of open recruitment. Every new hire was based on word-of-mouth recommendations. I would just put out the word that I was looking for someone to fill a particular vacancy, and somebody would bring in a candidate. I would then choose whom to employ based on a sense of trust, if I can use that word in a broad sense. This was an enormous disservice to the business.

It's not going to be easy to get the right candidate this way. People will simply steer their friends and dependents to you. They'll send their cousins, brothers, sisters, nephews and hangers-on, and tell you they're suitable for the job. It's not until you bring them in and put them to work that you realize they've been dumped on you. Zenon acquired a lot of dead weight in that way, which I eventually realized was hurting the company. It also did not help that many of these recruits came in through people I knew; these employees felt like they deserved special treatment.

(3) Senior management should have a proven track record, integrity and loyalty. In my experience, the recruitment of executives should not be subject to sentimentality of any kind. The focus should be on identifying an individual with a proven record in your line of business. The attributes of personal integrity and loyalty are also important. Positions such as CEO, COO and CFO cannot be filled based on emotions and relationships. The chief executive, for instance, must certainly have managed people and resources before, preferably in a big company. What business have they run? Where did they take the company? How have they dealt with crises? How innovative and creative are they? What are their values? Do they take pride in their work? Do they have a reputation for honesty and integrity? If there are any gaps in these credentials, think twice about installing them in your company's most important positions.

(4) Let a financially savvy professional get you a CFO. If you're borrowing heavily to finance your business, I have nothing against allowing the bank to appoint the CFO for you. This is not a typical recruitment method, but it is one way of putting yourself in check and allowing the banks to feel secure that their money is being well managed. It is a way of telling them you have nothing to hide. No bank will dislike the idea. It happened at Forte Oil. I invited Segun Agbaje, the head of GTBank, to nominate our CFO. I interviewed the candidate, Julius Omodayo-Owotuga, found him to be a straight shooter, and gave him the job. Your lenders will suffer heavily if your business collapses; they are major stakeholders. It is in their interest for the company to run well, and by allowing them to nominate a CFO you'll be reassuring them that their money is safe with you.

Yes, there is the fear that such a CFO may undermine you and work for the bank instead. For this reason, you should also have internal auditors, to provide a series of checks and balances. Indeed, Nigerian banks are in the habit of taking liberties with customers' money. They will overcharge interest and try to confuse you over what you have paid and what is outstanding. Many companies find it challenging to keep track of the details with their banks. In that regard, having a CFO from a bank is risky because of the danger of collusion. That is why your internal audit unit must be alert and diligent. At Forte Oil, we did not find any manipulation by the CFO. He was our inside partner, looking out for our best interests.

HOW I FIRE

I have never fired any employee and then regretted it. If there is justification for them getting the sack, there is no need to regret anything. Before I take any action, I think it through, and assess the decision based on my principles. I may sack someone over the phone, or do it in an instant, but I was never hasty in the sense of being rash. I am also aware that there are intrigues among employees, jealousy and backbiting and politics, with one wanting to ease the other out so that they can become the boss. I've always been conscious of this. However, once I have my facts and I am convinced, that's it. You're gone.

As mentioned, some candidates can talk a good game, but the problem starts with doing the job after you have engaged them. I remember recruiting a particular Zenon CEO I was excited about because he demonstrated excellent knowledge of the industry. Before I hired him, he had approached me with the suggestion that the company should get into engine oil. Being a chemical engineer, he had a background in engine oil production. When he came on board, I took his advice, and we launched Zenon Engine Oil. I gave him customers, but nothing came of it. He was all talk and no action. At Zenon, I fired as I deemed necessary. But with a public company like Forte Oil, there must be a board meeting, with directors voting on your wish to fire the CEO. That was a different ballgame altogether.

FIGHT TO GET EXCEPTIONAL PEOPLE ON BOARD

In headhunting, you must be aggressive. There was nobody I really wanted who I didn't fight for, and I eventually hired most, no matter how long it took me. When I was starting Zenon and asked Tunde Babson, the Manager of Flame Petroleum, to come join me, his first response was an emphatic no. I also headhunted Joel Tunde Falasinnu from Total to be AP's COO.

I tried to headhunt Tokunbo Amosu from Honeywell Oil and Gas for Zenon, but he turned me down. There were also some guys from Oando PLC, Chevron/Texaco and Mobil Oil who said no. Some were afraid they were going to leave a structured environment for a less formal one. What they did not factor into their thinking was that they could come and help me structure the business, which was what Akin did. Because of him, KPMG and PwC were later retained to manage recruitment for Forte. Most of those who turned me down ended up saying they wished they'd joined me. I always told them it was their choice; I did not feel slighted in any way. I just thought they missed an excellent opportunity, and I owed it to my companies to go after the very best people.

WHEN THE FIT IS NOT PERFECT, EXPERIMENT

We had four CEOs in three years at AP and seven CEOs in ten years at Zenon. One of the reasons I never gave up trying to recruit the right chief exec was that there was bank debt on the side. I wanted to succeed so I could repay the banks and take the business to the highest level possible. I had to run a relay race, management-wise. You pass the baton. If you don't see anyone to hand it to, so they can keep it going, you continue the race by yourself. The baton must not stop moving forward.

AP had several CEOs before we rebranded. When I took over the company as Chairman, Mallam Zira Maigadi was the CEO. He worked with me for a few months, until the third quarter of 2007. He had been instrumental in my buying the business, and I saw that he could also help with the transition phase, from the old AP to the new AP.

After him, I brought Joel Tunde Falasinnu in from Total, to become COO from the third quarter of 2007 through Q3 2009. It is a fascinating story.

I used to sell diesel to Total. In 2003, I told Tunde, "You know you're going to work for me when I acquire all these major marketers, right?" He laughed. It was an audacious statement. I was a diesel seller, running an upstart company, and already talking about buying a major downstream enterprise.

After I'd purchased AP, I had a meeting with Tunde in Abuja. "Come and run the company," I said. He declined. I offered him a handsome financial package, and in the end, he agreed to work for me for the next two years.

In quick succession after Maigadi and Falasinnu, I brought in Mike Ahme as COO, who served in that role from the third quarter of 2009 until December 2011, and Akin as CEO, who did so spectacularly well in leading the rebranded Forte Oil PLC.

In Zenon's 1999-2009 run, my CEOs included: Biola Ogunrombi; Pastor Oretope Paul; Dr Adeyinka Akinbami; Steve Cathay; Idowu Adebowale; Biola Babalola; and Akin Akinfemiwa.

ABOUT STAFF HONESTY AND LOYALTY

What makes me fire people?

Dishonesty is the primary offence. Indiscipline is another. Greed and selfishness are also high on the list. No matter how competent you are, the moment I uncover an act of deception, you're gone. How can you and I be in the room, sitting across from each other and discussing the fortunes of the company, when I know you are a common criminal in a shirt and tie? It would be impossible for me to keep you as an employee. Most of the people I've fired were not upright individuals.

Dishonesty, which stems from disloyalty, warrants immediate dismissal.

Loyalty should be a significant consideration in filling positions. We all tend to look at competence—which is non-negotiable, by the way—but a competent manager who is disloyal will still ruin your company. In my experience, loyalty is not a function of how long someone has worked for you, either. The time they've been with you can certainly be an indicator, as you know that these are people who have grown with the company and shown commitment. That's good, and it makes you more comfortable. However, loyalty can show up very early in an employee's tenure as well. They don't need to have worked for you for a full year before you spot it.

How does loyalty work? Loyal employees do not undermine you or the company. They don't badmouth or criticize you in front of others. When there are things they disagree with, they will find a way of telling you privately. They watch out for you and the business. They go the extra mile to make things right. They never seek to take advantage of you or the system. Instead, they want to see how the company can grow, how you can position it better in the market, and how to cut costs. They're ready to forgo their own comfort and privileges when necessary. They place the company above personal interests. If they want to leave, for whatever reason, they will broach the subject with you in confidence.

Disloyalty is not dissimilar to a cancer that will spread far and wide to ruin an organization. I had a CEO who snuck around behind us to ask one of our biggest clients not to buy diesel from Zenon, explaining that he had his own company that could supply them instead. How could you keep such a manager in your business, let alone your CEO? It would make more sense to shut down your company and apply to work for his. There are people out there who will do anything to grow their own business on the side, and chase you out of the market, all the while standing with you and smiling. If you don't know what they're doing behind your back, you'll wake up one day to discover that you don't have a business anymore.

HOW TO ASSESS LOYALTY IN AN INTERVIEW

I value loyalty because I want to be sure my employees have my back. I want to be sure I can rely on them. I think every human being wants to feel confident they're working with people who will look out for their interests. I always look for loyalty in addition to competence. It is said that loyalty is a value, while competence is a skill, so it is by no means a matter of either-or. You can train to acquire a skill, but a value is a personal ethic, which is not malleable. Getting both competence and loyalty in a new employee is the ultimate dream. Then, you can sleep with both eyes shut, knowing you are in good hands.

Unfortunately, you cannot gauge loyalty at the recruitment stage. There is a level of faith, or trust, required in deciding to engage or not. Still, there are some signs to watch out for at the interview.

A quick look at someone's CV will reveal how many places the candidate has worked at and how long they stayed on each job. There may be a red flag there, but that cannot be conclusive. People change jobs for various reasons. Perhaps they are not overly motivated, or the company is too limiting. Maybe they're looking for a place where they can express their aptitude with a sense of fulfilment.

Asking a few simple questions in an interview setting, and watching the person's body language, can be revealing. You can ask why they keep changing jobs, although you may not be able to verify their claims. A truthful candidate is more likely to answer probing questions quickly and confidently. An untruthful person would take their time, biting their lip and stammering on simple and straightforward issues, as they think about what to say. The way they speak about their previous work and bosses can give something away about their character. If you see signs of disrespect towards past employers—especially if it's with more than one—this is a concern. Most principled employees would avoid badmouthing even those who deserve it to a stranger.

HOW I NOTICED THINGS WERE OFF

I have had varied experiences with employees. I once had a senior executive who came highly recommended. I gave him a new car. The day after he got the car, he started misbehaving. He was chasing women and relaxing in my living room as if he were on a boat cruise. I asked him to go. I also had an employee who was too forward. Anytime we visited my billionaire friends, he would be the first to sit down, before the rest of us. One felt too big to help my family out with an assignment, and to me that was a sign of disloyalty, because he had gained from me far beyond what was his due. Little things like that get to me.

My key staffing mistake at Zenon was that employees were brought to me by others. I didn't follow industry-standard recruitment procedures or work with professional recruiters. I just put out the word that I was looking for a team, and folks started showing up at my doorstep. This was not a good move. I tried to assess people, to get a handle on their personality. If anyone attempted to carry my bag, I was always suspicious. That was a little too 'kissing-up' for me, although in African culture doing so may show that you respect your boss. I remain suspicious all the same.

One manager I hired came for the interview on a motorbike taxi. I did not do much due diligence before giving him the job, because I respected the person who'd recommended him. A car came with the job, and shortly after that, I was looking out my office window when he drove in. Someone opened the door for him, another held his jacket, and yet another person carried his bag. He strolled in majestically, just two weeks into the job. That is what power—or a twisted sense of it—can do to people.

HOW I TEST EMPLOYEES

As noted, I'm continually sizing up employees. When they come to my office, I may test them by giving them a sandwich. Instead of going off to quietly enjoy it, some will go around bragging to others that I'd given them a gift. I find out about this through low-key intelligence. You cannot trust such a person with sensitive information. The sandwich test showed me who could be trusted, and who would be likely to sell information to competitors.

My not being very formal had many advantages, but the downside was that there was no camaraderie or teamwork among the staff. It was everyone for themselves. Everybody was trying to be in the boss's good graces, to the detriment of the team dynamic.

WHY MY EMPLOYEES RARELY LEAVE

Overall, I would say I am a reasonable employer. I don't want people to work 24/7. I'm quite considerate in that regard. I believe people should only work eight hours at a stretch. Everything after that is eye service, which I can't stand. What am I doing that I cannot finish in an eight-hour day? I can understand that some deadlines require extra hustle, but this doesn't happen every day.

Remarkably, when people work with me, they rarely want to leave. Many tell me they like having a relationship with me, and that I'm not bossy. I do not expect to be treated like royalty, and I don't expect them to carry my bag or jacket. They also say I engage with them on their level. Of course, they're well compensated, pulling in above-average pay and fringe benefits. I buy cars and houses for them and pay school fees and medical bills for those who take their jobs seriously. When you do what makes your staff happy, those who have values will reciprocate. I also enjoy good relationships with my former employees. Many of them are still my friends. I'm comfortable calling them and asking them to help me out with things.

TAKEAWAYS

- When you want to hire, what qualities do you look for? If you had to choose between competence and loyalty, think about what you would settle for
- I made several mistakes in recruitment: I did not engage HR professionals and was too busy doing people favours
- Once I got it right, I started really cruising along. Hiring and firing must be handled properly

LESSON FIVE

CREATE A WARM WORKING ENVIRONMENT

I did not get many things right at Zenon, but there was one aspect no one could deny: we operated like a family. We *were* one big family. I could sense the loyalty, the commitment and the pride among my employees. At Forte Oil, we operated as a family as well.

Once you demonstrate loyalty and commitment to the cause, I will take it upon myself to give you the necessary incentives, to keep you happy. I want you to wake up in the morning and feel excited about coming to work.

Keeping the team happy should be uppermost in the mind of any entrepreneur. A comfortable, contented and driven team will deliver results. Notice that I never say 'perfect' team. There's no such thing. There will always be problems and challenges in any team, even the most motivated in the world, but getting people to cultivate that spirit of oneness can address a lot of issues and create a convivial work environment. The entrepreneur has to be deliberate about building team spirit, through their words and actions.

I had to change the vocabulary of the Zenon staff. I encouraged them to change 'you' and 'yours' to 'we' and 'ours' when talking about the company. I would correct them and say, "The company belongs to us all. Even your children's children can benefit from this business."

It's a collective spirit. I always let people know that it is not only me; that the credit goes to the entire team. They feel respected and appreciated. Every human being wants to be recognized and valued, no matter where they sit in the hierarchy. In an African setting, there are usually sizeable gaps between the top and lower positions. This tends to cut off the entrepreneur from team members who are on the lower rungs of the ladder. There must be a deliberate effort to bring everyone into the circle, to make them feel at home, to enable them to work comfortably from whatever position they occupy.

From Zenon to Forte Oil, we had in place numerous incentives to ensure they were pleasant, welcoming places to work. This gave us a significant edge over our competitors, setting us apart in many ways. Here are a few examples:

(1) Incentives promote loyalty and commitment. Incentivizing the team is critical to building dedication, commitment and camaraderie. At Zenon, for instance, all members of senior management got new cars. Their official residences were in Victoria Island. We made sure they lived in places befitting their status. Later, Zenon bought houses for them. There was a caveat, though: for anyone who got sacked within their first ten years, ownership of the house would revert to the company. If not, after that decade of service they'd get the titles to the homes signed over to them.

This system was not entirely free of drama, of course. We dismissed a manager for misconduct, but he wanted to keep the house I had built for him in the city of Lekki, which was valued at ₦480 million. We had bought the land and built it from scratch, complete with a swimming pool. It was one of the properties I handed over to AMCON to settle my debts in 2012. Surprisingly, the agency came back to me in 2019—seven years later—to say they could not take possession of the house because of legal issues. It seems that the former employee had gone to court, trying to retain the property. He was working for NNPC when I recruited him but was so unprofessional.

What this incident also shows is that being good to people does not mean they will be straight with you. There are all kinds of human beings, and you should never expect the same level of reciprocity from everyone. Doing so will just set you up for disappointment.

Zenon employees were well paid. Our salary scale was the best in the industry, even better than deep-pocketed Mobil Downstream. I had no regrets about paying them so well. I didn't want to hoard all the benefits; most of them worked as hard as I did. I wanted my people to be happy. Their official cars became theirs after four years. We took good care of our staff, but there were Judases among them. Once you can reconcile yourself to the fact that this is human nature, for better or worse, you are better able to handle any treachery.

(2) Incentives improve performance. Overall, our incentives led to better performance. You could see the smiles on the employees' faces. They never looked frustrated, which is essential for a smooth-running work environment. People want to be happy. Imagine that you have a car that regularly breaks down, sometimes in dangerous places. You can't do your work as you would like. If you have a reliable new car, you're eager to go to work in it; you even enjoy the commute. There is also the self-esteem and confidence that stems from working for a company that pays you a fantastic salary, gives you a new car and takes care of your medical expenses. I even flew certain employees abroad for treatment when they took ill. They were also getting fat bonuses. At the end of the year, I would say, "Here, go and share this ₦100 million as a performance bonus." The junior staff got a 400% bonus at Christmas time.

(3) An open-door policy encourages interaction and improvement. It was important that we had the ethos of a family spirit. At Forte Oil, we organized Christmas parties, which I attended. I deliberately didn't attend the staff's private parties, such as children's naming ceremonies, because I would have had to be at everybody's events. That would have been too stressful and demanding. If you attended one and not the other, it could create the sense that you have favourites. Being sensitive to this balance is essential. I had a good rapport with all the staff and maintained my open-door policy. The information exchange was a two-way street; I was a lot wiser for that. They had access to the Chairman, and I knew what was going on at ground level. Still, you have to recognize that even this is open to abuse. In Zenon, I noticed that because of this informal, family-like setting, some employees started coming in late. Some started dressing overly casually. In Zenon, there was nothing I could do. But in Forte Oil, they were far more disciplined. I had put a more formal, professional look and feel in place from the start.

(4) Extend a helping hand to those you value. Scholarships for children of longstanding staff won me their hearts. The kids of employees who have been with me for 20 years get scholarships. I am paying the school fees of the children of all the first-generation staff—through university, from a bachelor's degree to a master's or PhD. Only two of them have qualified so far, both drivers, but this motivates everyone to remain loyal and committed. A few of them enjoyed foreign training trips. At Forte Oil, some attended the Lagos Business School or headed to Oxford. We ran Forte Oil professionally, and provided well, so that employees were not inclined to abuse this generosity. It was no longer child's play; I had learned my lesson. Forte Oil was a public company, even though I owned 80% of its stock. We had to deliver value to our shareholders.

After I sold Forte Oil, the severance package for all those who did not want to stay on following my exit was mouth-wateringly huge. The CEO, CFO, Company Secretary, and my personal secretary were handsomely rewarded. They also sold the stock I gave them, reaping fat profits. If the people who are there now decide to depart tomorrow, it will be Ardova PLC, the company's new name since 2020, that must settle their severance package. That's the employment condition. This was part of why they were ready to work for Forte Oil—the way we structured our terms of engagement. Because I was not on a salary, I didn't get a single penny in severance. The company was going to buy me a bulletproof vehicle, but I declined. I rejected all perks. I did not even collect diesel. If the company gave me free diesel, the CEO would also take diesel. All of them would. So, I refused all the perks. I kept to my dividends.

(5) Free lunch is appreciated, and it enhances productivity. Forte Oil was *the* place to work. Everybody wanted a job there. All my friends' children wanted to work for us. The pressure was enormous. The salary scale was well above the industry average, but I told Akin to make it even more attractive. No oil company could pay what we were paying. One of the perks they loved was free lunch, every day, for everyone in the company.

There was a caterer. Frankly, I don't know how much it cost. I ate there only twice. The canteen was a bungalow at the back, and it was an excellent operation. They fed everybody. Also, there was free lunch at the depot. The CEO, CFO and everyone else ate there every day. In fact, I'd instructed the executives to eat there as a bonding move, to help sustain the family atmosphere. Previously, people had to drive far to eat because there was no restaurant of any sort nearby. They'd come back from lunch late because of traffic. It was too disruptive and stressful. Establishing a cafeteria on the premises was a good move. The staff appreciated it, and this too enhanced their productivity.

WHY I MEET POTENTIAL EMPLOYEES

At Christmas parties, I would give my employees the microphone to speak their minds. I encouraged them to open up and talk freely. If you think the company is missing an opportunity, speak up. Given the open environment we had created, they were not afraid to do so. But I made sure I did not undermine their bosses. If the CEO was firing someone, I didn't get involved. The chief executive had carte blanche to hire and fire. My only requirement was that I wanted to meet anybody about to be employed by Forte Oil before they started. It was vital for me to become familiar with them and size them up before they joined the family. We outsourced some positions, but when it came to staffing the management ranks, I talked to the applicant personally and did my assessment. I could tell many things just by looking at them: their personality, how forward they were, their composure and so forth. I'd ask probing questions about where they had come from, what they'd done, why they left their previous employer and what they saw in their future. Once they left my office, I would comment 'yes' or 'no' on each applicant. With this pre-employment exercise, I could put a face to every name. Even when I could not remember their name, I could identify the person as someone who worked for us, and this would help me guide the CEO in dealing with people and their activities. At the height of Forte Oil, we had more than 12,000 employees, including those employed indirectly, as contractors and subcontractors. With an average of 12 staff per station—a manager, pump attendants and security guards, working in two shifts—recognizing them all would have been impossible, but that initial face-to-face encounter was important to me and appreciated by all.

TAKEAWAYS

- Practice the golden rule: treat people well and you will most likely get loyalty in return
- Rewards—from simply expressing appreciation for contributors, to handsome salaries, perks and uncommon incentives—give a company the edge it needs
- Embrace openness and allow dissenting voices; you gain insight from others' perspectives

SECTION TWO

GROWTH AND EXPANSION

*FINDING FAME AND FORTUNE,
BECOMING UNSTOPPABLE, COASTING TO VICTORY*

LESSON SIX

KNOW YOUR MARKET

Our parents advise us to be thrifty and save when we start earning income. They tell us we should own property as soon as we can. They drum it into our heads that as a starting point, we should build a house for ourselves. They emphasize the significance of acquiring as much property as one can manage, wherever there is a favourable real estate market. They always stress that the best investment, the most rewarding legacy—apart from a cherished name and good breeding—is to leave property as an inheritance. They warn against living large, splurging on frivolities and chasing excessive pleasures. They always admonish us to live simply, far below our means, with warnings such as, "Don't eat with ten fingers!"

I took all this to heart. I did not go crazy with owning property. I learned about some aspects of the market early. I supervised building projects for my father. This was an education for me. My dad opened my eyes to the intricacies of construction. He filled me in on the ploys and tricks of the type of contractor who fleeces his clients—he called them *Baba Mukaila*. He described the bricklayers—the *Baba Mukailas* with their white skullcaps and acrid cigarettes—as a necessary evil because, in the end, they would deliver the goods, despite the trickery and deceit. Drama was never in short supply in the building trade.

I had a little construction experience when I embarked on having my personal house built, when I bought a plot of land on the street named for my father in 1996. A former employee of the G. Cappa construction company headed up the crew. The architect, Stephen Bola Oladele, was introduced to me by my friend Tunde. Oladele had designed his father's Queen's Drive mansion. The decision to spend extra to ensure a quality dwelling saved me a lot of headache and heartache. In 2000, when I relocated to a rented duplex on Victoria Island, I sold the house, which I'd had built for less than ₦11 million, for ₦40 million. As noted, that move cut my commute time and strategically positioned me closer to the captains of finance.

As fortune smiled on Zenon, diversification was next. Building a property portfolio came to me as naturally as breathing. Nobody prods you to start investing in property; it comes with the territory when you have extra income. As I've said, we are taught not to keep all of our money in banks, but to spread the risk across different sectors and portfolios. Friends and associates were constantly bombarding me with tips on land and buildings for sale, as they explained how lucrative real estate had become. Nigeria was experiencing an economic boom, and the population swelled in cities like Lagos, Abuja and Port Harcourt as Nigerian expatriates returned from jobs in Europe and North America.

There was also an upsurge in the middle class. After getting a good education, the upwardly mobile filled the ranks of well-paying jobs as start-ups blossomed.

My friends were heavily into real estate, building high-rises that were bursting with luxury apartments for rent or sale. My acquaintances Aliko Dangote, Tayo Amusan and Bukola Saraki were all getting rich off the go-go real estate sector of the Obasanjo years. They were pulling in huge rents and profits from sales. It was predictably the next step for me. As a younger man, I had adored my friend Tunde's father, Wahab Folawiyo. I was enamoured of his portfolio of beautiful houses in the Apapa neighbourhood of Lagos. I had the good fortune of interacting directly with this man, who was worthy of the moniker *Baba Adini*, an exalted chiefly title.

He advised me to diversify into real estate, and I decided to build luxury flats in the best sections of Lagos, Abuja and Port Harcourt. There was high demand for exclusive apartments, selling for US$2 million or more in the poshest parts of town. That niche market—the super luxury space—was my target. The mantra in real estate has always been location, location, location. In Lagos, the hot spots were Ikoyi and Victoria Island; in Abuja, it had to be Maitama. Port Harcourt was a different case: there, I bought a property that had been forfeited to the EFCC[10] by the previous owners. Apart from the fact that the choicest of locations attracted the highest rent, the next thing was not to compromise on elegance.

My target market was the cream of the expat crop and executives with exquisite taste, who were ready to pay for top-notch pads with luxurious finishing and furnishings. I hired Siji Dosekun Partnership, one of Nigeria's foremost architectural firms, for the design. For construction I turned to Cappa & D'Alberto, an old Nigerian construction company founded by Italian immigrants in 1932. I trusted them, knowing they'd deliver first-class buildings, and that I wouldn't be disappointed. Once a building in a good location passed the luxury and functionality tests, the rest was easy. Clients lined up, with their wallets in their hands.

My business model for apartment sales had me delivering a fully furnished flat for ₦80 million. On the rental side, an annual apartment lease would be about ₦16.7 million, which was equivalent to US$100,000 at the time. In five years, I'd basically made my money back, with a total income of ₦83.5 million. Meanwhile, I owned the building, essentially free and clear, and because I'd paid for first-rate construction and outfitting, it required minimal maintenance or renovation. Subsequent rent would be straight-up profit.

I founded a property development company, FO Properties, to exploit this market. At our zenith, we had over 150 flats and office complexes, and they were all occupied. In Lagos, they ranged from the Oando Building, a twin-block of 14 floors on Ajose Adeogun Street, to apartments on Cooper Road, Temple Road, Bayo Kuku Road, and Agodaba Avenue in Park View and several others. There were similarly nice residential and commercial spaces in Abuja and Port Harcourt. The property business in those days was sweet indeed.

But times have changed. The Nigerian market is a different story all these years later. Today, you need more than 35 years to recoup your costs. And, with a glut of properties and an uncertain global economy, deep-pocketed tenants have disappeared, leaving some of the buildings with just 25% occupancy. Rental flats go for as little as US$10,000 a year. I exited the market after I forfeited my holdings during the crippling recession of 2008 and my ₦220 billion debt-relief agreement with AMCON.

There are lessons to be learned from my experience in real estate. To succeed in the high-end property game, I recommend focusing exclusively on quiet, posh locations, insisting on beautiful architecture, and being willing to pay for first-class construction, with top-of-the-line décor. In my case, and among my friends who went big in real estate development, this proved to be a masterstroke, although the favourable economic environment of the time was instrumental in our success. If you want to succeed, you must know the market you choose to play in like the back of your hand. The dynamics of the sector should be your preoccupation, 24/7. If you don't stay on top of things, you will struggle.

These are my takes on making the most of any venture into real estate:

(1) Knowledge is the best starting point. Before you make a move into any sector, before starting any enterprise, begin by learning as much as you can about it. That certainly helped me in the real estate business, with FO Properties. And although I did not start Zenon with a formal feasibility study, I had a fair idea of the local fuel oil market. A few things were clear: diesel was in high demand and in short supply. As detailed earlier, my own experience spotlighted the gaps. I had to move my family into a hotel because there was no diesel to power our home's generator. It then took five days after I had paid for my supply to finally be delivered. And a broken-down old truck leaked fuel onto my yard. As soon as I decided to get into the business, clean it up and make diesel supply less cumbersome, I started calling insiders and consulting them. That led to the realization that the entire country depended on diesel, and this colossal market was woefully underserved.

After I started Zenon, I came to learn that all the textile factories sprawling across the Ilupeju, Aswani, Apapa and Oshodi neighbourhoods of Lagos lived on diesel. And most of the other prominent manufacturing concerns, which needed their factories operational 24/7, had a similar dependency. With the government monopoly unable to fill the need, the magnitude of the opportunity became apparent. The entire country was hungry for diesel to power homes, offices, factories, mills and fishing trawlers, as well as every sort of vehicle and heavy-duty equipment. That fired my passion.

(2) Knowledge gives you an edge. I quickly found out who had diesel to sell. It was the middleman who offloaded in bulk, who didn't get down into the nitty-gritty of delivering to end-users. They didn't want the headache of logistics, buying vans or drums, or investing in storage tanks. Many were content to look for bulk buyers—honest and trustworthy customers, with cash—to sell their allocation to and pocket the commission. And that buyer was me. All the hawkers of allocation papers needed was a connection in the NNPC—be it a girlfriend or an uncle, or someone with ties to the presidential villa or the National Assembly. I learned who wanted to sell allocation papers, and who, like Obat Oil & Petroleum, had the product in their tanks, ready for me to buy on a retail basis, in one fell swoop.

Sometimes, I would buy from importers like First Fuel's AbdulRahman AbdulRazaq, who at the time of this writing is Governor of Kwara State. I was lucky to buy large quantities of diesel from him, and he gave me generous discounts. There were only two independent retailers, apart from the majors. They were Flame Petroleum, which I mentioned earlier, and Sea Petroleum, owned by Senator Stella Oduah. Knowing where to buy allocation or bulk retail and cultivating a warm relationship with my suppliers and rivals, provided the edge that helped me become a prominent player.

(3) Knowledge affords you a more precise, long-focus vision. As the weeks rolled into months and years, I became a keen student of the diesel sector. This understanding of the market, and knowledge of my competition, helped clarify my vision. When I started selling to individual homes out of drums, my father was my first customer. I delivered ten 200-litre drums to his house in the Odoragunsin Ward, in the town of Epe.

Suffice it to say, the humble early days of riding in the van I've described set the stage for so much more. I learned the language of the trade and the metrics. If the volume a truck carried was 33,000 litres, I used to tell myself that one day, I would have ₦33 million, and then ₦33 billion, ₦330 billion, and eventually ₦3.3 trillion. I played around with the figures, amusing myself with endless multiples of the number 33.

From the earliest days of Zenon, I knew it was a business that required close attention. Though still a novice, hauling two drums in the back of the van, I was ready to figure it out and put in the hard work. I learned the processes and procedures, such as where to register the business and how to get a licence from the DPR, the industry regulators.

(4) Knowledge saves you resources and time. Being knowledgeable is essential, in order to know where to reliably get whatever you need, at the best price. It was easy to make a 200% profit if you knew where to buy. Diesel was then ₦12 per litre, and we were able to sell for as high as ₦25 or ₦30. Being grounded in the business further opened my eyes. After buying from First Fuel, I learned that Tony Onoh of Eurafric, with a depot in Ibakem that belonged to Mamemo Ibru, also sold bulk retail. I started buying from him, too.

An entrepreneur must be familiar with a wide range of supply sources to get the best bargain. It pays to know about market capacity, such as how much customers are consuming in aggregate, the low and high seasons, and much more. I met people in our industry who didn't know that 1,164 litres of oil make a tonne, which was the capacity of a shipload. Conversely, you needed to be able to divide the tonnage by 1,164 to get the number of litres in each shipment, and work through a series of other calculations from there. That was necessary to factor out what you'd be paying, your subsequent markup, how many customers you'd be able to service with that load, the profit you'd make, and so forth. That was the heartbeat of your business.

I learned that sales were high during the Christmas period, because households kept their generators running, and many people travelled across the country at that time in diesel-powered buses. During the rainy season, demand was low because public power often improved, with better performance from the hydro stations, which stabilized electric power generation.

The knowledge I acquired over time also led me to realize tremendous efficiencies, savings and profitability, as I acquired four ships in quick succession. These included: MT Sir Michael (8,500 tonnes); MT Lady Doja (17,200 tonnes)—a flat-bottom craft that was one of only five in the world (with the advantage of berthing in shallow waters); MT Nana (22,000 tonnes); and MT Zenon Conquest (10,300 tonnes). They all ferried diesel from larger tankers that could not berth at the port.

Understanding the market and my competition gave me insight into when to empty and when to fill tanks and ships, and when to sell. People paid in advance, and at one point I had ₦2 billion from depositors awaiting diesel. They liked to settle in advance because it was a first-to-pay, first-to-load proposition. I had built a reputation for trust, so people were confident that they'd get their product, as agreed. With the first-come, first-served promise, I was also giving them an attractive incentive to engage, pay and come back again.

USE TODAY'S ISSUES AS INSPIRATION FOR TOMORROW'S EXPANSION

The expansion of the business started with trucks, but we still grappled with irregular supply from tank farms and those peddling allocations. And only two companies always had diesel—Marca and Webeco, an oil and gas firm originally founded to provide the tar-like petroleum derivative bitumen for road construction. But Webeco, whose primary focus was not diesel, only had storage capacity for 5,000 tonnes, which wasn't as reliable a source as Marca, which could stockpile 20,000 tonnes. Many of the suppliers talked a big game, but dragged their feet in providing the goods, after collecting money for an essential commodity that was in high demand. Delays—often up to four weeks—stemmed from slow turnover by the NNPC, since the troubled refineries were shut down and the national oil monopoly had to import. Once you gave them a bank draft or cashier's cheque they could confirm, they promptly loaded your product. In just one two-month period, I did ₦600 million in business with them.

As described earlier, a seemingly trusted provider let me down at a crucial moment when they wouldn't take a personal cheque after the banks had closed for the day. That caused me to lose an order for nearly ₦20 million. After that, I knew I could no longer depend on bulk suppliers—I couldn't continue to rely on this unpredictable model. How could I subject myself to the whims and caprices of unreliable dealers? That led to me building the storage tanks I have detailed previously.

HOW TO KNOW YOUR MARKET AND COMPETITION

There are well-tested ways of knowing your market and competition, which vary by sector. For the segments I've engaged in, apart from the stock market (financial, petroleum, property and power), here are the methodologies I relied on:

(1) Study the basics and learn how things work. As soon as I entered the diesel market in 1999, its vast and lucrative nature was immediately apparent. It was clear to me that this was something I'd be involved in for a long time, potentially expanding into sales, transport and storage. And when the opportunities presented by deregulation became clear, I began importing, and layered on a trading company, shipping agency and insurance brokerage firm.

(2) Invest in information and intelligence gathering. News (and gossip) travels fast, and if you know where to go and who to court, you can catch wind of some incredibly valuable information for your business. I was friends with my bankers, and those who operated in the supply and distribution chains. I regularly interacted with tanker drivers at the depot, and essentially everybody else associated with the various aspects of my business. And they all had useful information.

News of Jean-Claude Meyer's cancer was not widely known at first, because he'd been abroad for about three years, but it eventually filtered into town. His company, Marca International, controlled the local market.

We'd had our ups and downs—he was an early supplier, who helped me get my business going, but we also clashed at times. When he passed away at age 47, his death created a vacuum. His son, Olivier, who stepped in to manage the business, wasn't interested in the oil industry. I sensed that if I offered him the right price, he would sell.

Marca's depot, built for ₦300 million, was then worth ₦800 million, and I offered the son ₦2.8 billion. The offer was too good to be true, and Olivier thought it was a joke. He took out pen and paper, scribbled out '2,800,000,000' and sat there counting the zeros.

Market intelligence had made me confident that he would sell. I'd also learned over the years that if an offer is high enough, people are willing to sell pretty much anything.

Olivier Meyer gladly accepted my offer, and I bought the Marca International depot with financing from Zenith Bank (and with subsequent support from Intercontinental Bank).

(3) Expert insight can set you on the path to greater success. When Zenon collapsed and I needed to start again by restructuring AP PLC, it was clear that I had to engage an expert. I needed the advice, counsel and guidance of a veteran in the oil sector. The brief was simple and straightforward: I wanted to basically sack myself, rebrand, start from scratch and do it right.

Who did I choose? Olumide Onakoya, who had for years been the MD of the Mobil Downstream operation in Nigeria. He'd been responsible for everything that happened between oil and gas production and the point of sale. And he went to work, detailing what we needed to start anew. He was surprised I was ready to pay ₦7 billion in severance packages to my old staff, but I knew what I wanted. He charged me ₦100 million for his services, and I was more than willing to pay, because I knew how invaluable his expertise would be. And it proved to be just that. From December 2010, when we rebranded as Forte Oil PLC, until the company's sale in 2019, we ran a professional and hugely profitable enterprise.

From there on out, it was all about market research, strategy and competent decision making. We didn't even consider bidding on the purchase of Geregu Power PLC in 2013, until the experts we engaged for US$13 million in research and consulting fees had rigorously examined what we should buy and the terms of any sale. Acquiring the 414-megawatt electrical power generator in south-central Nigeria's Kogi State has paid off handsomely.

(4) Study financial reports of public companies and follow their activities. Back then, publicly quoted companies were required to publish quarterly financial statements in newspapers, in addition to their annual profit and loss reporting. This public disclosure allowed me to learn all I needed to know about the oil sector and its top players. My major competitors—Total, Mobil, Texaco, Conoil and Oando—released their financial statements, and I studied them to see where the market was headed. I read the before-and after-tax profit details and scrutinized gross income and losses. To track the performance of banks, my friend Segun at GTBank showed me how to look for interest income when reading their financial statements. That is where they make money. CNBC, Bloomberg and other business media also provided essential insights into what everyone was doing, good, bad and otherwise. Dedicating time to following developments in the business world, and scanning the horizon for what lay ahead, opened my eyes to how the top dogs played the game.

(5) Keep an eye on the stock market. Daily monitoring of companies' share prices presented a clear view of their strengths and weaknesses. And over time, one could deduce whether they were on the path of profitability or loss.

TAKEAWAYS

- If you do not know your market and the competition, your business will soon be history. You cannot survive if you don't grasp the basics. That is the starting point. Knowing where the sector is heading, and spotting the opportunities, allows you to enjoy the benefits
- You can see clearly and plan well when you understand the language, terminology and metrics of the business. You stay abreast of what is happening and take advantage of the circumstances

- With concerted intelligence gathering, you have an edge over others, because you know what they're all up to. This allows you to get a leg up on the competition
- Expert knowledge saves you time, energy and money in the long run. Experts provide a long-term view of possibilities, to help your decision making
- Published financial reports, share prices, and company and sector news will sharpen your business acumen and help you anticipate developments

Nonetheless, a lot of short-term movement in the market is emotion-driven, and I fell victim to that. I bought shares based on relationships and continued to hold on to them when I should have sold. I paid dearly for my hesitation. As the pros do, I should have simply set a target of doubling my investment and exited while the going was good.

LESSON SEVEN

HONE YOUR USP LIKE A MAESTRO

I was making my name in the diesel business. Zenon was well received, and we'd cornered a sizeable percentage of the market, with public perception on the rise as our branded cars, cruising around the city of Lagos, advertised our services. Those whose businesses and homes depended on this fuel valued us beyond words. But the market was huge, and I wanted to increase our share of it. I was not motivated by greed. I had the product in mass quantities, at the best prices, and had the biggest clients buying from me in volume.

Zenon had developed an unbeatable customer service experience. Once you had a taste of our USP—our unique selling proposition—you became a faithful fan. We were there for you; the product was in your tanks long before your previous supply ran out. All at the lowest prices.

As noted earlier, we already had Dangote Group, Cadbury, Nestlé, WAPCo, Nigerian Bottling Company (with Coca-Cola as its cash cow) and Flour Mills of Nigeria as customers. But we had only a little slice of Julius Berger, the big structural engineering and construction company, which consumed up to ₦1 billion (about US$10 million at the time) worth of diesel a month. We wanted a bigger slice of that pie, and got to work on a deal.

Known for building most of Nigeria's infrastructure since going into business in 1965, Julius Berger practically controlled the top of the construction sector, building roads, bridges and skyscrapers for state and federal governments, and private agencies that serviced the government and for-profit organizations. The company delivered the best and the most durable works and was in high demand. With an abundance of heavy-duty equipment, cranes, tractors and trucks requiring diesel, in addition to their offices and operations sites, its business would be remarkably lucrative. Julius Berger could comfortably sustain a diesel-supply company on its own. You could go to bed, sleep soundly, dream merrily and wake up rich.

By the time I started formulating plans to win a fair share of this business, Total, Oando and Mobil were already big suppliers to Julius Berger. The ultimate win would be to become their exclusive diesel supplier. I had witnessed the headaches caused by the *Baba Mukaila*, those unscrupulous construction contractors my father had first warned me about. Apart from hungering for the big contract, I knew I had to get a first-rate construction company to build my office building on Victoria Island and my house in Ikoyi. They were massive projects that I couldn't afford to gamble on. The office was designed by a German referred to me by Julius Berger and the house by an Italian, Massimo Vallotto.

Once I made up my mind that it was better to spend more and sleep soundly, with the guarantee of well-finished buildings, I opted for Julius Berger for my own construction needs and set up a meeting with their procurement manager. I bounced the big idea off him. "If I give you the contract to build my office and house, will you let me supply all the diesel you need?"

He was immediately excited, because the terms of the proposal were compelling, and my personal projects would attract other high net-worth home-building clients. The diesel contract was enormous, worth ₦3.5 billion (US$35 million at the time). In the end, I faced no serious opposition. I had as much diesel as they wanted, my prices were the best, and my service and support were first-class. What's more, my USP—which we'll talk more about below—towered above all others.

I was ecstatic when we signed the contract. It had a 20-year maintenance clause for the buildings. I paid the deposit and, in turn, received exclusive rights to provide Julius Berger's diesel supply of some ₦1 billion a month. I was winning on many fronts, making money with their business, and getting buildings with their elegant, signature finish. Once the contract commenced, it was a mutually beneficial engagement. Both parties were quite happy.

A few months into the deal, I suggested a barter arrangement. I told the manager, "Since you owe me money for the diesel we've already supplied, let's net off from the contract cost, and after that, we can operate on a barter arrangement."

He thought he'd misheard. "You mean the diesel you've delivered should serve as payment for the buildings?" "Yes," I replied.

In less than a week, this was approved. There was no better guarantee that I'd provide the construction giant with its full supply of diesel. This far exceeded what I had planned or could have imagined. That was the hand of God at play. To show good faith, I locked up a tank solely for Julius Berger and instructed my people, "Never sell that product to anyone else, no matter the temptation." Any time this client wanted diesel, we had a more than ample supply ready and waiting for them. We also delivered to them anywhere they wanted in Nigeria, in trucks and barges.

At the time, Zenon was bringing in between four and seven ships' worth of diesel a month, so there was no question of any shortfalls as Julius Berger worked on major construction projects at a rapid clip. On their side, the customer had locked in the contract cost. It was fixed, no matter the vagaries of the market. The deal was the unusual breakthrough we all pray for in our businesses. It grew from a 35% chunk of our business to 90% of our total volume, pulling in around ₦3.3 billion a month. Our USP was sharply honed, and we continually explored additional advantages we could deliver. We were laughing all the way to the bank.

The concept of the USP was introduced by American advertising pioneer Rosser Reeves in the 1940s, although it was given that name much later. That came in 1961, again from Reeves. He stated that the object of advertising is to conclude a sale by showing the value of your product to consumers—the one reason they should buy your product and not your competitors' offerings. The concept was expanded into a broader business concept by Theodore Levitt, a German-American economist, to comprise all that differentiates a company's product from that of its competitors, such as price, being the first of its kind, quality or the solutions it provides. It encompasses everything you're offering that the competitors cannot.

From Femco to Centre Force, Zenon, AP, Forte Oil and Geregu Power, I learned that successful businesses thrive based on the unique value they deliver. In my case, this was the wholesome customer service experience we provided. We always strived to exceed expectations, to give more than we promised, and to be respectful and friendly. To that end, here are my biggest tips:

(1) Low pricing will entice customers to try your product. To make consumers look our way, we promised attractive prices and ready supplies, and we delivered without any problems. Those who gulp diesel in large volumes always look for bargains. Provided the product is genuinely sourced, not adulterated, readily available and meets their specifications, a lower price will give you an advantage. Zenon had the best rates because of the huge volume we handled. We were also in control of the supply and distribution chain, with our trading company and shipping agency, insurance and trucking business, storage tank farm and four ships.

By scaling up my capacity, I could take less profit and pass better prices on to my customers. I was not greedy, so I worked with tiny margins that others would have struggled with. As business boomed, I invested in supply chains that gave me better control of availability and pricing. And with deregulation, I mastered the intricacies of the industry to my advantage. I could lower prices at will. As I've described, I soon controlled 93% market share, and even the majors, like Total and Oando, bought diesel from me. They became middlemen.

(2) Prompt delivery and efficiency are always appreciated. Cash flow sustains businesses. You must generate sales so you can cover your production costs, and whatever is left is profit. In a bulk commodity business, without selling sizeable quantities, the business will be in jeopardy. And to conclude a sale, you have to offer your customer more benefits than your competitors. One of the advantages I offered was unfettered access. Customers could reach me, or any of the staff who serviced the account, at literally any time, knowing that the product was just a few hours from their tanks.

Prompt delivery and efficiency were key selling points. If I had a 10 am delivery scheduled, we were sure to be there before that time. I ensured that the truck was loaded the night before, and that the journey started early, to beat traffic and unforeseen problems. If, for any reason, we couldn't make it on time, we kept customers abreast of the situation, apologized sincerely, and provided a new delivery time. This flow of information gave the customers confidence and peace of mind. They knew we were dependable and that they could count on us. We would always be there for them.

To win the confidence of big consumers of diesel, like the manufacturing plants that can't cease production, because of the cost and pain associated with having to restart machines, we sent dozens of diesel-laden trucks to their factories, even prior to specific orders coming in. The Zenon trucks lined up at designated spots, in full view of the factories, ready to discharge at the word 'go.' From Cadbury to Nigerian Bottling Company, we developed a reputation for being visibly there, ready to deliver an unceasing supply of diesel.

(3) Personal customer relations go a long way. One way to improve the customer service experience is to personalize your interaction with clients. Early on, I learned the value of personally courting and wooing customers. I sharpened that skill as I grew into the business of selling diesel.

In those earliest days, riding along in the van with my driver, I interacted with the security guards or anyone else who took delivery. We chatted, got to know each other, and came to have that up-close, in-person relationship. As the business grew, I taught my staff how to speak to customers, win their confidence, and smooth out the relationship with those who paid us money for our product and service. My employees knew how to open closed doors and speak to those in charge of procurement.

They knew what price and conveniences to offer. They learned to maintain cordial and professional working relationships with those who were important to their work.

(4) Quick decision-making aids service delivery. Because I was the sole owner of Zenon, I had the advantage of being able to take swift decisions that gave me an edge over my more bureaucratic, inflexible competitors. I could make a big decision and begin executing it immediately. I could change the price in an instant, or quickly divert supplies to a customer with an urgent need.

Neither Chevron, Mobil nor Total could act as quickly. They had more rigid, cumbersome processes to follow, with formally regimented decision making. Sometimes they had to get approval from headquarters in the US or France on a particular matter, which could take days or weeks. These multinationals had a board of directors in Nigeria, but the majority of their shareholders were abroad and major decisions emanated from there. Even when my petroleum business became more structured, with Forte Oil PLC, we still cleaved closely to the concept of streamlined decision making. My managers were well aware of the way I reasoned. They could make independent decisions, based on my philosophy and style, while taking full responsibility for their actions.

(5) Make use of payment incentives where possible. Once we began dealing with larger volumes, our objective was clear: become the sole supplier of every substantial diesel consumer. Given our size, we had to service those with high consumption, or our business model would fall apart. To land those massive companies I've mentioned, we had to offer more value than our competitors.

We started by providing 30-day credit when the product was not scarce. It became a standard incentive for big, reputable companies. They would pay, so why not extend a credit line to make Zenon a more attractive supplier? Others couldn't take that risk, out of fear of some catastrophic breakdown or because it would jeopardize their short-term cash flow. Sometimes, if the competition matched our credit incentive, we stretched the terms out to 90 days. It was a win-win: we had to sell the product that was being continually replenished in our tanks, and we kept our major customers happy.

(6) Hire focused, motivated go-getters. We ran a company driven by targets. The sales team, with new cars to facilitate their pitches to procurement managers, had goals to meet and used all the resources at their disposal to win sales. I regularly spoke with the head of each department, explaining my vision of how we would conquer the market. If there was a particular segment or client we were targeting, we researched their payment style first, and if they were worth getting, we moved in.

We had personable men and women on the sales team, who worked hard to bring in new customers and win accounts away from our competitors. And they did. Our company's stellar reputation for price, abundant inventory and prompt, efficient delivery made their jobs relatively easy.

(7) Don't neglect branding. I have always been passionate about sales—the whole process of making your pitch, winning over customers and closing deals. And one of the best ways to sell more is to work on the public's perception of the company. It's easy to get prospects to buy your product when they know of your positive image and trust you to deliver on your promises. To this end, the unique Zenon name generated curiosity and exciting buzz, fueled by our beautiful logo, with the 'O' replaced by a drop of yellow, orange and red oil.

When we rolled out our new Volkswagen cars onto the roads of Lagos—Audi A8s, Polos, Boras, Touaregs and Golfs, emblazoned with our logo—they were hard to miss. Even if you weren't a customer, Zenon had claimed its spot in the public consciousness. It had a recognizable name, and its business was known. When we started acquiring our DAF trucks, they too were difficult to ignore. With ample word-of-mouth on our commitment to excellent customer service, our branding made the job of selling diesel easier.

Budding entrepreneurs would be wise to remember that you enhance such perception further if you create an air of myth around your persona. You are not supposed to be like an open book—people might take advantage of your predictability or take it for granted. Instead, position yourself where you want to be seen, avoid overexposure and sell a little mystery. Being unpredictable also helps in negotiations. No one should be able to tell what you will settle for in deals. If they do not know, they're likely to offer more, to ensure that the deal you're working towards is worth your while.

(8) Invest in youthful management with a vision for tomorrow. The emergence of Forte Oil from AP taught us a lesson the hard way. Forte Oil had to start out on a clean note. I changed the name to two words, with initials that unmistakably match mine, and it was clear that I had to give it my all to ensure that the enterprise succeeded.

Part of the fresh start was bringing in a young team with a clearer vision. They understood what they needed to do to rebuild, move forward and succeed. We started by rebranding the stations, making them more colourful to attract customers. We then introduced 24-hour service in some of the stations. We also engaged a brand ambassador to propagate our USP.

With the above steps, our 2% share of fuels and 3% share of lubricants in the downstream sector grew to almost 20% in fuels and 14% in lubricants, as we climbed from the bottom of the ladder to number two in that space. In 2007, when we bought it, AP had about 270 stations. We'd go on to build that out to more than 480 locations. The business evolved to include FO Solar, petrol, aviation fuel, engine oil, property, upstream oil services, AP Ghana, diesel and Geregu Power.

As mentioned earlier, we paid US$13 million for expert analysis before purchasing majority shares in Geregu Power PLC in 2013. We had to be sure of what we were buying. The consultants advised us to drop the idea of acquiring distribution companies—DisCos, as they are known in Nigeria—and buy a GenCo, a generation company. That saved us some heartache and billions in additional outlay. We'd also learned a lot from the recession-related debt calamity of 2008, which so disastrously impacted Zenon. Instead of borrowing, we chose equity investment from my foreign partner and the State Grid Corporation of China (SGCC/ SMEPC). SGCC/SMEPC initially acted as consultants but later became equity partners. The only loans we got amounted to about ₦50 billion from commercial banks, and another ₦10 billion from the Bank of Industry,[11] at a single-digit interest rate. (Both loans have since been repaid in full.) We again had the presence of mind to have our loans converted to Nigerian currency by the Central Bank. That saved us the pain of precipitous devaluation, from US$1/ ₦197 to US$1/ ₦360.

Retaining the management and staff we inherited allowed for a smooth takeover. We then retrained and re-orientated the team to create a new culture of performance. The crew were all former Power Holding Corporation of Nigeria personnel who knew the job. After retraining, the management style changed as we reengineered processes and assessment metrics. The financing structure was different because we retooled to plough all the money back into servicing our debt.

HOW BUDDING ENTREPRENEURS CAN DEVELOP A WINNING USP

(1) **Integrity is everything.** A new entrepreneur, aspiring to make a name and fortune, should focus on honing three selling propositions: integrity, integrity and integrity. That's the first (and second and third) and most important thing. It opens doors for you. To succeed, and do so in a big way, you need people and banks. People will partner and do business with you; banks will finance your ventures and help your enterprise expand. Once it becomes known that your word is your bond, you can go places. If you aren't considered dependable and trustworthy, you're guaranteed to *not* go far in business.

Some businesspeople are crooked, taking advantage of customers and banks, and only appear successful. At the end of the day, they fail. Everything collapses, as they cannot sustain whatever gains and advantages they had. Integrity is paramount to enduring success; it is woven into its DNA. Integrity will propel you, with the help of people and financial institutions who are downright eager to be associated with you.

(2) Work harder, and smarter, at selling what is in high demand. It takes more than hard work to succeed when you're starting out and trying to grow a business. First, it is crucial to choose or develop a product that's either in high demand or that has a solid niche market with high returns. Once you have a product that can generate enormous income, you can take advantage of the high returns to turn your life and business around.

But that demands more than hard work. Apart from putting in long hours—a hard-driving entrepreneur's workday can be as long as 12 hours or more—you have to *work smart*. Yes, you have to put in the hours, but more importantly, you must use your time wisely. It's all about concentrating on the critical elements that can give your business a boost. You have to know what everyone else in your sector knows, and then figure out those key differentiators that nobody else has thought of. You must source, internalize and process information that will help you. If you sleep too long or party too hard, the days will fly by, and the weeks will pass, and you'll find that you've gotten nowhere. You must be keenly tuned in to information that will assist your growth and put it to good use.

(3) Take time off to reflect and meditate. This may sound counterintuitive, given what we just said about keeping your nose to the grindstone, but you also need to take time off from your regular workday to reflect and meditate. You might start with half an hour every day, when you're able to be alone in a quiet spot. This is for you to mindfully assess your position, concerns and future. This spiritual exercise clears the mind, centres you and rejuvenates the soul. You can then slowly increase the duration of these exercises, until you can take at least a week off to recharge and reset. The more time you spend on your own, the more creative inspiration is likely to come to you.

Even now, I still take time off from my daily schedule to be mindful and meditate. Every month, I take about a week off to clear my mind of all the clutter, plan and strategize. I'm not distracted, and I can think. I exercise, meditate and reflect. And I have time to read. I've read books about trailblazers as diverse as Howard Hughes, John D. Rockefeller, Colonel Sanders, J. P. Morgan, Aristotle Onassis, Adnan Khashoggi, Andrew Carnegie and Dale Carnegie. These private, thoughtful sessions give birth to visions, ideas and plans that I then perfect with my team. I also make sure to write things down. I've always kept notebooks where I jot down thoughts and ideas.

(4) Capitalize on opportunities. There are always opportunities lurking just round the corner. If you watch keenly and listen attentively, you will become aware of your ideal next business direction. When you work hard and work smart, avoiding distraction and frivolities, you're more able to key into these opportunities. You can see how to minimize your costs, and add extra value to your customers' experiences, all to your benefit. Knowing what to do to control the supply and process chains relevant to your business, and deciding what to outsource, becomes clearer and easier.

TAKEAWAYS

- Identifying a winning USP is vital to business survival and success, and knowing what works will give you an edge. I remember how we did two things to improve the business we attracted at my father's Impact Press. I convinced my dad to employ a white man in the sales department. Due to various historical and social factors, Nigerian clients at the time seemed to prefer white executives over black professionals. It was a reality every pragmatist needed to take into account. And, we printed a sample cover of a foreign magazine. We then showed customers the original magazine and our production, asking them which was of higher quality. Most chose ours over the original. When we told them their first choice was our work, they were already convinced of our capabilities. My wife's dry-cleaning company also employed a white man at the beginning, as finicky clients of that era were more likely to find such a person more trustworthy. For every business, you have to know the USP to develop, and the advantages of exploring it to the fullest.
- Pricing is the most significant USP you can adopt to win over customers. With a lower price, most will give your product a try. And because Zenon took advantage of large volumes to even out differential and losses from pricing lower, we quickly attracted customers.

- We could deliver as promised, on time, with better efficiency, providing a customer experience that was difficult to replicate.
- We were just a phone call away from our customers, who had 24-hour access. We maintained a personal relationship with those who aided our sales and prosperity.
- Our fast decision making improved our chances of quickly acquiring available supplies, because we could lower prices in an instant. It even allowed us to offer 30-or 90-day credit.
- We had the advantage of a focused, youthful team with a clear vision, to lead us into a beautiful future.
- With a winning name and logo, displayed on vehicles seen out and about in our market, branding helped position the company and generate sales.

LESSON EIGHT

HAVE ROLE MODELS AND MENTORS

I adored my father. When I think about him, I always feel a smile forming on my face. I remember his determining presence in my life, his soft and gentle admonitions, the lessons and aphorisms that escaped his lips. To this day, they lovingly ring in my ears. As I matured in business and in life, I eagerly embraced his advice and gingerly walked in his footsteps. This proved helpful beyond estimation when I found myself mired in seemingly insurmountable problems. My admiration for my father, his life and his legacy, is immense.

Throughout my life, I've had the good fortune of meeting and interacting with illustrious people of means. I rubbed elbows with those who possessed enormous wealth, power and influence. I learned from them at close quarters, one-on-one. Yet, my father was on another level. He lived simply, honourably and humbly, to an almost embarrassing degree. Despite all the opportunities along his path, and the blessings the Lord showered on him, he remained untainted. And he was successful by any measure. My dad was quite simply a teacher like no other. Patient and circumspect, he always looked at the bigger picture.

My father—the larger-than-life journalist, public relations guru, printing entrepreneur, philanthropist, reluctant politician and ninth governor of Lagos State—left a substantial legacy that is impossible to ignore. He taught me virtually everything that has defined my life. More than anybody else, he mentored me prudently, allowing me to make mistakes I could learn from. He planted confidence and self-belief in my young and impressionable mind, and gave me wings to soar. I feel lucky to have learned from him and grateful to have been so close to him, studying the ways of the world and how to stay many steps ahead. I was a dutiful student of the Sir Michael Otedola School of Life.

He had under his belt so much knowledge and insight, gained after surviving treachery and betrayal. It was a long journey, from his days under the titan of politics and public administration, Chief Obafemi Awolowo, for whom he worked from 1959-1964; to his time at Mobil, from 1964-1977, from which he retired and later became a consultant to after losing his gratuity (an end of service lump sum payment) to a dishonest friend. He went on to establish Impact Press, and work as a reputable printer after getting a loan from Union Bank and starting his life afresh; and on to politics, from 1991-1993, where his deputy unsuccessfully connived to have him removed from office.

Through it all, my dad maintained an equanimity only surpassed by his unwavering kindness.

At this point, it's a good idea to define mentors, protégés and the concept of mentoring. One should keep in mind that mentors are different from role models. For me, a mentor is an older, successful player in your field of interest who teaches and guides you regularly on the rules of the game and its tricks. You must meet periodically, where the mentor will take you through the routes to success and back alleys of failure. The mentor is the one who imparts knowledge, and the protégé is the one who receives it. Both ultimately learn from one another.

On the other hand, role models are inspirational figures you might study and emulate, to try and replicate their achievements and success. They do not have to enjoy any personal relationship with you, and you've likely never even met. The term role model is of more recent vintage than many think. It was coined by the American academic Robert K. Merton, considered the founding father of modern sociology, and became popular only in the 1970s.

The mentor brings many attributes to the table because he walks the talk. He guides patiently and teaches sympathetically, ensuring that you process and learn before moving on to the next stage. But the protégé also displays some qualities that make the sessions worthwhile and rewarding.

(1) Mentors will help you along the way to success. My father efficiently performed the role of a mentor, perhaps unconsciously at first. Recall how he nudged his friends and associates to let me cut their nails. And how, when I asked for one of his briefcases as my school bag, he obliged. There were countless other examples, all helping to move me forward, propelling me towards my destiny.

Discerning but easygoing, his support when I opted out of high school softened my grieving mum's heart. She was inconsolable when she learned I wasn't going back to school. In her eyes, I was jeopardizing a future that was all but assured. "*Olorun l'omo ise asela*," my dad reassured her. Only the Almighty knows which endeavours are rewarding. He saw what no one else perceived. My mother only calmed down when she grasped how comfortable and unperturbed my father was with my decision.

As described earlier, the only subjects I'd paid any attention to through secondary school were business-related. I was fascinated by factories, and how machines worked together in perfect harmony to produce goods. I was also enthralled with private and public companies, pondering the history of retailers like Sears, Roebuck and Co., and looked forward to lessons in commerce. In hindsight, if I'd gone on to the University of Lagos or the London School of Economics, would I be where I am today? I could have studied mass communications and followed my father's path. But God has his reasons and looks at things differently. He does not rate graduates higher than non-graduates. He blesses whomever he pleases.

A degree is not a criterion for success before God. He gives you a purpose and expects fulfilment. He can only direct: "You, go into the military and fulfil your mission." "You, go into the business space and change lives and fortunes." Many wealthy Nigerians—from Chief Adeola Odutola, the first president of the Manufacturers' Association of Nigeria, and Prince Samuel Adedoyin of Doyin Group of Industries, to Alhaji Razak Okoya of the Eleganza Group—did not attend university in those days. Blessed with inherent intelligence, a capacity for enduring a punishing schedule, feverishly discerning and hot in pursuit of opportunities many could not see, these moguls set themselves apart despite their background.

I later found out how many successful people around the globe don't have degrees. I was pleasantly surprised that being university educated hardly counts as a requirement for conquering the realm of business.

Reading about these game changers warmed my heart:

- John Davison Rockefeller (1839-1937) was considered America's all-time wealthiest man, with a net worth of US$418 billion in 2019 dollars. The founder of Standard Oil Company went to work at age 16. At its peak, his company controlled more than 90% of the US oil market. It later split into 34 entities, including ExxonMobil and Chevron Corporation .
- Henry Ford (1863-1947), with no formal education in engineering or business, built his first car in 1896. He left the family's farm at 16 to become an apprentice in a Detroit machine shop. The revolutionary industrialist, who pioneered mass production in assembly lines, transformed global transportation.
- Soichiro Honda (1906-1991) quit school at 15, becoming an apprentice auto repairman in Tokyo. He spent six years learning the trade and returned home at 22 to start an auto repair shop. First producing piston rings for Toyota in 1937, he founded the Honda Technical Research Institute in 1946, and in 1948 produced motorized bicycles with his Honda Motor Company. Motorcycles followed in 1949, and cars in 1963.
- Raymond Albert Kroc (1902-1984) dropped out of high school at 15, and during World War I became a Red Cross ambulance driver. He joined the fledgling McDonald's hamburger stand business in 1954 and opened his first McDonald's in Illinois in 1955. In 1961, he bought the company from founders Richard and Maurice McDonald, for US$2.7 million. He transformed the brand, turning it into a global behemoth, with 2021 revenues of US$23.2 billion.
- William Henry Gates III (born 1955) is from Seattle, Washington, where his father was an attorney. He studied law at Harvard but dropped out

after two years. The co-founder of Microsoft, with its transformational technologies, would become one of only three people in the world whose net worth exceeded US$100 billion.

I could go on listing the successes of other dropouts: Richard Branson, Larry Ellison, Steve Jobs, Jan Koum, Michael Dell, Mark Zuckerberg and so many more. The point is that I was in good company, without even realizing it. While formal education is certainly a valid choice that works for many, it is by no means a requirement for getting ahead in business. However, I do recommend having at least one mentor, and learning from them as much as you can.

(2) Mentors give you hands-on, real-world experience. At the time I dropped out of school, these illustrious men and their achievements were not points I could advance to convince my mum. No one I knew personally had chosen to leave school and pursue a different course. My classmates were already in upper sixth form, set to sit for their A-level exams, ready to sail through university and settle into respectable professions. It was unthinkable for the son of educated parents to even consider dropping out. It was *hara-kiri*—ritual suicide.

But my mentor, my father, was understanding and patient with me. He frequently praised my emerging business capabilities, through my childhood and teenage years. And all I wanted was to understudy him and assist in all the ways I could. In fact, he'd already recruited me when he began his public relations stint with Mobil in the late 1970s. I doubled as his assistant and driver as he worked at the Victoria Island head office of the oil giant. From our house on the mainland, I used to drive him in his Mazda, dropping him at the office by 9 am and picking him up at 5 pm every weekday. We commuted in the erratic Lagos traffic, during which he never stopped opening my eyes and mind to life's possibilities as he regaled me with stories and lessons.

He wanted to keep an eye on his restless protégé, as well as save time and money, by enlisting me as a driver. As I've noted, he'd lost his savings to a dishonest friend with whom he had partnered.

And now, he was back treading on his home turf. After ferrying him to work every day, I stayed in the car, listening to music on the radio and learning about the entertainers of the day from presenters like Benson Idonije, who had been the first manager of Afrobeat superstar Fela Aníkúlápó Kuti. As my father worked with his erstwhile Mobil colleagues, Ogbeni Oja Bayo Kuku and Chief Godwin T. S. Adokpaye, I thought about my future and slept. I did not know what lay ahead.

My life took a different turn, and I entered a more joyous phase, when my father set up Impact Press. I was fascinated by the whole process and thought I had found my forte. I was enthralled by the big German-engineered Heidelberg machines—the single-colour KORD and two-colour SORDZ printing presses—as they were being assembled.

Seeing my interest, my dad was more than willing to pull me under his wing and assign me all sorts of errands and duties. Every day, for far longer than a three-year university education would have demanded, he taught and guided me, mentoring me with more discipline and insight than a business degree could have provided.

As the floor plan was plotted out—the mount bases for the machinery were positioned and the presses were assembled, part by part—we worked all day and slept in the office, excited to see each piece take shape. We hardly went home at all in the beginning. We'd wait in the office as workers from R. T. Briscoe, an industrial outfitter, installed, tested and tweaked the equipment. If a part was missing, or they needed to engineer a workaround, I'd dash across town to Briscoe's offices to fetch this or that.

At times, we rushed home to freshen up, pick up our breakfast or lunch in a basket, and hurry back to the business on Randle Avenue. Sometimes I'd pop out to Kas Chicken on nearby Itire Road to pick up meat pies and soft drinks. Before long, Impact Press was ready to roll, and we commenced business.

(3) Protégés should be willing to put in the work. As my father's on-the-job trainee, and as a budding professional, I was ready to play any role required. I'd do whatever was needed to help establish a thriving business that would put food on our table, clothes on our backs and improve our quality of life. My father knew he could count on me, and because I adored him to no end, I was the obedient and dutiful child who stood with him come rain or shine. I juggled the duties of labourer, driver, account clerk and cashier, estimator, marketing officer and, later, office manager.

At the time, we had an import license—a government permit allowing goods to be brought into the country—authorizing ₦200,000. I was a loader and packer, offloading paper from vehicles, arranging it in orderly batches on my head and moving it inside, along with other workers and one of my sisters. At times I had to sprint home, where we had storage space in the back, to collect reams of paper urgently needed at the press. On Sundays, I'd move the reams required for the week's jobs from the house to the press. My father found many ways to save money, with me facilitating a lot of those shortcuts.

In the early years of Impact Press, I also served as an estimator/cost analyst, providing customer quotes. I learned all the costs, involving paper weight and quantity, ink and other variables that added up to the total cost for various jobs. As we worked on almanacs, we dreamt of big companies hiring us to produce their calendars.

My duties as account clerk and cashier included keeping the register stocked and paying in cash as my father serviced the start-up loans he'd taken from Union Bank. I also served as the storekeeper, keeping inventory and dispensing production items such as rollers, blankets and inks. What's more, I was sometimes the purchasing manager. I still remember the first generator I was tasked with buying from Stag Engineering, for ₦29,000.

Since they had installed the printing equipment, R. T. Briscoe was also our go-to company for most press supplies. Over time, I worked up requisitions and placed orders for more than a thousand different items. Those were good old days, when there was an abundance of honesty and trust, and things were done with a handshake. That spirit of confidence and fairness is sorely lacking these days, with deception and fraud all too prevalent.

As the years passed, I took to sales, convinced that regular cash flow from big businesses that print yearly calendars would bolster our bottom line. My father saw my talent as a negotiator and encouraged me. He was obviously pleased as I succeeded in bringing in one new account after another. After that, it was easy to convince him that I could be a sales consultant, earning a 10-15% commission. I was tired of being a regular employee on a fixed salary. I wanted more for myself and for our family business.

And the sales and marketing push paid off handsomely. I landed many new calendar jobs, in part thanks to a tactic I described earlier: printing a replica of a European magazine, which potential clients thought looked better than the original. True, there were some jobs I could never get, like the annual calendar for Folawiyo Group, a big industrial concern. Its founder, Chief Wahab Folawiyo, preferred to print in Germany. His son, my friend Tunde, could do nothing to steer the contract our way.

(4) Mentors treat you with warmth and respect. The print shop set in motion a different relationship between my father and me. We were inseparable—I was literally always around him, at home and at the office. I came to see that we shared similar traits, especially a lowkey, quiet manner. When we turned out the lights at the office each day, usually around 7 pm, I'd gather things together and we'd drive home. We'd then watch television and discuss the day's business, and so much more, as my mother prepared dinner. We would eat together and continue chatting into the night. Dad told me stories from his life in London. He reminisced about Regent Street Polytechnic, where he graduated in 1958. He'd talk about his journalism years, at *St Pancras Chronicle*, *The Guardian* and *The Times*, where he rose to a sub-editor position. He regaled me with stories from his days as editor of *Western Nigeria Illustrated*, after he'd returned to Africa from the UK in 1959. He recalled his relationship with Chief Obafemi Awolowo and his colleagues at the Western Nigeria Broadcasting Service (1961-1964), before he joined Mobil.

My father was a contented man, never interested in bribing anyone or unduly influencing any business activity. To him, I was not only a son, but an able protégé, collaborator and friend. He respected my views and never belittled me for any immaturity or naiveté I might have shown. He respected my opinions and carefully considered any insight I ventured to offer. He cherished my foresight as well, as many forward-looking things I envisioned eventually came to pass.

More than anything, he mentored me and coached me in what separates the gentlemen from the men. He frequently sang, "He who goes a-borrowing goes a-sorrowing," and did everything in his power to avoid taking loans. Ours was a life of frugality, bordering on stark austerity, while he settled his debt with Union Bank.

(5) Mentors don't just tell you; they show you. Another important thing I learned from my father was that I must always keep my word. He stressed that faithfully keeping your part of a bargain separates beautiful souls from greedy, ugly people. Keeping one's word, one's bond, was never negotiable, even if it resulted in a considerable disadvantage.

"Hard work pays," he preached. "There is dignity in labour." And he led by example. As he went from retiring from Mobil, returning there as a consultant and ultimately setting up the printing business, I witnessed his code of honour in everything he did. It was a powerful learning experience, as I internalized this way of dealing with people—his way of living—and went on to abide by those standards of personal honesty and integrity.

For him, delaying gratification was second nature. He personified that principle, which separates the thrifty investor from the careless spendthrift. He saved the way a squirrel buries nuts in good times to cope with lean periods. He denied himself the luxuries he could have afforded to secure a better future for his family and associates. With the little he had, he was still generous and happily supported many. He was the picture of simplicity in all things, from his attitude and bearing to his physical possessions. He had only two cars for most of his adult life—a Mazda for work and business, and a Mercedes that he drove on Sundays and special occasions. His sartorial taste was simple and elegant, and his eating habits uncomplicated. He advised me to drink water and never soft drinks, and that beer was better than sugary beverages.

"You don't need bad friends," he warned, as I watched a series of betrayals by his close friends and allies. He shunned frivolous social events, choosing a more solitary existence, at home with his family. "Being alone, thinking about a better tomorrow, is far better than gallivanting at society events or beer parlours, engaged in meaningless discussions," he told me.

Time and again, I saw first-hand that no matter what life throws at you, you can shake off misfortune and begin anew. Before my eyes, and throughout my life, my mentor reinvented himself as he moved from broadcasting to public relations, and from printing to politics. He never groused over misadventures or misfortunes. He was quick to turn rotten luck into fruitful endeavours. He never dwelled on the past, but always learned from it all before moving on.

I was privy to his ill-fated ₦2 million investment in a friend's fluorescent lighting company, then the equivalent of US$2 million. I was the one who delivered the cheque to his friend, which then disappeared into thin air because the devaluation of the currency at the time saw the business collapse. But it did not damage their friendship. He also showed me how to spread my portfolio and keep my savings in different banks and countries, to manage risk.

His relocation from Victoria Island to the less exclusive Surulere district, where he established the press, had the look of a downgrade in living standards, but it did not seem to faze him. He powered through with a cheerful disposition. My friends lived like kings, ensconced in luxury, but they never laughed at the changes in our family's circumstances. My dad's humility and unassuming nature was always apparent, no matter whom he was dealing with.

His way with his employees, whose livelihood he provided, was a lesson in modesty. That rubbed off on me from a young age. At Impact Press, the staff were like a family. They didn't see me as the boss's son. I interacted freely with them—we ate together, shared stories, laughed and worked through our low points together. In fact, I'd hired most of the largely Ghanaian workforce myself before the government-ordered expulsion of undocumented immigrants in 1983. My father also ensured that I worked my way up the ranks, unlike the children of business owners who springboard to the top without any experience or qualifications.

His strict adherence to schedules and appointments was endearing. He didn't tolerate tardiness and was always ready for any engagement ahead of time. I picked up his habit of never keeping anybody waiting. Instead, I would be there early for an appointment, waiting for them. I can't imagine being deliberately late to show how important one is. Because my schedule is meticulously organized, sometimes a quarter of a year ahead, I live by that credo.

WHAT'S IT LIKE TO HAVE PROTÉGÉS?

I have protégés, too—my children. I find time to share with them the lessons my father taught me, as well as things I have picked up along the way. Sometimes we take time off, away from Nigeria, and go through nuggets of wisdom that can make a difference in their lives. Just as my father instilled in me self-belief and confidence in the face of life's hurdles, I have also imbued in my kids the courage to conquer. I remember our time together in Monaco, in the summer of 2019, where we bonded through hour after hour of mentoring.

I invest in my protégés in other ways, too. My father lent me the £250,000 that scaled up Zenon's business, and I've provided my kids with financial support to keep their dreams alive. I bankrolled the first DJ Cuppy and Davido show (my musician daughter and her friend) with ₦10 million, when they were just 16. It flopped. A handful of older people came—the former Cross River State governor, Donald Duke, was there with his wife, Onari, as was lawyer and powerbroker Jide Coker—but young people didn't show up, and the hall was practically empty.

"Papa, people aren't coming," my daughter lamented.

"Open the gate and let them in for free," I replied. It was a lesson in tenacity and perseverance, and today they're both successful entertainers.

SEEK INSPIRATION IN ROLE MODELS

I mentioned earlier that I took an early interest in pioneering businessmen, and these role models taught me a trick or two. I lionized my friend Tunde's dad, Wahab Folawiyo, and was privileged to study him up close.

As a young lad, I remember counting postal orders, used as a means of payment at the time, well into the night with Tunde.

In my adolescence, I asked the elder Folawiyo about how they did things in his early days, what it was like at the ports, how difficult imports were, and whether they had to pay bribes. I was focused more on the challenges his business faced, so I could learn how to avoid pitfalls, and I benefitted from his wealth of experience. After he passed away, I learned even more about Yinka Folawiyo Group from Tunde.

Another business luminary who piqued my interest was Greek shipping magnate Aristotle Socrates Onassis. He was one of the world's most eccentric and inspirational billionaires, and married to Jacqueline Kennedy Onassis, the widow of US President John F. Kennedy. In fact, Onassis's love for the sea and sun—and of Monaco in particular—drew me to that Mediterranean principality, where I now spend time every year.

As a teenager and young man, I began tracking successful people, following their stories through newspapers, books and magazines. I soaked up everything I could about the lives and careers of industrialists Amzat Beyioku Adebowale and Bode Akindele, who treated me to dinner and business lessons in Lagos and London. I studied Alhaji Razak Akanni Okoya, whose Eleganza household goods factories I visited along with Eddie Otudeko, his son-in-law. I also spent time with Prince Samuel Adedoyin, founder of the Doyin Group conglomerate, who later bought diesel from me. I also adored the industrialist Aliko Dangote, and once persuaded my father to accompany me to Dangote's house to see his Rolls-Royce.

WHAT I LEARNED FROM CHIEF MOSHOOD ABIOLA

My first memory of the winner of the annulled June 1993 presidential election, Moshood 'M.K.O.' Abiola, is from around 1971, when his son Kola was my classmate. Chief Abiola was a dutiful father. He wasn't rich or important back then, and it was common knowledge that his family was always his top priority, which remained the case after he'd found wealth and fame. His first wife, the late Alhaja Simbiat Abiola, was a close friend of my mother's.

Over time, I studied Chief Abiola's life in politics and philanthropy, and his habit of building up other people. That trait was evident in the encouragement he offered when I was a budding entrepreneur in the early 1990s. His tenacity, fairness, wisdom and good heart were all things I tried to emulate.

I got a taste of his magnanimity and kindness when I was organizing a memorial concert for Nigerian statesman Obafemi Awolowo and wanted Chief Abiola to be involved. His grandson, my friend Segun, convinced him to come, despite his political differences with Awolowo. He and his wife danced to the performances and made a ₦100,000 contribution to help underwrite the event. At the end of the evening, he took me aside, commended me for the concert's success and called me 'a great man.' That did so much for my confidence.

The following year, when I tried to persuade my father to go into politics, he dismissed the idea, saying it was not an honourable pursuit. He cited Chief Abiola's experience in 1983, when he wanted to be the National Party of Nigeria's presidential candidate, but was rejected, despite all his hard work for the party. I kept pestering my dad until he finally agreed to run for the governorship of Lagos, and the rest is history.

I had yet another upbeat encounter with Chief Abiola after my father was elected. The outgoing military governor, Brigadier General Raji Rasaki, suggested that dad recover from an exhausting election campaign at the Lagos State guest house in Ikeja and that nobody was supposed to see him. I went to visit him there early one morning and found Chief Abiola and his wife waiting in the living room. "Great man," he said, "where is your daddy?" Once again, this great man had called me 'great man.' After Chief Abiola and his wife left, I enquired of my father why he gave Chief Abiola and his wife an audience with him when nobody was supposed to see him. My father said to me "Femi, there is a difference between power and money; money will always bow before power".

After the election's annulment by military strongman Ibrahim

Babangida, my father said he believed Chief Abiola would have been a great president, even though he was in the Social Democratic Party.

I believe my inclination to study the wealthy and successful paid off handsomely. And today, I am humbly grateful that people say they count me among their role models. It is for them that I write this book, in an attempt to help them with what I have learned.

TAKEAWAYS

Succeeding is easier when you find an experienced mentor who's willing to impart the wisdom and knowledge that formal schooling cannot provide. It's almost like having a steadying figure hold your hand and lift you through puddles or guide you across a busy road.

With the benefit of hindsight and having learned from mistakes and obstacles that marked their journey, their insight can save you time and money, quickening your growth and success. Here are some of the ways that can play out:

- Sometimes a mentor can help open doors that would otherwise slam in your face
- Mentors give you advantages that depending solely on yourself wouldn't be present. You learn from their successes and failures, and adjust your journey accordingly
- From teaching timeless qualities and attributes to laying a foundation for breakthroughs, mentors and role models enable self-discovery and enlightenment
- From my father's mentorship, I learned honesty and integrity, contentment, thrift, the power of saving and investment, humility and punctuality, simplicity and hard work
- My dad taught me to treat all people with respect, to be personable, to keep my word, to face life courageously, and to be ready to deal with setbacks and start anew
- My role models' paths to success helped me understand right and wrong choices. Their life stories showed me how to seize opportunities and cope with inevitable misfortune

LESSON NINE

MAKE YOUR LIFE SIMPLE

The dream was vivid and alive, playing out in living colour. The images and sounds were distinct, loud and clear. I woke up and knew I had to remember it all—to process its details and analyse what it meant.

This dream was significant, as it painted a picture of the man I would become. "You will become great," my dearly departed grandfather declared. "Cleanse your mind and body and wear white attire every day. It will define who you become, my grandson. Let everything sparkle and shine but be neat and simple."

I was barely in my twenties, still working for my father's printing business. Like most young people, I was caught up in the latest trends and fads, eager to fit in with my friends and impress the girls. I craved clothes that were fashionable and of the moment. This was difficult, though, as I lived with my parents and had little money to spend. Yet, I heard my grandfather's message loud and clear. And because I have always been spiritual, with a seeming ability to predict the future at times, I appreciate the notion of prophecy. This intuition can come from various sources, and dreams are one such avenue.

I started looking for the best way to wear all-white clothing and saw that traditional Nigerian attire would be the way to go. I would adopt our country's time-honoured native wear—the two-piece *buba* and *sokoto* outfit of long, round-neck shirt and matching pants.

I bought enough brocade fabric, the textile commonly used in the country's southwest at the time, for two sets of the outfit. My *bubas* were cut just below the elbows, a kind of short-sleeved top that allowed me to work unencumbered, and with which I could easily see my wristwatch. The *sokotos* were basic, cut to ankle-length, with a drawstring instead of a belt. And they were beautifully white.

This was all I wore for months. I wore one set while the other was washed, dried and ironed for the following day. My new dress code took family and friends by surprise. They wondered what caused such a radical change from regular, colourful, contemporary garb to the more sombre and austere ensemble. They considered it dull and monotonous. But I'd made up my mind, and I knew what I wanted—their snide remarks didn't get to me. My objective was to be as clean as possible and avoiding stains as I kept to my busy schedule was a constant preoccupation. As long as I could keep my clothes neat and presentable with the resources at my disposal, I was OK.

By the time I turned 24, I had introduced matching shoes and *aso oke* caps, the traditional Yoruba headgear, to the ensemble. It was the musician Fela who inspired this colourful addition. But I ditched the handwoven fabrics two years later, when I wanted to project a more serious image. Still, there would be no room for bright, trendy styles or flashy accessories. I wore only black or brown shoes, mainly loafers.

I have opted for simplicity in every aspect of my life. If something will free up more time, make me more productive and efficient, and allow me to live a more enjoyable and fulfilling life, I will do it. As I've said, my dad influenced that pursuit of the simple things. His lifestyle was so shockingly unassuming that people tended to undervalue him. He was easy-going, without a hint of self-importance, even as the governor of Lagos.

Minimalism helps you avoid decision fatigue, and that's exactly what it did for me. Just as Apple's Steve Jobs always wore jeans and a black turtleneck, and Facebook's Mark Zuckerberg has his uniform of jeans and a dark grey T-shirt, Albert Einstein favoured grey suits to minimize the time needed to decide what to wear each morning. Over the years, I have developed a model for simplifying my life, and I'm continually perfecting it. This clean, uncluttered approach has improved my life in so many ways and made me a better person.

These are my thoughts on keeping things simple:

(1) Minimalism can teach you discipline. Some of my friends were troubled by my 'boring' choice of monochromatic clothing. I told them it projected seriousness and professionalism. The military was in power in Nigeria at the time, with soldiers in well-starched uniforms everywhere, and I drew a parallel to my streamlined work uniform.

'Less is more' was my motto. It has always been. In my opinion, people look far better when they are dressed elegantly, in simple garments. My style is even more austere than the dark, sombre suits of the corporate world. My tops have hidden buttons and no embroidery. I put on the same kind of design in brocade day after day.

In early 2017, I replaced my baggy shirts and trousers with a slimmer version, with the tunic's sleeves now at wrist length. I'd stopped wearing watches in 2016, because mobile phones of course have an ever-accurate clock. Meanwhile, my friends always struggled to adjust their sleeves, waving their hands when talking so you could see their status-symbol watches. I did not need to gesticulate.

Dumping wristwatches made me see life differently—even observe its reality more closely and intensely. It felt like dispensing with what is not essential. I am so comfortable in my skin that I no longer care who wears the most expensive timepiece or who has the most impressive watch collection.

I was crazy about watches for 27 years and had 89 in my collection. These included a Chopard, several Rolexes, and models made by Piaget, Baume & Mercier, Vacheron Constantin, Patek Phillippe and others. I have a diamond McLaren watch that came with the Mercedes-Benz I bought in 2004, one of only 200 produced. When I began making money, my dream was to have 365 luxury watches, one for every day of the year. I shopped around the world for the finest watches; it was a preoccupation during trips abroad. Looking back, it was all so unnecessary.

I should add here that I do not wear my white native attire when I'm abroad. I've always worn very different, colourful clothing outside of work and away from Nigeria. It has to do with the message it's sending out, of course. Can you picture me wearing my *buba* and *sokoto* brocade in London? It would be too awkward and attention grabbing, for all the wrong reasons. It's important to consider what the cultural standards and expectations are wherever you're visiting, and that extends to what you're going to wear. It's great to stand out if it helps with what you're trying to accomplish, but make this a conscious decision and not an embarrassing accident.

A few years ago, I decided to become more stylish, mainly because of my children. I shopped around for a look that would suit my simple style, and American designer Tom Ford fit the bill. Now, every quarter, the label supplies clothes and accessories appropriate for my lifestyle abroad and the weather there. I have a stylist who coordinates the ensembles—I'm shown images of everything and give my approval before these bespoke clothes and accessories are shipped.

My butler arranges them in my wardrobe, and I refer to the photos as a guide for how they are to be matched and worn. And so, as was the case during my all-white phase, I don't have the hassle of having to pick what goes with what.

For social events in Nigeria, I now wear an *agbada*, a flowing robe, with the *buba* and *sokoto*. I launched this new style at the suggestion of my acquaintance Aliko Dangote, when his daughter Fatima was getting married to Jamil, son of the former Inspector General of Police, Mohammed Abubakar, in 2018. Sofisticat, the designers of my kaftan and trousers, made the *agbada* and cap. Now, I have some in my wardrobe for inescapable social events.

(2) Spend time only with those you appreciate. I do not surround myself with too many friends. Fake friendship is a burden, because you end up associating with people who are just there to use you for their own purposes. That's why old friends are usually better than new ones. You will have grown up together, learned to appreciate one another's idiosyncrasies and respect each other's space. You truly know them, their character and their values.

There have been friends who disappointed me, in little and big ways, in business and other matters. Loyalty is scarce. Some friends are greedy and will not think twice about cheating you. But I have friends I've known since my days at the Staff School, and good neighbours in Surulere and Victoria Island. Those are my oldest friends.

(3) Tone down your social activities. One of the ways I simplified my life was by streamlining my social calendar. I've turned down invitations to many events that had no value or meaning to me. They would have been a sheer waste of time and energy. I often do not know those organizing an event, either socially or professionally. Random people drop invitations at the office and expect me to grace their functions. If I were having a birthday party, they wouldn't make my guest list. I have never met or spoken to these people; we've had no interaction whatsoever. My friends know to tell me months ahead about social engagements, so I can consider adding them to my schedule.

I attended assorted parties and events years ago, but when I eventually cleared the decks, I found that I was able to focus 100% on my business. From the start of Zenon, I was simply not accessible for a period of about six years. The only people I was in touch with had to do with my business—those with an allocation of diesel to sell, bankers, and people linked to supply and demand chains. And, of course, I was there for my family. That lifestyle stuck, mainly because I am a loner at heart. I enjoy my own company and use the time by myself to reflect and meditate. That makes me more efficient and thorough, centred and peaceful.

(4) Simplifying allows you to delegate. As you delegate to others, assigning activities tailored for maximum results, you become more efficient. One of the advantages of simplifying my life was the realization that I should only do what I cannot entrust to others, and only if that helps achieve the goals I have set. This delegation frees up so much time that it improves both the quality and the quantity of what I can accomplish.

At Forte, following the reorganization of my business in 2010 and the appointment of Akin Akinfemiwa as CEO in 2011, responsibility for running the company resided with him. He proved to be so competent that my life became dramatically easier.

I have one personal secretary in Lagos, who organizes my schedules and business engagements. I have butlers in London, Monte Carlo, Dubai, Abuja, and Lagos who run my homes. All these employees, with their clearly defined responsibilities, contribute to my life of simplicity. A few years ago, I promoted one of the butlers in Nigeria to the position of deputy house manager. He was in Year 2 at the University of Lagos then and has ample time for his studies because I'm hardly there these days.

I've had a butler to look after me throughout my adult life. That started shortly after I moved out of my parents' house in 1987 and rented a bungalow in the residential area of Surulere. My first butler, who came from Cotonou in the Republic of Benin, started in 1988. In 2019, I started toying with the idea of a chief of staff, and then hired one. The experiment did not last more than two months. I believe you should only do what works for you, rather than blindly following others' recommendations or approaches. After all, I still need to be actively engaged in organizing my life, to keep my brain busy.

(5) Simplifying frees up time for what excites you. Once you clear away the clutter in your life, you can do things that are special to you. Because of my lifestyle and my decision to only involve myself in concepts and ideas that advance my goals, I have more time to concentrate on what is important. Looking after my wife and children is what motivates me. And then, one of the pursuits that makes me happy is philanthropy, which I'll discuss in the pages ahead.

TAKEAWAYS

Carefully choose the activities that dominate your life so that only what counts remains. Hold onto what improves and fulfils you and cast the rest aside. Spend your days on what gives you joy.

If you want to excel, you must be selective about what you spend your time on. Simplifying your life should not be negotiable, for so many reasons:

- It allows you to focus on important things that will make you more successful
- It saves time, energy and resources, and gives your life more meaning
- You are more at peace, only participating in endeavours that mean something to you
- You delegate more, and those you delegate to can work more efficiently
- You are removed from the drama of fake friends, and enjoy more rewarding relationships with people you care about
- Minimalism in your attire sends out the message that you are sensible and focused, and speeds up getting ready in the morning

SECTION THREE

REACHING THE TOP

CONQUERING THE WORLD UNDER MY FEET

LESSON TEN

DON'T FOOL AROUND WITH YOUR HEALTH

My father had always been healthy and agile. Though not an exercise freak, he was trim and always appeared fit. He was moderate in his eating and drinking. His modest, unrushed approach to life and deliberate pace even led to the saying 'Baba go slow' when he was governor of Lagos. His easy-going manner gave no hint that a life-altering stroke would hit him at the age of 71, in 1997.

He had managed his high blood pressure for decades, taking his medication and having regular checkups. On one of his visits to his doctors, he was put on a daily aspirin regimen, to reduce the risk of heart attack or stroke.

Little did we know that some of the last batches of aspirin bought for him in Nigeria were counterfeit medication. They were just chalk, pressed to look like aspirin. In reality, he was not getting his medicine, and the stroke hit without warning.

We had to fly him to London for treatment, and he endured the long Swiss Air flight via Geneva, as the Nigerian military junta had banned British Airways and its direct flights.

I accompanied my father on the trip and witnessed his pain and distress at being helpless. In London, I was there by his side for seven months as he underwent physical therapy. Recovery was slow. As his primary caregiver, I pushed his wheelchair from his flat to treatment at Wellington Hospital every day, and back again afterward. He sat silently, almost completely immobilized. He had to be helped with even the simplest things that we all take for granted.

The experience shook me, as I watched the pillar of my life, a strong man who'd taught me most of the things I know, confined to a wheelchair and a life of dependence.

More than anything, physical wellbeing is fundamental to living fully. If you're not fit and sound, your ability to work, play and go about your day-to-day activities is hampered. No matter how brilliant, educated or endowed you are, your performance is limited if you're nursing an ailment. It's therefore important to ensure that you treat your body carefully and give it all it requires, from exercise and quality food and water, to medication, rest and sleep. More specifically:

(1) Health is wealth. No maxim captures the essence of good health better than 'health is wealth.' An idiom in the Yoruba language drives this home: *Ilera l'ogun oro* (sound health is the key to riches). You can't be rich in any sense of the word without good health. One's physical wellbeing warrants the utmost care and attention. Ralph Waldo Emerson, the American philosopher and poet, put it succinctly: "The first wealth is health." If you're not hale and hearty, you cannot fully attend to your daily business and earn a decent living, let alone become successful and prosperous. Work is exhausting for those who aren't up for the fight.

As you make your bed, so you will lie in it. If you're under 40, you can get away with eating junk food, drinking without care and sleeping little. But as you approach your 50s, you should be at the pinnacle of your profession, and you should start slowing down. You're not getting any younger, and you need to take better care of your body. If you fail to listen to the music your body sings, you may end up laid low by an illness that no degree of success can reverse.

You don't want to have to conduct your business from a hospital bed, with family, staff and business associates parading in and out. You must be smart enough to appreciate that health truly is wealth and be proactive. From what I have seen, the best way to guarantee good health is by modifying your lifestyle. It is mainly about what you eat and drink. What you ingest is what you get.

(2) Your body can take more battering at a younger age. The early days of Zenon were frenetic. It's surprising that I never broke down while building the business. From 1999-2004, I would only sleep two hours or so a day. I had no choice. I described earlier how I spent full days at the office before driving to the depot, where I'd supervise the offloading of diesel through the nights.

The vision was mine, and I needed to drive it. No one could represent my interests better than me. Remember the Ocean Challenger story, where I acquired 5,000 tonnes of diesel off a ship, at a profit of ₦500 million? Who else could have swooped in on my company's behalf to offer a better price than the competition, and cut the bank draft at 8 in the morning? Nobody.

My father's stroke jolted me awake. I was 35, and Centre Force was doing well, but it struck me that ill health could impact anyone, even when you're successful and better able to manage it. The key is to start preparing early, because you *will* grow older and weaker, and the excesses of youth will take their toll. No matter how much energy you expend earlier in life, you won't be able to do the same in your 50s and beyond. So, prepare to slow down, and observe a healthier lifestyle.

(3) Manage your health challenges well. I have only been hospitalized twice as an adult. Other than that, I've been blessed not to experience any real health scares. We have high blood pressure in our family which can lead to serious health issues. All these conditions can be managed and controlled, thanks to better awareness, simple lifestyle changes and advances in healthcare. Apart from taking any necessary medication and exercising, you should eat well, choosing a nutritious diet that's rich in fruit and vegetables.

You don't need to employ a nutritionist—that's not necessary. The main idea is to reduce salt, sugar, carbohydrates and red meat. They're the killers, especially in old age.

(4) Invest in your physical wellbeing. As my business was becoming more successful, I knew I could afford better medical care elsewhere in the world. Before then, I'd taken out a policy with the health insurance company Bupa. It covered transportation for treatment when necessary. However, as I became more successful, I could pay my way anywhere if I had a problem. I undergo yearly medical checks in London and see my doctors without fail. The annual checkup involves a few tests, and every five years I undergo more involved testing, including a colonoscopy.

I also have a team of doctors who advise me on the things I should do and things I should avoid. For instance, they guide me on what to eat and not eat.

I have learned how to manage my hypertension, stave off prediabetes and keep my blood sugar at an optimum level, maintain my ideal weight of 80kg, and exercise faithfully every morning to burn 700 calories.

(5) Eat well, exercise, sleep and drink plenty of water. Good food is essential to sound health, as is regular, moderate exercise, eight hours of restful sleep a night, and drinking plenty of water, while avoiding overindulging in alcohol. I eat only twice a day, and relatively lightly. I have stopped eating breakfast; when you don't eat early, your digestive system is empty, and your organs are well-rested from the previous day. I eat my first meal at lunchtime, and have dinner at least three hours before bedtime.

When I turned 28, I was diagnosed with hereditary high blood pressure. I take medication for that every morning, and although the doctors now say that I can go off it, thanks to positive lifestyle changes, I'm not ready to. I'm convinced that it continues to help.

(6) To live long, don't abuse alcohol. I stopped drinking alcohol around mid-2017 when I realized there was nothing to gain. I asked myself what benefit I got from it, examined the effects it had on me, and concluded that I neither needed nor wanted it in my life. The day after any particularly exciting party I'd attended, there would be eight or nine people waiting for me in the office. I had given them appointments that I didn't clearly recall. The next morning, as they repeated their hard-luck stories, I would instruct my accountant to hand them money.

Because I drank throughout my adult life, I'm in a good position to comment on alcohol's effects—on me, at least. I had been a beer drinker before moving on to brandy. My tastes were expensive. I enjoyed high-end liquor, including outrageously overpriced bottles of cognac on trips abroad with friends and family. There was vodka. There was champagne.

When I look at the lifestyles of some of Nigeria's wealthiest men of my father's generation, who lived into their late 70s and 80s, I realize that they did not drink. Alcohol is a killer because we never really drink in moderation. As we sit with our friends and start carrying on, the drinks keep coming.

TAKEAWAYS

As I've noted, I have learned to exercise, maintain my weight and keep my sugar intake low. I try to sleep more than eight hours a night, drink plenty of water, avoid alcohol, eat two healthy, nutritious meals a day, never miss my medical checkups and abide by the doctors' recommendations.

Never fool around with your health because this is the only body you have. Here are some thoughts on that:

- Health is wealth. Without sound health, your chances of succeeding if you are still alive, are limited. Once weakened, you lack the capacity and stamina to explore opportunities, seal deals and put in the hard work
- Growing old is assured. It is wise to prepare for it by working on your wellbeing while you're able to
- Your youth is the only time your body can withstand sleep deprivation, long hours, excessive partying and alcohol without real consequences
- Actively manage your health and invest in healthcare. All that some conditions require is simple attention. Go for the best cover you can afford
- I'll say it again: eat well, exercise regularly, get enough sleep and drink plenty of water

LESSON ELEVEN

PAY A PREMIUM IF NEED BE

Before 2013, when the government of President Goodluck Jonathan decided to privatize Nigerian power sector companies, I knew nothing about the business. I knew printing and publishing, having managed my father's company for years. I could talk confidently about presses, plates, paper and ink. I could discuss lithography, colour separation and the other esoterica of the trade. Having run a finance company, I also knew about personal loans and advances, lending rates and collateral. And, I knew about the downstream oil sector, and oil trading and shipping, from my Zenon, AP and Forte Oil experience. I could also discuss property very comfortably. I could even analyse politics and economics. But power generation? That was a new world for me.

However, I was lucky to know Chris Adeyemi and Taj Giwa-Osagie, who heightened my interest in the power sector. My instincts nudged me to diversify, move into the space and conquer yet another world.

What did I do to get off on the right foot? For the first time, I would engage consultants before starting a business. The entrepreneur puts in labour, and the capital, but they can't do everything unilaterally. The entrepreneur works on the synergy between all the factors that drive success. They bring together the right elements, including smart people. What they lack, they can buy. The rise and fall of Zenon taught me a lot. I was not going to settle for anything less than world-class again.

Before venturing into the power sector, I decided to engage the best in the field, from wherever in the world they resided. And that meant paying a premium. As I've described earlier, that included US$13 million in consulting fees. For that piece of work, we hired China's SGCC/SMEPC, the largest utility company in the world, with assets of over US$585 billion. It covers 88% of China's national territory, providing power to more than 1.1 billion people. It also owns assets in Australia, Brazil, Greece, Portugal, Italy and the Philippines.

After several meetings in China and Nigeria, we negotiated the consultancy contract, which was discounted from US$16 million. We made a US$4 million down payment, and work began. A team arrived in Nigeria and spent about six weeks visiting and studying the power generation and distributing companies that were up for sale. After extensive research, they recommended that I focus on acquiring Geregu Power PLC, because it was a new plant with easy access to gas. They advised that the other plants were old and would require considerable time and enormous resources to get them functioning properly.

They dissuaded me from buying the power distribution company I'd initially had in mind, Ikeja DisCo, because I would have had to replace the transformers, put in an additional $400 million in capital investment and wait 13 years before breaking even. I set my sights on Geregu, and we notified the Bureau of Public Enterprises that we were withdrawing our bid for Ikeja DisCo.

My foreign partner asked, "How can we pay these guys US$13 million for consulting?" I explained that it was the only way to move on; we needed that expert research, advice and counsel. He covered his share of the outlay, and was happy in the end, as we got tremendous value for money. I later bought him out.

If you look at some of those who bought power entities, they would have been better off had they engaged the calibre of consultants that we did. They gave us a clear-eyed view of the terrain. The companies who dove in without the foresight that our consultants provided ended up struggling with hefty loans and little revenue, while I ended up buying the newest, best plant.

The country's president, Goodluck Jonathan, was eager to get the power sector up and running, and was worried when we pulled out of the Ikeja DisCo deal at the last minute. He called me, sounding concerned. "Femi, my brother, why are you pulling out?"

I went to see him, explained that I'd changed plans based on expert advice, and was buying into the sector with a different acquisition. That put his mind at ease, and I had no doubt that I was on the right path. It is important to state here that I do not consider Ikeja DisCo, which I'd opted out of buying, a bad company. It was just that we had to know what we were getting into, and concluded they were not for us.

For an entrepreneur starting a small business, there often isn't enough money to pay for premium staff or consultants, although scale and proportion are relative. Nevertheless, if you want to acquire a company and big money is involved, you invariably must pay a premium. It doesn't make sense to end up in a mess because you were pinching pennies. The right experts will give you an idea of where you're going from the outset. There is value in research and planning. That was the advantage we had going into the power business.

The lessons learned from my two experiences with engaging experts—to start with a clean slate from Zenon and AP, and to strategize my involvement in the power sector—were illuminating. This is what I can share with you, to help you along your journey:

(1) Do not be afraid to start anew. As I've described, I brought in Olumide Onakoya, the former MD of Mobil Oil Nigeria PLC, to help me restructure after Zenon collapsed. I had once visited him years earlier, at a time when I owned a 9% share in the local Mobil operation. I told him, "I am going to buy this company." They were not interested in selling, and he later retired from Mobil.

As my restructuring consultant, Onakoya interviewed the staff, designed the salary structure, and got people from Mobil to train them. Before the debt clearing house AMCON came in and made the exercise moot, the banks had even agreed to advance us more funds. As we were now involved with the acquisition of AP, I asked Onakoya to put the old oil company on sound footing. I laid out my vision and told him I didn't want to retain any employees who didn't align with that future. The whole place was rotten, tripping over red tape like a government bureaucracy. Onakoya told me that liquidating the workforce would be costly. It was indeed. I ended up paying ₦7 billion to finance severance packages, and everybody jumped at the buyout offer. We sacked everybody in AP and Zenon, and I brought in a new team. The consultancy fee for the Zenon job was ₦100 million, and ₦150 million for AP, but it was worth it.

I wanted a clean break with Zenon. When something has collapsed, you dust yourself off and start over again. It is like a car that's been in an accident and is badly smashed up. You let go of the old wreck and buy a new car. Of course, when you completely reset, the reworked operation doesn't look the same, and it doesn't necessarily require firing the old employees. As noted earlier, when I took over Geregu, I didn't sack the staff I'd inherited. I decided that all the team needed was reorientation. They just needed to discover themselves. I gave them the opportunity, and it worked.

(2) Experts cost a lot. I had no qualms about spending so much on consultants to advise me on Zenon and AP. That's how I am; I don't mind spending money to achieve what I want. Some people ask, why pay more if you can spend less? I simply don't think that way.

When I set my mind to accomplishing something, I put my best foot forward, and expert assistance can be a big help. If I'd hired someone sub-par, just so to pay less for the restructuring consultancy, I could have gotten terrible advice and found myself back at square one. Good things are costly; that is an absolute.

(3) You must separate ownership and management at some point. Having an expert hand at the helm is essential. I've described how I was no longer CEO after restructuring Forte. I couldn't ignore my consultants' recommendations after paying them so much, and they advised stepping away from day-to-day operations. The time had come for me to end my lone wolf business style.

I no longer went to the office as I used to. I would stay in my own private office, elsewhere in the building where Forte was headquartered.

That was the extent of my involvement. They knew that the owner was up there, on another floor, but that was all. I never signed a cheque; I never made a management decision. I attended board meetings four times a year and conferred with the CEO if he came to me with an issue. That is a key advantage of being a proper public company: corporate governance.

When you put people in positions of trust, and they're trustworthy, you can let go and let them be. It was always my idea to give them independence, and the consultants made it easier for me.

(4) You can't get far without structure. The experts taught me to do things properly. Drawing from their vast experience, we developed job descriptions and came up with performance-based bonuses to motivate the staff. They set up the structure and the mechanisms and put corporate governance guidelines in place. When I ran Zenon, I would call the assistant depot manager and give him instructions. By the time the manager got back, the assistant would be doing something different from what the manager had told him to do, because he'd be following my orders. This created problems between them. The assistant would have to pick between his manager and the company owner, which caused all sorts of trust and coordination issues. The consultants made me aware of how dysfunctional that was.

In nine years at Forte Oil, I literally only spoke to three people—the CEO, the CFO and the company secretary. It was nothing like Zenon, where I had everyone's phone numbers, down to the tanker drivers. Despite my good intentions, that had created many problems within the organization.

(5) Everything has a price if you are willing to pay. As I've said, I abide by the principle of not fretting over the cost of quality. I think that everything is for sale if you're willing to overpay. If you came to me and said you wanted to buy Geregu, I would sell it to you for the right price. For me, there's no sentiment attached to ownership. Mark my words: the owners of the world's biggest enterprises would sell in a minute if a buyer was willing to astronomically overpay.

Paying a premium for quality applies to staff as well. You have to offer more money for the right employees, especially if you're poaching them. I remember how I lured Joel Tunde from Total, to become COO and Executive Director of AP in 2007. Years before, in the early days of Zenon, when I was just a buyer of his firm's diesel, he'd laughed off my first offer of employment. The day I approached him to work for AP, a member of the Nigerian House of Representatives, Samuel Bamidele Aro, was with him. When Tunde was alone for a minute, I told him, "If you resign from Total tomorrow, I will give you a great financial package and incentives." He consulted with Aro in private and came back to tell me that although Total had promised to make him MD of Total Ghana, or ED for Nigeria, he would become my new COO.

TAKEAWAYS

- Sometimes, the difference between succeeding and failing can be down to how much you're willing to pay for expertise
- If you neglect to do your research, or fail to choose the best in the field, you aren't saving costs, but setting yourself up for failure
- Make sure your company structure is optimal
- Entrepreneurs, remember quality costs money

LESSON TWELVE

LIST YOUR COMPANY, WATCH YOUR LOANS

Zenon was cruising at a high altitude, at a very fast clip, but moving ahead on an even keel. We manoeuvred through our share of turbulence and reaped the rewards. The supply and distribution chains were working in harmony. I was doing well—far better than I could have imagined when I'd entered the diesel market. My primary objective was to keep busy. I would provide for my family while I enjoyed the little extras that come with modest success. I never knew I could get so big, so fast, selling fuel.

But God and fate favoured me. I was grateful but still hungry. I was anxious to conquer and soar. I wanted more. I was looking for ways to do my business better and better. We were big, and already had created Sea Force Shipping (2001); Atlas Shipping Agency (2001); FO Properties (2003); Fineshade (2006) and acquired Nigerian National Shipping Line (2007).

We'd also acquired majority shares in Visafone Communications Limited (where I was the second largest shareholder); Zenith Bank Plc (where I was the second largest shareholder); UBA Plc (one of the fifth largest shareholders); First City Monument Bank (one of the fifth largest shareholders); Stanbic IBTC Bank; Oceanic Bank International; Intercontinental Bank Plc; GT Bank Plc (one of the fifth largest shareholders); Africa Finance Corporation; (where I was the largest individual shareholder); Access Bank Plc; Bank PHB (one of the fifth largest shareholders); Mobil Oil Nigeria Plc (where I was the second largest shareholder); Chevron Nigeria Plc (where I was the second largest shareholder); I was hugely involved with Transcorp, a mega-company founded by a group of businessmen as a Nigerian play on the South Korean *Chaebol* trading community concept. And, I was involved in NITEL, the privatized national telecoms company, and the Port Harcourt and Kaduna refineries.

The reality that I had reached and surpassed my objectives set me thinking I could aim higher and test new ground. In 2007, I began to toy with the idea of listing Zenon as a publicly traded company. As soon as I knew it was a possibility, I started consulting and eventually invited in experts to look into my books and advise me. I wanted to divest 49% of Zenon and still hold controlling shares.

The consultants looked through my books, analysed the pattern of profits and growth, and valued the assets. They arrived at US$1.2 billion as the value of the 49% I wanted to sell. We conferred with the banks, and they were ready to underwrite that amount, giving me the cash balance for the unsubscribed shares.

As the discussion to issue the stock moved ahead, with all the details laid bare, I got cold feet. The more they told me about becoming a public limited company, the more convinced I was that it wasn't for me. The prospect of putting together a board of directors that was subject to approval by the Nigerian Stock Exchange, holding regular board meetings and annual general shareholder meetings, filing closely scrutinized quarterly financial reports, and so much more, set me thinking.

I knew I was not yet ready for such rigorous corporate governance, so I suspended the project. I backed out of listing Zenon in 2007 for three reasons:

(1) A limited liability company enjoys independence. I loved the freedom of owning our independent company. The other directors were my wife and children. I had the independence to run the company freely; no one breathed down my neck or questioned my decisions. I was the boss and did things my way. Although I had an MD and top management staff, they worked for me, followed my directives, and rarely took issue with my plans and decisions. If I wanted to raise or lower the price of a product, I didn't need their approval. I expanded the business on my terms. Going public meant the free rein I enjoyed would end. Even minority shareholders could raise issues that I'd be required to deal with. I was not ready for that.

(2) You need to adapt your idea of ownership. I wasn't prepared to let go of being an unsupervised owner. I had experienced the sweet joy and adulation of running companies for a decade-plus, with more than four years at Centre Force and almost eight years at Zenon. And I had become used to being—and being called—boss.

More than that, there was the whole ego angle that was associated with owning a company. I was still attached to the idea of outright ownership. Diluting it with other stakeholders made me uncomfortable. Once I divested, I could no longer lay claim to being the owner. I was a control freak who enjoyed leading from the front, dictating where the company should head.

(3) A public company involves transparency and corporate governance. Being listed required meticulous observance of rules and regulations, stipulated by official bodies that supervise companies. At the time, this long list of directives and stringent penalties for noncompliance was downright scary. It meant I would have to conduct business in a strictly prescribed manner. Our results would be published in the newspapers—revenue, profit and loss statements—for all to see. That was too much for me to bear.

I have no regrets about refusing to list Zenon; I wasn't ready for the responsibilities that came with being a public company. It's true that when I reflect on the calamity ushered in by the 2008 recession, where I lost practically everything, I wonder if having gone public would have saved us. Perhaps. A competent CFO, who would not avert his eyes from the loans and our exposure, may have seen the signs and prevented the ensuing catastrophe. I'll never know for certain.

What I am most thankful for was the timing of my woes. My world collapsed when I was about 47. I tried to cut my losses, sell my bank shares and leverage the oil prices, but couldn't save myself from ruin. But I was still relatively young and agile, which helped me rebound.

Once I'd abandoned the listing, fate again dealt me a good hand. Because Zenon had been so quickly and hugely successful, I looked for ways to go further in the business. My understanding was that the major oil companies, especially Mobil and Texaco, would leave once the variables in the sector changed. The diesel business was already evolving, and with the electric power sector set to pull itself together, I could sense that fuel demand would dwindle. If the government's plans for the electricity sector came to fruition, and with the abundance of gas in Nigeria, diesel would no longer be in such high demand. My eyes were set on acquiring a major player, and I invested heavily in the stock of those companies. As detailed earlier, by 2007 I was the second-largest shareholder in Mobil Oil Nigeria PLC, with 9%, and held a 14% share in Texaco's Nigerian operation, as its second-largest shareholder. The foreign owners held 60% stakes in each of those companies.

I tried to talk the foreign owners into selling, but they declined. I continued with my plans, hoping they'd change their minds.

One Sunday morning, I was reading *ThisDay*, a local paper, and came upon an interesting interview with the Managing Director of African Petroleum. I thought to myself that it would be nice to meet this Mallam Zira Maigadi. I wanted to size him up. I reached out to him, and he came to see me. We had a lengthy discussion about the industry and about life.

Four days later, he called me, sounding distressed. Maigadi said he urgently had to see me. I explained that I was in the capital city of Abuja. "No problem," he said. "I'll head to the airport now and catch the next available flight."

As soon as he arrived, he told me that a company was going to buy AP, and the unions were opposed to it.

I went to see Nigerian President Obasanjo, to discuss the fate of the company. After additional consultation, I ultimately bought ₦17 billion worth of AP shares, followed by a complete takeover and Rights Issue, underwritten by a consortium of banks that raised ₦52 billion because of the confidence they had in me. And then, we rebranded to Forte Oil PLC in 2010.

I have owned private limited liability companies and presided over the boards of public limited companies as an executive and non-executive chairman, and the differences are so apparent. The advantages of listing far surpassed those of operating an LLC.

A listed company brings many benefits to stakeholders, from major investors to minority shareholders, from the board to management, from employees to consumers of the products and those in the supply and distribution chains. Everyone benefits far more because of the rules enforced by the regulatory and supervising authorities, and the resources at the company's disposal.

A whole new world of opportunities opens wide for listed companies. Here are seven of those I find most important:

(1) Listing provides the expertise of a board. A diverse board of directors brings years of experience to the table. The board is the engine room of every publicly traded company, and in Forte Oil we brought in men and women from varying backgrounds—high-calibre people of discipline and integrity who'd made a mark in their professions. With these clearheaded overseers, I could no longer just do whatever I wanted, despite controlling almost 80% of the company's stock. By 2017, our Board included Akin Akinfemiwa (CEO); Julius Omodawo-Owotuga (CFO); Nicolaas Vervelde (CEO, Nigerian Breweries PLC owned by Heineken); Dr. Mairo Mandara (Founder and Board Chair of Girl Child Concerns and Senior Fellow at Children Investments Fund Foundation (CIFF); Dr. Salamatu Suleiman (Former Minister of Women Affairs and Social Development and currently ECOWAS Commissioner for Political Affairs); Christopher Adeyemi (Partner of a London-based Law Firm); Anil Dua (CEO West Africa, Standard Chartered Bank, former Global Head, Project and Structured Finance, Standard Chartered Bank) and yours truly. The board helped redefine the company and put it on the path to stability and growth.

(2) Listing gives you better access to funds necessary for growth. Listed companies raise funds through IPOs, as AP did in 2007. Banks underwrite and sell the shares, helping you raise money to run the company instead of borrowing. Shares are then tradeable on the floor of the stock exchange every workday, with shareholders cashing in or out as they please. This freedom to buy and sell gives the company respectability.

(3) Listing curtails the ego of the majority shareholder. Unlike a limited liability company, partnership or sole proprietorship, where the owners can in theory get away with anything, PLCs are not run that way at all. There are clearly spelled-out rules for arriving at decisions that management committees, the board or the general body of shareholders must ratify. Unlike in Zenon, where I could lower or increase diesel prices with a phone call, in Forte Oil, management met to decide on such things, and referred certain matters to the board. At Zenon, I decided on salaries and emoluments. At Forte Oil, there was a committee that took on that role. It was an entirely different ballgame.

(4) Corporate governance fortifies the company. Eagle-eyed regulators protect stakeholders' interests, and best business practices are encouraged, to the benefit of all. No group or individual enjoys special favours, and the entire country benefits as the appropriate taxes are assessed and paid. Nigerians are better off because of Forte.

(5) For PLCs, risk management is a top priority. In a public company, there are better methods of identifying, evaluating and prioritizing risks. Coordinated activities address how resources are applied to avoid risks and amplify opportunities. The board and management meet regularly and can better assess uncertainty in the financial markets, anticipate problems and take action to avoid or minimize risk. They identify opportunities on the horizon and strategize how to leverage and profit from them.

(6) A PLC is more likely to outlast the competition. With the wisdom of the board, experienced management and diverse shareholders, it is easier for a PLC to outlive its owners, and the less-organized competition. The sponsors don't have to run the company; a talented group of resourceful professionals manage it. Once the salary and emoluments are right, and managers are given clear and measurable goals, the company can operate profitably for decades. This allows owners to pass their holdings down generationally, while others in the industry fold.

(7) It is easier to sell at a premium as a PLC. The majority shareholder can exit the company, cashing out as I did from Forte in June 2019. Because we operated transparently, obeying all the rules and regulations of the Nigerian Stock Exchange and the Securities and Exchange Commission, dutifully filing our very favourable financial reports, we were well prepared to sell. Finding a buyer was not difficult, and we sailed through all the rigorous checks by international banks, agencies and lawyers. It would have been far more difficult to sell my privately held Zenon, with all its irregularities and problems obscured down in the weeds.

INSPIRING PUBLIC COMPANIES THAT I ADMIRE

There are several PLCs that I've long been fascinated with, domestically and on the international stage. That's particularly been the case with companies that boast world-class boards, such as Nigerian Breweries, Nestlé, CAP PLC and Guinness. I admire Apple because it is awash with cash, hence my strategy to be cash rich. As noted earlier, when I was young, I adored Roebuck and Co. and Mercedes-Benz Group.

Many public companies have lasted for more than a century. Ansaldo Energia, the Genoa-based firm I signed a maintenance agreement with in 2019, and the biggest power company in Europe, was founded in 1853. Look at JP Morgan, Hilton, Mercedes-Benz, Rolls-Royce, Nestlé, Guinness, Heineken—they've been up and running for many generations.

The Hilton Hotels Corporation chain was founded by Conrad Hilton in May of 1919, in the small railroad town of Cisco, Texas. Today it operates more than 5,700 properties in 113 countries, spanning six continents. However, the Hilton family no longer owns the business; it was taken public in a December 2013 IPO.

The Mercedes-Benz trademark was registered in 1902 by Emil Jellinek, whose background before entering the auto business was in insurance, stock trading and diplomacy. But the company itself has its roots both in German engineering company Daimler Motoren Gesellschaft, founded in 1890, and in the work of auto designer Karl Benz, whose 1885 vehicle made history by featuring the first internal combustion engine in a self-propelled vehicle.

Another legendary carmaker, Rolls-Royce, came to be in 1904, when factory owner Henry Royce and car dealer Charles Rolls forged a partnership in Manchester, England. They unveiled their first car just a few months later, at the Paris Salon exhibition. Rolls-Royce Ltd was incorporated in 1906 and is today owned by BMW. It also manufactures aircraft engines, while remaining a leader in the luxury auto market.

Meanwhile, Guinness Stout was introduced in Dublin, Ireland, back in 1759. It made its way to Nigeria in the 1940s, and in 1963 the first bottle rolled out of the Ikeja plant, the first Guinness brewery outside of the British Isles. Guinness Nigeria PLC, which was listed on the Nigerian Stock Exchange in 1965, is the sole beverage-only company in Nigeria, producing and selling spirits, beer and non-alcoholic drinks, including Smirnoff Vodka, Baileys Irish Cream, Harp Lager and the African favourites Malta Guinness and Orijin.

All of these companies have benefitted greatly from being superbly managed, publicly owned enterprises.

WATCH YOUR LOANS LIKE A HAWK

My father never ceased drumming it into me: "He who goes a-borrowing goes a-sorrowing."

As I've said, dad always lived far below his means and only took a loan once, to start Impact Press. And he did not rest until his last day on the job.

In our private moments, he warned me never to use a personal house as collateral. This admonition stuck in my head. It is impossible to run a business without loans, be they from family, friends, associates or financial institutions, but there are rules to that game. You must deny yourself luxuries, avoid frivolities and never show off until you've paid off the loan. You must always deal in trustworthiness. Without trust, you cannot go far.

I enjoyed having a line of credit long before I established Zenon. In the early days of Centre Force, I took my first loan from Société Générale Bank of Nigeria, where my friend Bukola Saraki was an executive director. I applied for a ₦1 million loan to finance a project, and quickly paid it back. Over the years, I also borrowed ₦5 million, ₦30 million, and later ₦300 million, all of which I dutifully repaid.

The advance from my father at the beginning of Zenon was repaid early, and I've mentioned Zenith Bank and Intercontinental Bank financing my acquisition of Marca's 20,000-tonne fuel tank farm. A consortium of Nigerian banks, alongside BNP Paribas, gave me a trading loan of US $2 billion that I liquidated during my AMCON tribulations, and I also got a turnaround loan from GTBank through a recommendation from its MD, my friend Segun.

I've told you how I acquired Geregu Power with more equity, along with the Chinese utility SGCC/SMEPC and my foreign partner, which was promptly repaid. We got an additional loan from the Bank of Industry to refurbish the plant, which was handily repaid. Having said all that, I could have borrowed so much more through my long career.

No matter how tempting and accessible loans are, you should take them wisely. Have the discipline to only do so when you definitively need them to grow your business, after weighing the costs and benefits.

At Centre Force, Zenon, Forte Oil and Geregu Power, I found loans to be useful, utilizing them sparingly to grow the companies. That taught me a lot about borrowing, including the following:

(1) Banking can be a slippery slope if you don't know what you need. Banks continually bombard you with sales pitches once you have an enterprise with a cash flow. They offer you all sorts of incentives, and once you take the bait, they never stop. Before you know it, you become so trapped in contracts and obligations that you risk losing it all. You need to know when to step on the brakes. Since the loans are protected by collateral security that surpasses the value of your indebtedness—your property and assets—the banks have nothing to lose. You have everything to lose.

(2) Do not fall into the temptation of lifestyle loans. In my country, there are many who take loans to underwrite a luxurious lifestyle, with all the toys and comforts, never intending to pay them back. They structure things to satisfy risk assessors and bribe bank executives. During the diesel boom days, the marketplace was uncontrolled. I saw people walk into one bank and take ₦3 billion loans. They'd end up suffering losses of ₦400 million or more when the chickens came home to roost. But because the banks anticipated recouping ₦6 billion, they never did proper risk assessment, and bribery was involved. This same bank would go on to approve another ₦15 billion in lending.

Of course, customers who defaulted would then disappear. In some cases, the collateral was a new business's supposed product, which never materialized. Wily fraudsters forged letters of credit and fake shipping documents. And with bribes, and connivance on the part of the authorities, these loans were eventually written off.

Others don't get their numbers right. They take loans and begin to count how much money they could make, calculate profit and start to live like kings. They get credit to the tune of ₦100 million and hope to make a profit of ₦30 million. They spend the projected windfall, and if things take a downturn, they run into big problems.

I took trading loans, opened letters of credit, bought ships and paid the banks as I received payments, all aimed at growing my businesses. I have never borrowed to burnish my lifestyle. You would be wise to do the same.

(3) Know when and where interest rates are too high. Interest is so high in Nigeria that it's tough to do any profitable business with loans. At 24%, you're carrying a staggering weight. If you borrow ₦1 billion today, your interest obligation is immediately ₦240 million, before you even utilize the money. The only sectors that can still manage such high rates are cement, telecoms and power generation. No other industry can make money with such a burden; you'd just be slaving away for the banks. Rates obviously vary from place to place, and they rise and fall over time. So, do your research and figure out whether taking a loan will help or hinder your business.

(4) Keeping an eye on bank charges is challenging. I touched on this earlier, but banking charges and fees are challenging for an entrepreneur to monitor and stay on top of. We need experienced internal auditors and accountants to keep an eye on fees. If you're not diligent, a ₦100 million loan can increase to ₦110 million, just due to these charges. And there are unusual, buried fees that only sharp-eyed forensic auditors can readily discover. Zenon was not structured—I ran it by the seat of my pants, and there was no reconciliation of figures—but Forte Oil was different. I had by then employed an experienced CFO and internal auditors who would spot errors immediately, because we reconciled the accounts every day. This is a key advantage of having a public company.

(5) Consider every option. You should make sure you know the lenders and the products they can make available to you well before you make your decision. For instance, check whether you qualify for single-digit loans at an alternative financial institution, like Nigeria's Bank of Industry. And be sure to denominate your loans in your local currency. You cannot control devaluation and currency fluctuations, which can kill you.

TAKEAWAYS

A PLC has an edge over all other types of companies. The advantages to having this sort of structure are many-fold:

- Listing gives you the advantage of having a diverse board, with years of expertise, that will change the company's outlook and afford it a better chance of growth
- Between IPOs and traded shares, cash to grow the business is readily available and easy to access
- The ego and the excesses of a majority shareholder are toned down, and everyone wins, thanks to rigorous corporate governance, rules and regulations
- Apart from being easier to sell, because of the transparency demanded by regulators, a PLC has a better chance of outliving its founders

Watching your loans is easy when you are disciplined, care about your good name and are thus motivated to pay off everything as soon as possible. Loans are difficult to track when you don't pay attention, and don't have sharp auditors on the lookout for manipulation.

To make the right choices, consider these steps:

- Get internal auditors, recruit a capable CFO and do daily and weekly reconciliation of bank transactions, capturing credit, debit and all other charges
- Never divert loans to bankroll your lifestyle. Do not spend projected profit. Pay off your debt first, before you start living like a king
- Never delay payment of loans, because interest will compound. Pay it all down as fast as you can
- Make sure you've considered all financing options, to find the one that best suits your situation

LESSON THIRTEEN

LEAVE FAMILY OUT OF YOUR BUSINESS

Although my wife and children have been directors of my businesses, I generally advise caution when considering working with family. In the booming glory years of Zenon, from 1999-2007, my children were in school and too young to work for me. The eldest was a teenager and the youngest still a baby. So, their working at the company was clearly out of the question, even though I had made up my mind long before not to bring any family member into my business. I had seen the ruins friends' offspring had made of their empires and read how institutions were battered to their knees by family scions.

I did make an exception in 2007, when I acquired majority shares in AP. The takeover was rancorous and stressful, at one point nearly even costing me my life. On 15 July 2010, in the thick of the ordeal, I was in an elevator that fell violently after ascending to the top of our Broad Street headquarters on Lagos Island. I was stuck in the lift for about an hour and a half with six other people, all of us badly bruised and battered. The president of Nigeria at the time, Goodluck Jonathan ordered an investigation by the Inspector General of Police. The IG's investigative team discovered that the lift had been sabotaged, and arrests were made.

Because of the pressure of keeping an eye on my ₦17 billion investment, having resolved to work there every day from 8 am to 1 pm, and resume at the Zenon office from 2-7 pm, I knew I needed someone to help me out at

AP. I figured that only a trusted family member could handle this. There was no better ally than my sister Lola, who had worked at Commerce Bank, Zenith Bank and FCMB. She was experienced enough to take on the role of Finance Manager, and later Director, keeping a watchful eye on the cash register. I reckoned she would relieve me of the stress of having to constantly look over my shoulder. She would stay with me until the firm's management underwent a restructuring several years later.

Looking back at my time at my father's growing printing business, despite my fascination with machines, lack of desire to return to school and desire to assist my dad, I had lost interest by 1987. I managed to hang on there for four more years, scaling back to the commissioned marketing consultant role I described earlier. Still, everyone seemed to think I was fit to take over the press, and probably expected me to do so.

They'd seen me stare, wide-eyed, as reams of blank paper were fed in from one end, slid through rollers and ink, and clean, colourful images appeared on the documents at the other end. The cutting, trimming and stitching machines held me spellbound, as did the packaging apparatus. But in the end, after working in almost all the departments, I got tired of it all. It was a passion that had burned bright at first, but it wasn't my calling. I decided that it was better to have my own business, to pursue my own dreams and vision.

If I'd stayed on there, what would have become of the business after my father passed away? I wasn't an only child. The possibility of rancour and rivalry was there, simmering under the surface, and I knew a bitter workplace fight would tear the family apart.

Just over a decade later, with the rebranding of AP to Forte Oil, and our slow but steady rise to profitability, my wife Nana began to press me to bring my daughters into the business.

It started with Tolani, who had then finished her first and second degrees at the university of St Andrews in Scotland. Nana didn't see why I couldn't hire Tolani. "Put the children in the business, Femi. Let them keep an eye on things," she'd say. I would explain to her that that sort of thing never worked. "It's old thinking," I argued. "I've studied business empires where scions took over and ended up ruining everything. The children rarely developed the company beyond where they come in. They usually wreck it! It has zero advantages. Look at my contemporaries: where did their kids take their businesses? Most of them destroyed those empires."

The pressure was intense, but I was unwavering. I did all I could to distract Nana and the children from the idea. All of them envisioned becoming CEO of Forte Oil, and they didn't let up for years. Tolani was the first to approach me, after her mother had surfaced the idea, and asked when she could join the company. Ifeoluwa was next—she wanted to be CEO straight away. She went on to take a course in the oil business at Oxford University, as well as a programme at Mercuria, an upstream oil giant with interests worldwide. She thought that would help change my mind. Temi, too, used to ask: "Papa, when am I going to wear a suit and come and work in the office?"

Eventually, I sat my children down, explained to them that Forte Oil was my vision, and impressed upon them that they would not be able to run the business.

I had made up my mind on two things when I was setting out in business. One, I was not going to have friends or enemies. I was only going to have competitors. And two, no children or family would ever work for me.

There are a thousand and one reasons why having family in your business is a bad idea. Here are just a few:

(1) They usually lack the required experience and skills. Succeeding takes years of dreaming, planning, working hard and learning along the way. That learning process involves falling flat on one's face, getting up, and then trying again. And again, and again. As a business struggles and survives, it takes more years of hard work and good luck to break through. They do not teach the experience gained on the job and on the streets in any classroom. The skills you acquire aren't buried in books. No matter where you educate your children, they'd still need years to learn the skills and experiences necessary to contribute to the family business. Joining the company as an executive director wouldn't cut it. Quick promotion to

CEO certainly wouldn't put the company on the path to greatness.

(2) It is neither their passion nor calling. The children who stepped into their fathers' businesses were likely railroaded or smitten by ego. I've seen successful people tailor their kids' upbringing and education to the family business, despite the offspring's evident lack of interest. Sometimes, selfish desires propel them. When deep interest and genuine passion are missing, and the next generation takes the helm, the company stands no chance. Without the calling, failure is all but assured. It takes more than curiosity, or wanting to please daddy, or thirst for riches, for a business to succeed. In troubling times, and the darkest of days, when you struggle and fret and lose sleep, only the deepest passion keeps you going.

(3) It causes unhealthy rivalry among siblings. With more than one child, who becomes the MD of the company? What criteria would one use to pick the CEO? Will it be education, interest, experience, age? Rivalry would be sown in the hearts of siblings as they battle for control of the soul of the company, and whoever is picked to lead the family business becomes an enemy of the others. I have seen this happen time and again. And can you imagine how vicious it becomes if the children are from multiple marriages? It would be a relentless, withering fight. I sincerely preferred that my children find their voices elsewhere. They did, and now, everybody's happy.

(4) It encourages indiscipline. Family members can try to play on a father's sentimentality if he's the head of a business. You'll really see this if it involves children with ego issues. And once you can't enforce discipline because someone feels they're above the law, the company slides into unruliness. Let's say a family member insists on disregarding schedules and violating company policies. Resentment arises, and the staff will grumble, shining a light on how unsuitable the family member is in their role. Those with good conscience will resign and pursue their fortune elsewhere, while the sycophants will stay, fostering greater discontent. At the end of the day, the company loses.

(5) They are rarely prudent. Children of business owners are usually after the spoils. They can see perks as an entitlement and splurge on frivolities. Or they may take risks with the company's money. It happened to me: I once took money meant for Impact Press salaries to a nightclub and sprayed the Juju star Sir Shina Peters with the cash. I was overwhelmed with his praise-singing, and the propulsive, upbeat music, and lost myself in the moment. Needless to say, I regretted it come payday.

Of course, there are exceptions to every rule. On rare occasions, sons, daughters, nieces and nephews can pull off successful turnarounds and improve on the accomplishments of the founders of a family business.

Some conditions I've listed below make such transformations possible:

(1) A relative in your company should work his or her way to the top. Children simply cannot step into the shoes of their parents after a few years of tutelage and encouragement. And they certainly shouldn't be allowed to join as executive directors. They should start in an entry-level position, grow along the way and be promoted based on merit. If they show an interest in the business, they should serve a requisite number of years at various levels, and prove themself, qualifying for sequential promotion, as any other able-bodied employee would. They should be industrious and learn the ropes one rung at a time, in one department after the other. These years of experience will pay off in the long run, especially when the protégé learns the tricks of the trade directly from you.

(2) Relatives can help your business if it aligns with their passion and calling. A child should have the necessary passion and energy for the business. It should be clear from the onset how much time and effort he or she is ready to invest. Their buy-in and commitment is easy to discern—the glint in the eyes, the ceaseless energy, the extra hours of toiling, the mastery of the lingo and metrics, and much more. When the flames of passion are genuine and enduring, recognizing a child with a calling becomes easy. Remember my love of printing? It didn't last. God had a higher plan for me. It takes years to find out if the passion is indeed authentic and enduring, and even longer to confirm whether it is a true calling.

(3) Take care when planning succession or wealth transfer. The same caveats apply when the entrepreneur is thinking far ahead, to matters of succession and wealth transfer. For that, it is appropriate to appoint one's siblings or children to the board, to ensure a smooth transition and protect their inheritance. But the family member must be suitable for the task, equipped with a good education, level-headed demeanour and years of experience.

When I am reflecting, I sometimes think about big businesses I grew up knowing and admiring. One of them that's still alive and well is Leadway Assurance Company Ltd, started by Sir Olusola Hassan Odukale. His son, Oye Hassan-Odukale, carried the enterprise many notches higher in his three decades there, taking the company public and rising to the position of MD, a post he held from 1994-2019. Oye was well suited for this role, with bachelor's and master's degrees in business administration from the University of Houston. His younger brother, Tunde, who also climbed up the rungs, became MD of the now publicly listed Leadway Assurance PLC. The 55-year-old Tunde joined the company in 1999 and has a bachelor's degree in Pure Mathematics and a postgraduate diploma in Actuarial Science. Again, here was a member of the founding family quite well suited to his role. So many other companies from back then are either dead or struggling.

In the end, I have some general advice on how to approach your children's dreams and aspirations:

(1) Encourage each child to find and pursue his or her passion and calling. I have long encouraged my children to chart their courses and live *their* dreams, not mine.

I got my daughter Tolani a job in London, but as time went by it became apparent she was only interested in singing and interacting with musicians. After a few years at her regular job, she was listless and unhappy. She summoned enough courage and laid it on the line. "Papa," she pleaded, "I want to sing." My reaction: "No problem." I encouraged Tolani and gave her my blessing. I just thought, let this girl go out and follow her muse. Once she's street smart, and immersed in her chosen field, she can apply her knowledge and see where it takes her. I encouraged my children to pursue their passion and find their calling and assured them they could always count on my support. I was not embarrassed when they chose entertainment. I was elated.

Ifeoluwa is now an international DJ, and Temi is an actress and lifestyle entrepreneur. They are doing their jobs professionally, with staff on their payroll. I get them to do monthly accounting, with a profit and loss report, because they're running businesses. You should never force your children into your mould, or attempt to remotely control them.

(2) Avoid any appearance of favouritism. It is difficult to convince your children that they are equally loved when one enjoys more attention and holds a high position in the business that provides the lifestyle they all enjoy. The seemingly favoured sibling will generate jealousy and animosity unless they all possess a significant degree of maturity. Why create room for acrimony and bickering with even a whiff of favouritism, especially in a family business?

(3) Allow them to benefit from your business success. Don't be hesitant to provide your offspring with a superlative lifestyle, even if they don't work for the company. A successful entrepreneur's family can enjoy a great life. You can put them on an allowance, give them grants to pursue their dreams and loans to help grow their business. Recall that a loan from my father gave Zenon a big boost. Likewise, I give my children loans to support their endeavours, and all of them owe me money. I have a loan book where we record the transactions. I also give them allowances for upkeep, and some of their bills are taken care of, allowing them to devote more energy to their vocation. My children are happier pursuing their destinies than they'd be with a force-fit into my endeavours. Although they're still finding their feet in life, I tell them that if they'd worked in Forte Oil, they would have destroyed the business and sacrificed the opportunity to live their dreams. I would rather have them follow their own paths and learn what life is, through their own unique lens. Today, they are all comfortable with where they are.

... BUT FAMILY TRULY COMES FIRST

I got married and started my family in September of 1992, when I still served as my father's assistant. But by the time Zenon kicked off, it was impossible to be the father I wished I could be. I was so preoccupied with building the company that I allowed the workload to creep into my weekends.

On Sundays, when Nana succeeded in dragging me to church, I disappeared to the depot after the service. I supervised the construction of diesel tanks and ate in my car. Time was scarce and diesel was scarcer. The workers needed motivation, and my presence sped up the projects. I needed to stay on top of things as I had ships being loaded with product on the high seas. Where would they offload? Would everything go smoothly? The earlier my employees topped off the tanks, the better positioned I was to make a killing in the market. My excitement was infectious, and it drove the workers.

When we conquered one project in the distribution chain, we had to tackle another in the supply chain. Commissioning the tanks, ordering the trucks and ships, and building the business was so exacting that I was hardly ever at home. I did not have time to socialize, and you wouldn't see me anywhere but at the office, at the house for brief periods, going to or from the depot, or out of town. I was neither available nor accessible. I was married to the business.

The Zenon operation got so big that Jacob Ajekigbe, the MD of First Bank PLC, was alarmed. "Young man," he said, "you are amassing all this money..." He was astounded at how huge the diesel business was, and how much of it I was cornering. At the height of Zenon, I had more than 150,000 tonnes of storage capacity. Nana was also growing her dry-cleaning business, Garment Care. She could hardly complain that I was hardly home when she found herself in a similar position.

It was then that it dawned on me that I did not know my children well enough. I felt that I needed to make amends as quickly as I could, or it would be too late. After all, I had made so much money already, and the business had stabilized. And so, I started spending more time at home, bonding with my children, and going out and about as a family. And when the time came to send them abroad for their education, I knew I could not invent excuses for not seeing them for long periods. That was when we started a 90-day vacation experiment. We travelled around the world, from Africa to Europe and North America, and the children sometimes came back to Nigeria as well.

With Forte Oil—with a competent board and agile management, and time on my hands—I began to sit and talk more with my kids, asking about their dreams and ambitions. I wanted to make them comfortable in my presence and encourage them to express themselves freely, which is a trait I learned from the Afrobeat star Fela.

You have to be keenly interested in your family, concerned about their welfare and wellbeing, tuned in to their dreams and ambitions, and aware of all the challenges life throws at them. Without bonding, the opportunity to do so is lost, and they'll find solace and succour elsewhere. More often than not, if that's not with you, they'll seek it in the wrong places, with the wrong people. A father must be more than a figurehead—he is a provider, guide and protector. His broad shoulders are the beams that support the house.

These are just three of the many reasons why family comes first:

(1) Family is all you have at the end of the day. After a long and trying day toiling in the trenches, you return to a cozy home, filled with love and warmth, and enjoy the evening with your adoring family, because they're all that you have. Through thick and thin, in prosperity and pain, they stand by you. You can stop being the CEO, but you will always remain a husband and father. When tragedy strikes, family will rarely abandon you, and when riches land in your lap, they stay faithful and real. You can count on family.

(2) Family enhances your work-life balance. Balancing one's professional life with personal, social and family life ensures a pleasant existence and helps alleviate stress. Devoting time to family, and engaging in activities that enhance your joy together, gives the entrepreneur more stamina, inspiration and resourcefulness to succeed. To avoid the burnout and illnesses that the busy lifestyle of an executive can bring, it's important to spend quality time with those near and dear to you. Compartmentalizing the various areas of one's life leaves room for a healthy balance.

(3) Bonding provides a better platform for mentoring. Growing out of long years of toil, experience laced with disappointments, failure, struggles, survival and success attracts admiration and respect from those who look up to the entrepreneur as a role model. And passing on stories of such a harsh and beautiful odyssey to your children colours their lives in brilliant hues. They can relish anecdotes, lessons and tales first-hand. Mentoring the children, as I have done, holding weeklong sessions at a stretch, is a good foundation that helps build their future. They seek my opinion on basic challenges and complicated issues, as I point out opportunities and offer suggestions on how to do things better.

PAMPER YOUR CHILDREN—WITH SENSE

When it became public knowledge in September 2020 that I'd bought each of my three daughters a Ferrari Portofino, it 'broke the internet,' as they say. There were millions of comments, from those who said this was the way to go, from friends who said I'd put them under pressure from their own children, and from those who charged that I had over-pampered my daughters. Some said I went against tradition, because our society does not value female children as much as their brothers.

But as should be crystal clear by now, I always do things as I like. I invest in knowledge. As a wealthy entrepreneur, I must say I did not just wake up one day and decide to buy Ferraris for my kids. A lot of thinking went into it. I have decided to share my thoughts on this because I find them valuable.

I'd made the decision years earlier, in March of 2018. My daughters are entrepreneurial, in the creative arts, which is a world with its own tastes and standards. I looked at the way the industry works, in terms of branding, and said to myself, "I need to encourage these girls." When you look at artistes—the way they dress, some with ten necklaces, gold, diamonds—you realize that gives them a boost in their art. So, I said, what can I do to elevate the profiles of my girls? That's branding.

An anecdote that reconfirmed my business instincts earlier on in life occurred sometime in 1996. I recall that I was finishing my first home in

GRA Ikeja and was looking for someone that makes beautiful wrought iron furniture for my swimming pool. Someone recommended a young, savvy up-and-coming businessman then as one of the best in that sector. I called him up and invited him over for an assessment. I recall he arrived at my house in an old Volkswagen Jetta. He subsequently gave me a bill of ₦965, 000 for the job which was a lot of money then. It didn't take me time to realise that I could take advantage of him. I offered him ₦400, 000 as my final offer. He hesitated and we bargained for a while until he reluctantly agreed to accept ₦500, 000 for the job. Because I liked his countenance and personality I decided to share a lesson in business strategy with him. I asked him if he knew the reason why I priced him the way I did. He looked at me with bemusement and said no. I then shared with him one of my mantras. I told him that in business "perception is reality." The way people perceive you is the way they relate and treat you. I then told him that he gave himself away when he drove to my house in an old Jetta. I recalled telling him that my perception of him then was that he was still struggling with business and would gladly accept my offer. I told him that if he had driven in a brand new Mercedes I would have treated him differently. He took my advice in good faith and to back up my assumptions then, I offered him my Mercedes Benz E320 Brabus Cabriolet at a huge discount with a promise that it would impact on his business positively and years later, he confirmed that it did. That young man then is Mr Anselm Tabansi, the founder and CEO of Svengali Designs Limited, one of the foremost furniture manufacturing brands in Nigeria today. That encounter in 1996 led to an enduring friendship that has lasted for 29 years.

The second reason is that my daughters can sustain their lifestyles. As I have noted, I regularly look at the cash flow from their businesses, and that convinced me that they could manage the cars by themselves. I made the first insurance payment, and they pay for the subsequent ones. There is thus a level of responsibility and commitment that came with this gift. If they were doing 9-to-5 jobs and wouldn't have been able to cover the insurance and pay for maintenance of the cars, I would not have bought Ferraris for them. They would have needed to keep coming to me for one thing or the other concerning the cars, and I would not have set any of us up for that.

The third reason is that they're good girls. In their industry, there are a lot of wayward characters who get deeply involved in drugs and other nefarious activity and have no respect for anyone. My daughters are well behaved. To start with, they don't do hard drugs, which is such a relief for a parent. Also, they listen to me. We've stayed very close. I could not have asked for more from them. I counsel them about life, offer them advice and try to guide them. They respect me and show a high level of responsibility. Not many wealthy individuals can say that about their children. In a way, therefore, buying them the cars was my way of rewarding their good character.

I always liked Ferraris as a young man, but my parents could never have afforded one. I now had that ability, and I went to a Ferrari dealer in London and ordered three. The salesman there was incredulous, stammering, "Excuse me, sir?" I repeated that I wanted three Ferraris, and promptly paid a deposit with my credit card.

The cars resonate with the girls' entertainment industry vibe. The sound of a Ferrari's engine is something to behold. From gentle purr to hearty growl you hear every bit of its 600 horsepower. No Rolls-Royce or Mercedes comes close.

My daughters were quite excited when I told them on the phone what I was doing. When Ferrari started building the cars for me, the girls went to the showroom to pick their colours and interiors. I'd initially wanted the gifts to be a surprise, but since they had to personalize the vehicles, that wasn't going to be possible. It takes about a year and a half to build the bespoke car, a delay that was stretched out by the COVID-19 crisis.

When I told my wife what I was buying for the girls, she said, "Femi, Ferrari?"

"Let them enjoy their lives," I told her.

One of them said, "But you just bought us Range Rovers."

"Don't worry," I told her. "I'm happy that I'm able to give you everything I want to give you while I'm alive. All these things I am giving you are to show my love and appreciation for you while I'm still here."

Including taxes, the Ferrari Portofinos cost £270,000 each. For the three, the bill came in at £810,000.

At the apartments I was buying for them, the garages would now need to accommodate two cars, so the properties needed a bit of reengineering.

How much you pamper your children depends on what they are doing. If a child has proved to you that he or she can survive alone, that they can put things together to earn one naira, that's it. The sky's the limit for them. I also look at it this way: tomorrow, they can always sell the car and use the proceeds as capital for their business. It's an asset.

What I have discovered is that for many wealthy people, the children inherit the money when their parents die and go crazy. After a couple of years of living large, it's all been frittered away. If you're going to pass an appreciable amount of money on to the next generation, you have to prepare them for it.

Wealth can be a funny thing. When you're alive, you derive happiness from sharing your money. You give other people gifts, like cars or whatever. It brings you joy to be making others happy. You obviously won't experience this emotion when you're dead. And once you're gone, you lose control over what the kids do with the money that has been left to them.

DON'T FORGET TO WRITE YOUR WILL

They don't spend money in heaven. You can't take it with you!

These words still warm my heart. As I matured in life and business, and became aware of certain realities, I came to terms with 'the inevitable.' And one thing I always remind myself of is that death can come at any time. Preparing for the end by writing a will, so that the beneficiaries of one's assets are clear, and one's wishes unambiguous, is a duty we owe our family.

I have seen seemingly happy and closely-knit families at war over the assets of their late breadwinners. The bitterness and anger expressed by feuding spouses, siblings and extended family—who often hang their relatives' dirty linen for all to see—offends decent people. On occasion, the prolonged acrimony carries on in the courts for decades.

As soon as I turned 31, knowing that I had amassed appreciable assets, the time had come to prepare a formal last will and testament. I called my lawyer, spelled out my wishes, listed the beneficiaries and executors, signed the document in the presence of witnesses and had it notarized. It felt good to get that taken care of. Over the years, as fortune smiled on me, I rewrote my will twice, when I was 49 and then again at 55.

An entrepreneur must plan, be methodical and deliberate, and avoid putting those he cares about in an ambiguous position. He or she should prepare an atmosphere of friendliness and peace for those he calls family. One can do this once they're over the legal age, and of sound mind, and have the document kept where the executors can readily access it.

There were four primary reasons I wrote a will, even back when I didn't have a tremendous amount of assets:

- A will clearly expresses your wishes for how you want your wealth distributed, with no lingering questions or potential points of dispute. A lot of planning goes into writing a will, and it shows that you are organized and pragmatic
- The will gives you the satisfaction that all you laboured for will not go to waste or into the wrong hands, and that those you care about can enjoy your wealth undisturbed
- Psychologically, a will reinforces the notion that you cannot take anything with you upon your death. It's a powerful reminder of that, which is an incentive to better plan your life and have your affairs in order, especially as you grow older
- It puts wealth accumulation in perspective, giving you the latitude to make decisions about what risks to take. It allows you to ask, "Is it worth it at this point in my life to invest in this line of business and take more loans, or is it better to retire and enjoy the little I have?"

If you do not write your will, and die intestate, the distribution of your assets is left to the dictates of the law. The state decides who gets what, which may not match your intentions, and it can all lead to a very nasty, prolonged fight.

MARRIAGE MAKES OR MARS

Marriage—and in fact any exclusive, loving relationship—is the centre beam that stabilizes both partners. It's like a solid foundation, buried deep in the ground, that keeps a house standing, ready to withstand the harsh elements. Married life provides the backdrop for a mature life, with happy children and an all-round fulfilling existence.

Those who marry their soul mates have found the wind behind their sails. Being with Nana has been more than a blessing for me. This is because:

(1) Peace at home provides fertile ground for business to bloom. Nana has given me a peaceful and comfortable homestead, which makes striving hard as an entrepreneur possible. Since our wedding 30 years ago, I have risen high, fallen low and soared again, and my wife has shown nothing but support through it all. I've had time to focus, and pursue my dreams and vision unwaveringly, thanks to the encouragement, love and stability she has provided, through turmoil and triumphs.

(2) A happy partner looks after the children well. Because Nana is a generally happy person, she has taken good care of our children, and she's close to Tolani, the daughter I had before I met her. She has dedicated her life, like all good mothers, to ensuring the comfort and wellbeing of her family. Nana is the pillar that our family leans on, in good times and bad.

(3) Your spouse can be your good luck charm. Spouses can be the bringer of good. A husband or wife amplifies your fortune and multiplies your joy. Tied by fate, it is one's spouse more than any other person who determines if the partner will laugh or cry in life. Your spouse's destiny is intertwined with yours, and whichever is more dominant tends to lead the way for you both. One can't overstate how important it is to carefully select the person you want to spend the rest of your life with.

Marrying the right person means a lot to a partner who aims high. In choosing a spouse, it pays to keep the following in mind:

(1) Marry for love, but with your eyes wide open. They say love conquers all, because you'll be able to resolve all issues together, big and small, when the ties are strong. Nevertheless, your eyes must be open wide to the reality of who it is that you're choosing as a partner.

(2) Put romance in your marriage and find time for fun. A partnership that works is the result of preparation and effort. You must make time to feed love, trust and warmth. Supply the ingredients that make a relationship blossom and give each other treats and memories that make being together not just bearable, but longed for and irreplaceable.

(3) Allow your spouse some financial independence. Let your better half be financially buoyant and independent. Let them run a business or practise their profession and encourage them emotionally and financially. Set them up with a financial stake if you can, as I did when I gave Nana a loan of ₦40 million to start Garment Care and she dutifully repaid it in full in four years.

TAKEAWAYS

The love and support of family can make or break an entrepreneur, as it can fundamentally make or break you as a person. Along the way, there are a few things I recommend you keep in mind:

- Marry for love, invest time and energy in romance, and support your partner financially
- Family always comes first—cherish, pamper, love and support your children and your spouse
- Let your children find their own path and calling, instead of bringing them into your business, which seldom works out
- Pamper your children, but don't overdo it
- Make sure you write a will and update it when necessary

SECTION FOUR

COLLAPSE AND REBIRTH

WHEN IT RAINS, IT POURS

LESSON FOURTEEN

RECOGNIZE YOUR LIMITS, CUT YOUR LOSSES

The collapse of Zenon was the best thing that ever happened to me. I'm of course only saying this with the benefit of hindsight; it was disastrous at the time. As I've noted, the Zenon model was bound to crash at some point. I was making so much money that I'd downplayed the red flags. The diesel market was shrinking. Manufacturers were switching to gas. Several gas-to-plant projects, which cut diesel out of the equation entirely, were coming on stream. To make matters worse, the Niger Delta Boys, a violent criminal gang, started refining diesel from stolen crude oil. They incurred little or no cost and flooded the market with cheap, substandard product.

It was inevitable that a business centred around diesel would go downhill. It was not sustainable. As I've alluded to, I used to tell people that Zenon reached the heights it did because the country was not functioning well. The government didn't fix the power sector. If it had, the requirement for diesel to power homes and factories wouldn't have existed in the first place. Factories could also run on gas. Or electricity. Only diesel-powered buses and vessels on the high seas would require the fuel, so only they would be our customers. I knew the whole power supply picture in Nigeria would eventually improve, because many development projects were under way, and diesel's domination of the energy market was not going to last forever.

I say that the collapse of Zenon was the best thing that happened to me because of the lessons I learned. I plummeted to the lowest point of my life, experienced humiliation, saw others for their true colours, and paid heavily to get out of debt.

I built a new life after rebuilding my business empire from the ashes of Zenon and am entirely free of debt. I was lucky that all of this happened when I was 47 years old. Some people experience such severe challenges in their 60s or 70s, when a downfall like mine would be completely and permanently crushing. They go to their graves broke, broken and depressed. I experienced the worst and moved on. You do not start learning your lessons in your old age. That is not the best way to exit this world.

One of the most important, and hardest, lessons in business is knowing when to cut your losses. You must recognize your limits. You have to grasp what's working, what's not and have a sense of what might (and might not) be the solution. You have to keep asking what you want to get out of life. You also have to reach a stage of contentment without becoming complacent.

As an ambitious and driven businessman who did everything to dominate the diesel market in Nigeria, it may sound incongruous for me to preach contentment to any entrepreneur. If I was content, why did I keep pushing until I'd cornered 93% of the market? Why did I keep driving hard until the empire collapsed? And then started all over again?

I can preach contentment today because I have achieved it. And this is what it has taught me:

(1) Take an inventory. It's good to start small, but not right to *think* small. It's good to dream big and pursue your dreams. There's nothing to be said against ambition. There is everything to be said against a lack of enthusiasm and against complacency. But you have to know when to take a loss and move on. If you don't stop when the writing's on the wall, you risk losing it all. Sometimes, you need to stop, catch your breath and see if it makes sense to head in a new direction. Maybe that calls for taking a sharp pivot or reversing course. Speeding recklessly ahead, without ever hitting the brakes, can kill.

In football, when you've scored two goals and keep charging hard, hoping to obliterate your opponents, you also run the risk of getting snookered at the back. We've seen teams cancel out two-goal deficits and go on to win the game. You're rushing all-out to defeat the other guys, rather than defending the advantage you have. When you do that, your opponents—who have read you and can sense your vulnerabilities—will hit back. Before you know it, you concede one goal. You want to go out and make amends, and then you're hit with the equalizer. You become jittery and fatigued. Your opponents get a fresh run of adrenalin and keep coming at you. By the final whistle, you have lost the game.

You will discover that keeping what you had would have been better than pushing for more and losing everything in the process.

(2) Monopolistic pursuits can be your downfall. My desire for a monopoly wrecked Zenon. I plunged headlong into debt and lost it all. Yes, you are allowed to fail, but don't lose everything. If I had not experienced that loss, I would not have learned contentment. I would still be a raging bull, charging at everybody. Today, I'm happy to take it easy. I am delighted to survey the landscape, calculate my risks, know my limits, cover my flank, protect my turf, and—when it clearly makes sense—to cut my losses. Contentment is so important, but they do not teach it in a classroom. You need to experience life's quandaries to understand what it means.

Take a look at your life. In your quiet moments, ask yourself what your legacy will be, what you want in life, what makes you happy. You have to put all these together to arrive at the destination of contentment. It's at this stage that you realize that most of the things you wanted in life are not necessary. You must know when to slow down. You cannot keep going into debt, having sleepless nights and battling high blood pressure because of a desire to conquer by any means possible. There is no gauge to determine when you get to this stage, but if you're a self-reflective person, a simple check-in with yourself will tell you when you are crossing the line.

(3) Age helps you to embrace contentment. In my case, as I believe happens with many people, age helped me become contented with my life. The energies and desires you have in your 20s, 30s and 40s naturally diminish. By the time I got out of the Zenon disaster, my priorities had changed, so I looked within myself and reshaped my values. I asked myself what I wanted in my life and concluded that I wanted to be happy—very happy. What makes me happy? Giving. I found that I'm happiest when I give, in ways that help alleviate poverty and suffering. I want people around me to be happy. Seeing others happy makes me all the happier. That is what contentment brings into your life. It connects you with your surroundings and your community, and you see that life is about so much more than personal attainment.

There was a time when I'd deluded myself into believing that happiness came from downing bottles of alcohol and smoking. I've described the negative effects that had. If I drank to excess, which I certainly did, I'd start cancelling essential meetings and appointments, or showing up late, because of drinking's impact on my physical wellbeing and state of mind. I couldn't keep going like that. It's not as if stopping drinking and smoking is a piece of cake; it takes strength and conviction. To this day, there are times when I'm around a bar, and see people partying hard, and still feel enticed. But I'm strong-willed. I quit smoking and drinking at the right time in my life, and there's no turning back.

(4) You ought to know when to stop the bleeding. When I talk about cutting your losses, I mean that you should stop doing the things that are obviously making you fail. If you're losing money or going deeper into debt, why keep going down that rabbit hole? We've talked about how entrepreneurs can be driven by ego and keep at it despite all the red flags. They care more about what their contemporaries and competitors would say than what's best for them and their ventures. You have to be pragmatic, regardless of any overblown ambitions and projections. A time comes when you have to stop the bleeding so that you'll have enough vital lifeblood left to see the next day.

It also depends on the individual. Entrepreneurs typically believe they will succeed, so to a certain extent, losing money is no big deal. They can lose money here and make money there. If you are decidedly not ready to lose money, you can't be an entrepreneur. You'll lose it at one point or the other, but you have to know when to abandon a losing proposition and move onto something else entirely. Just recognize when it makes sense to let go.

I knew when that time had come for me. After all, I left the diesel business. You keep trying until you find your grip on a particular market. But you must know when enough is enough. You have to know where to draw the line.

WHAT MY SECOND-HAND CAR EXPERIENCE SAYS ABOUT CUTTING YOUR LOSSES

In 1983, I bought an Audi 100 GLS for ₦8,000. After spending ₦32,000 purchasing new parts and fixing it, virtually spending more time at the mechanic's workshop than on the road, I decided to sell it for ₦12,000 two years later. And I moved on.

I cut my losses. I accepted it was no longer efficient spending. I didn't need to keep losing money just because people would laugh at me if they thought I'd made a bad decision. Some entrepreneurs keep borrowing just to put up an appearance. But every entrepreneur must ask a series of probing questions. When am I going to be free from debt? How long can I live this kind of life? When will I stop being a prisoner to the banks?

Some entrepreneurs can't stop borrowing; they keep worshipping at the feet of the banks. If you don't reach the point where you ask yourself the hard questions, and face up to reality, you'll never get out of debt. From one business to another, you'll keep borrowing. You have brought the bankers into your life, and they'll forever be on your case. It will be as if they're sleeping in the same room with you—a constant, menacing presence.

It takes a lot to decide that you have had enough, that you've made your mark and you now want to go enjoy yourself. That is the contentment stage. And it's wonderful, once you know how to let go and embrace happiness.

ANOTHER CASE STUDY: THE US$600 MILLION JP MORGAN DEAL I IGNORED

The world is awash with opportunities, but you should never grab blindly. Explore and leverage every break that falls into your lap. Even the most successful entrepreneurs can't stop seemingly juicy deals from slipping through their fingers. Nobody wins all the time, no matter how savvy or blessed they are. You win some and you lose some. What is important is to win more than you lose.

Sometimes, deals that appear lucrative or prestigious will generate huge losses. If you're attentive enough, you will find that many ventures are not worth your time or energy. I came to learn that through the story of JP Morgan's US$600 million offer. Mr Olaolu Mudasiru of Vetiva Capital Management Limited approached me with a US$600 million offer from JP Morgan.

In 2007, I was one of the largest single investors in the Nigerian stock market, with considerable stakes in oil, telecoms and banks. In most of the sectors I played, I was the number one or two stakeholder, and Zenon was cruising along smoothly, with an extensive portfolio. So, it was no surprise when a representative of JP Morgan called to book an appointment to review and offer consultation on my holdings. After a meeting in my office, I forwarded an email that laid out my stock ownership.

The proposal they came back with was simple: JP Morgan wanted to buy all my shares on the Nigerian Stock exchange for US$600 million, with the exception of my stake in African Petroleum, which I'd just bought for ₦17 billion.

Soon after, Olaolu Mudasiru of Vetiva Capital Management Ltd approached me with a similar proposition.

The conversations were short and sweet. "Sorry, gentlemen," I advised both parties. "I'm not selling."

I chose not to cash out of the stock market for four reasons:

(1) It's not just about money. The shares were worth more than gold to me. I enjoyed having interests in the most lucrative sectors of the Nigerian economy and contributing to their growth. It was not only about money. It was personally fulfilling to provide funds to companies delivering essential services to the people of my country.

(2) You shouldn't settle for less than your worth. They grossly undervalued my portfolio. I would not sell for US$600 million—not even for US$2 billion. In 2007, my three billion shares in Zenith Bank were worth ₦180 billion, which was equivalent to about US$1.5 billion. If they'd done the assessment correctly, they would have found that my portfolio was worth well over US$3 billion, minus my assets abroad.

(3) You can say no when you don't need the money. The truth was that I did not need that big payday. I had many things going for me—my business was doing well, and I had just acquired a majority stake in African Petroleum PLC. I could raise money from a consortium of banks, as Jim Ovia, the founder and then MD of Zenith Bank, demonstrated when he helped arrange the US$2.8 billion trading loan that Zenith Bank, Access Bank and Oceanic, among others, provided to Zenon.

(4) A profitable investment is worth holding onto. My portfolio was profitable, and the companies were paying dividends. They paid dividends and bonuses frequently. The returns were well worth my investment.

If the JP Morgan offer had been a fair reflection of the portfolio's value, maybe I would have considered selling. But there was of course the possibility that I would have then invested the proceeds in other businesses and lost it all. True, I could have done so and doubled my money, but one never knows.

BAD DECISIONS: THE BANK SHARES

Before Zenon went into a tailspin, I had bank shares that I wanted to sell to clear up my debts. I'd bought them during the banks' drive to meet the Nigerian Central Bank's minimum capital requirement of ₦25 billion, between 2004 and 2005. If I had sold them off at the time I wanted to, I wouldn't have had any debt whatsoever.

I would have cut my losses on the shares and moved on, but I was deceived into holding onto them. The way I was then, I would have built the debt up again. Debt is such a sweet seductress. The illusion of ownership seduces you, and you forget that this is money you owe to others. It looks like easy cash being thrown at you, and you start to obsess over how to spend it.

I was going to get out of Zenith in 2007, when the share price was at ₦60. I was the bank's second-largest shareholder, after its MD, Jim Ovia. I would have made money if I'd liquidated at that point. Jim persuaded me not to sell, telling me it would appreciate in value, and I'd make more money.

That was the first time I saw Jim drive himself in a car. He pulled up to my house in a Mercedes G-Wagon. "Femi," he said, "we own the bank together. Don't worry—the share price will soon climb to ₦100. Don't sell." I listened to him, which was a mistake. The share price continued to tumble. Jim eventually bought the shares from me at ₦12. That was a massive hit. I had a similar experience with Tony Elumelu at UBA, which, incidentally, was my first foray into buying shares. I wanted to get out and he said I shouldn't, assuring me that the price would rise. They didn't, and I took a big loss. But I did sell my FCMB shares. Otunba Subomi Balogun, the bank's executive chairman, was very understanding. He said that when he needed me to invest, in 2005, I had obliged him. Now that I wanted to sell, he bought from me at a better price, unlike Jim and Tony, who'd persuaded me to hold on.

I was also lucky to sell shares in the bank Stanbic IBTC, which I had bought for ₦1.4 billion. Founder Atedo Peterside invited me to lunch with his Deputy MD, Sola David-Borha, and the two persuaded me to invest. A few years later, he was selling his shares and advised me to do so, and I sold at a profit, reaping ₦1.7 billion.

On the other hand, Intercontinental Bank took my shares as partial payment for money I owed them. Francis Atuche at Platinum Bank also took some to reduce my debt. Access Bank and GTB did likewise. What's more, I sold a portion of my shares in African Finance Corporation, where I was the largest individual shareholder, to reduce my debt. Access Bank and UBA seized my shares in African Finance Corporation for a total of

₦6 billion, paying ₦3 billion each. Wondering what these stock market adventures have taught me?

(1) Learn to spread risk. As I have said repeatedly here, there are things about being an entrepreneur that you can't learn in the classroom. You need to go through it. If you're wise enough, you will pick up on lessons that will shape your thinking. For one, it's difficult to recognize your limits until you enter a hole. You won't even know these limits exist or that you're about to bump up against them. It is like someone who drives at 180 kilometres per hour, thinking himself a Formula One driver. It is only when he crashes that he'll accept his limits. 'Experience is the best teacher' is an old maxim that never goes out of date.

(2) Don't keep all your money in one bank. I know from experience how unwise it is to put your money into a single financial institution. I also wouldn't consider keeping my money in one country. If you spread the wealth, and Bank A collapses, Bank B will not necessarily fail. But if Bank B does as well, that doesn't mean Bank C will go under. You spread your risk. If this country plunges into turmoil, others won't. Sovereign nations keep foreign reserves in other countries, and in different currencies, for a reason. That's why people insure, for protection from these sorts of calamities. As they say, don't put all your eggs in one basket.

(3) Consider my 60/20/20 rule. To better spread your risk, and protect yourself from the devastating blows of recession, devaluation and mismanagement by institutions and countries, your net worth should be spread across organizations and nations as follows: 60% in cash; 20% in property; 20% in stock. This is what I do, and it has served me well, giving me peace of mind.

(4) Know your limits, and what defines them. Knowing how far you are willing to go, and what you think you're capable of, helps you find solutions to overcome those limitations. I partnered up with industrialist Aliko Dangote to buy refineries. I'm not afraid to enter into sizeable transactions, but I have learned to bring in partners as a form of insurance. That is another way of managing the risks you take. I invited Dangote and the conglomerate Transcorp to bid for the Port Harcourt and

Kaduna refineries with me in 2007. We formed the Blue Star Oil Services Consortium, with Dangote controlling 51%, Transcorp 10% and me 20%, with plans to list the rest on the stock exchange. That's why there are partnerships—people come together to pool resources and dilute the risk. I could define my limits, and in this instance, it came down to available cash. If I had all the necessary money, I wouldn't invite anybody to join me in buying the refineries. But no bank would have gone there. I had to be pragmatic.

Knowing your limits affords you the wisdom to know what to do at every point to achieve your objectives. In addition to the refinery acquisitions, Jim Ovia approached me to partner with him in bidding for the rights to an oil block, a piece of land where petroleum can be extracted. The Port Harcourt and Kaduna refineries project failed, and we lost heavily. Though our money was refunded (US$561 million for Port Harcourt and US$160 million for Kaduna, for a total of US$721 million), I lost US$17 million in bank interest, and legal and consultancy fees.

(5) Seeking outside help can pay off. A few years before the government announced the privatization of the power sector, Chris Adeyemi—whom I've mentioned earlier, as my lawyer and confidant, who I made a Director at Forte Oil PLC—had been telling me about the opportunities that would present. He'd painted a very promising picture of having a hand in electricity generation and distribution.

On a journey to London in June of 2009, when I accompanied then Nigerian Vice President Goodluck Jonathan to an event chaired by the politician Baroness Lynda Chalker, Chris invited me to a meeting with his brother-in-law, Taj Giwa-Osagie, and an Irish associate who was interested in investing in Nigeria. The Irishman had worked at three top accounting firms—Arthur Andersen, Deloitte and Ernst & Young—and knew a lot about the power industry. We met at the London Hilton on Park Lane. Chris insisted that this was someone I needed to meet. The wheels of the power sector's privatization were already in motion, and my interest was piqued. We had a fruitful conversation, and I returned to Nigeria intent on getting in on the action.

Dr Jonathan became President of Nigeria in May of 2010, and in August he formally announced the privatization of the sector. We awaited the details and got ourselves ready to invest in the industry. I recognized that to succeed in such an enterprise, having a foreign technical partner and investor was an absolute requirement. I knew I needed partners with years of experience and a depth of expertise. Apart from the wealth of know-how they'd bring to the table, they would also put in equity and save me from borrowing.

Between January and June 2011, Chris and Taj researched the biggest power companies in the world. They combed the internet, looking for companies to partner with in Europe, the US, the United Arab Emirates and China. They eventually settled on Amperion from Greece and SGCC/SMEPC in China. They exchanged dozens of emails and had scores of conference calls with the Chinese company, and we were introduced to Amperion by Taj's associate. These efforts laid the foundation for the partnership, and we were invited to China for further talks in June.

And so, Chris, Taj and Mike Ahme, my Zenon COO, joined other partners and lawyers in travelling to China for the first presentation to SGCC/SMEPC. I remember telling Chris on the eve of the trip, "Don't come back with a no." The negotiations were tough. The Chinese were thorough and methodical, and at one point walked out. When they returned, our team resolved the areas of conflict, and eventually left with a signed memorandum of understanding with SGCC/SMEPC. The success of the trip was reassuring and convinced me that we could play big in the sector, with the big Chinese enterprise in our corner.

Our partnership with Amperion of Greece involved meetings in London, and some very tough negotiations. They visited Nigeria, and things seemed headed in the right direction, but they pulled out of the deal after we'd already created Amperion Nigeria, the holding company we'd use to acquire Geregu Power PLC in 2013.

When our Chinese partners visited Lagos after inking the agreement, we knew we had a solid partnership on our hands. What they saw impressed them, and they promised to deliver on their part of the bargain. I then flew to China—the first of my four trips there—and that cemented it. A visit in June of 2012 was one of the most significant. We negotiated and signed the share purchase and shareholders' agreement with SGCC/SMEPC. In July 2013, I was part of President Jonathan's delegation on an official visit to China and facilitated an informational courtesy meeting between him and officials of SGCC/SMEPC.

The most exciting part of the partnership was the consultancy to determine what to buy from the various Nigerian generating and distribution companies, and at what price. As part of the opportunity-scouting consultancy we paid SGCC/SMEPC for, more than 50 Chinese technocrats came for the due diligence, visiting every one of the companies that were up for sale. From Ibadan to Abuja, Geregu to Ilorin and more, they scrutinized everything. It was money, time and effort well spent.

(6) Know when to move on. I opted not to buy Chevron's Nigerian business for US$700 million. When Chevron Oil and Gas Ltd put the country's Texaco distribution and retail operation up for sale in 2009, I already held a 13% stake in it and offered US$300 million for the business. It wasn't enough. The consortium of MRS Holdings and Petroci Holding Company eventually bought the majority stake, for US$700 million.

I dodged a bullet there. Imagine if I had bought it for what was eventually paid. My debt would have been how much now? It would have been astronomical. It was one of the instances that convinced me that you don't always win, and that that's not always such a bad thing. You must know when to take your loss and move on.

(7) Know what works for you. I've described how bored I'd been in school, and that dropping out and helping with my father's business was the right thing for me. It nearly killed my mother, but I had to follow my instincts and my convictions. I wanted to take charge of my life.

(8) Timing is incredibly important. Whether it's in business, or in our personal lives, moving on requires wisdom and the right timing. You have to know when to change course. My first registered company, Centre Force, could have been a big finance house or even evolved into a bank, with branches around the world. I can't say. Car supply contracts and quick loans were no longer attractive to me, and I just moved on.

TAKEAWAYS

- There is a time to be born, and there's a time to die. In between, remember to live
- Every entrepreneur must assess the state of play in their business and know when to slow down, speed up, change gears, reverse, stomp on the brakes or make a U-turn
- Your ego must not stand in the way of doing what's right
- Many entrepreneurs have run into troubled waters, and failed, because they didn't know how to recognize their limits or cut their losses
- Know what works for you, and try to figure out the right timing

If Zenon hadn't collapsed, I'm sure I would still have gone on to do something else. AP put me on a bigger playing field, although there was no chance of becoming a monopoly there, as was the case with diesel.

LESSON FIFTEEN

MASTER THE ART OF REINVENTION

My friend Wale Tinubu, MD of Oando PLC and once a fierce competitor, calls me 'the master of reinvention.' I've been called that by other friends and associates, particularly after the sale of Forte Oil PLC in June 2019.

Some still cannot fathom why a Nigerian would sell a viable business that had been returning such huge dividends. Its owner was not old and couldn't possibly have been considering retirement. The firm was not mired in debt, nor was it in any other sort of trouble. To this day, the sale—an exacting process that took 16 months, with more than 4,000 documents exchanged—is a subject of curiosity and perpetual dissection in boardrooms across the country.

For most of my adult life, I have believed in, and successfully executed, strategic reinventions. One of the beauties of life is the human race's capacity to adapt and change and start anew. Evolution even teaches us that you adapt or die.

I have been lucky to know how to envision, plan and accomplish my reinventions. Sometimes, I've failed when I did not get the timing or process right, but most times I succeeded, with all the elements coming together to elevate me to victory. From one business to the other, I have been strategic in my planning, and surgically tactical in execution, as I've moved on to the next stage.

My journey to the top tier of my chosen fields has convinced me that if you don't reinvent yourself, you wither on the vine. I have seen the troubled fate of those who ignored the need for reinvention and have felt the excitement that comes with witnessing ingenious evolution and change. I never tire of citing the example of my friend, Aliko Dangote, who's mentioned many times in these pages. He started as a small-scale cement distributor, moved on to become a significant force in commodity trading, and later positioned himself as a colossus of industry, owning sugar, salt, cement and flour factories. And now, he's a petroleum products giant, with the world's second-largest fertilizer plant and the largest oil refinery in Africa coming on stream. I have called his US$19.5 billion, 650,000-barrel-a-day integrated refinery and petrochemical project—which is spread across 2,635 hectares on Lagos's Atlantic coast—'the eighth wonder of the world.' I've also called it 'Dangote's Wonderland.'

In just over 40 years, the Kano-born and Lagos-based businessman has become a phenomenon, celebrated around the globe. He is an example of how no great leader, in business, politics or any endeavour, succeeds without an ability to change course and refocus efforts when necessary. I am fond of the football metaphor of versatile coaches, with dozens of game plans and strategies, picking and choosing from them depending on the opponents and reality on the turf. When their team is leading, they know which tactics to deploy to stay ahead. When they're losing, they know to substitute tired legs and players who aren't on their best performance and bring on attentive playmakers who will implement the game plan.

In moving from the printing business, to working on my father's political campaign and as adviser to the governor, to my new life in a variety of business ventures, I was reinvention personified.

And that dovetailed into the personal brand. I described earlier how I've enjoyed changing my look through the years, with my all-white attire, updating the *buba* and *sokoto* to a slimmer kaftan, abandoning watches and adopting Tom Ford's international mix of formal and casual ensembles. The image I projected changed along with my vision, as I introduced glasses and a beard to my look.

The face of the company is critical; it gives the enterprise an identifiable look and feel and inspires confidence among its stakeholders. Public perception is crucial when you're considering and planning reinvention. I calculate everything I do; nothing is random or arbitrary. I don't just do things. I plan my moves meticulously, looking many steps ahead, and execute them painstakingly. And I am happy with where that's taken me, and grateful for where I am now.

It's clear why we entrepreneurs need to reinvent periodically. Here are my top reasons:

(1) Reinvention saves you and your business from failure. As years roll by, tastes change, technology reshapes the way we do things, and corporate leaders have to continuously adapt their products and services to fit the times. If they don't, revenue and market share will dwindle, and collapse is assured. Those who are smart will rebrand and repackage, or go into a new line of business entirely, to meet consumers' expectations and satisfy demand.

An entrepreneur who knows his or her market and competition, and all the ingredients that go into a successful endeavour, will plan for five or ten years ahead. They must detect dangers and see opportunities from afar, and continually sharpen their senses. In Zenon, I spotted the patterns of diesel demand. I plotted what I needed to do to grab a massive chunk of the market and invested in the distribution and supply chains. Going forward, I established companies at home and abroad to benefit from lucrative, untapped opportunities.

(2) The thrill of a fresh start is a great push. Reinvention is a tonic, providing fresh stimulation that any businessperson can benefit from. It redirects his mind to look for better value for the consumer and expands his perception of what can drive demand. This elixir keeps him awake and alert, sharpens his vision and provides insight, which leads to a more satisfying customer experience. A great example of this is my company FO Properties, the purveyor of those elegantly finished apartments, appointed with luxury furniture, in the most exclusive parts of town, that I mentioned earlier. Without new thrills and excitement, every day becomes uninspiring drudgery. And without that passion, inertia and backsliding are sure to follow.

(3) Routine is the enemy of growth. No matter how successful a product has been, it eventually appears tired and boring to consumers unless it's frequently tweaked, updated and injected with fresh value. Buyers desire newness in their purchases, which is often achieved through repackaging. People look for more modern and easy-to-use models, systems and designs. The consumer's experience must be gratifying. When we rebranded to Forte Oil, the service stations were remodelled, pumps modernized and employee uniforms updated. Some stations even started operating 24/7. When customers are bored with a brand, reinvention will renew their interest and keep the revenue flowing.

LEARNING FROM YOUR MISTAKES

Mistakes inevitably happen in business, and result in losses or reversals that are usually reparable. They crop up unannounced but can sometimes be anticipated. If you study the economic environment, the sector and your enterprise itself, you'll be better positioned to watch for potential missteps before they occur. Some experts can accurately forecast the economic outlook by analysing trends and activities. Companies recruit competent analysts to strategize, spot developing problems and complications, and take the appropriate steps before they do any damage. But when you're enjoying massive success, over a long period, it's easy to ignore serious problems until the business collapses. And if you are a control freak, you probably won't have the mentality to rely on the expertise of others or be proactive in anticipating and addressing problems. I was that guy. No need to call in experts to pore over the economic outlook when the business is doing fabulously well, I always thought. That was the story of Zenon.

In less than a year after starting the diesel supply enterprise, it had transformed my life beyond my imagination, and I took my eye off many issues that eventually combined to kill off the company. I paid dearly for ignoring the fundamentals that strengthen enterprises and render them more professional. Whatever form a business adopts—sole proprietorship, partnership or limited liability company—you must never ignore the basics.

There were some big mistakes that conspired to wreck Zenon. This is what I learned from them:

(1) Running a business without a structure is a bad idea. A company must operate within a clearly defined framework, from the rules of engagement to its operational procedures. There should be an employee manual, job descriptions and guidelines on what to do in various situations. There are certain positions required for a company with Zenon's volume of business to function correctly, and those roles were missing in our case. One of these was a CFO. Because I wore all the hats, Zenon could not protect itself from external and internal abuse. For one, we never assessed risks comprehensively before taking loans. Nor did we monitor the fees and interest attached to our bank loans. We ignored these gaps and management errors to our detriment because Zenon was making money, and at the time that seemed to be all that mattered.

(2) You should populate top management based on merit. My recruitment method was a bit unorthodox, and partly owing to that, those who filled the senior management positions were not professional enough to cope with the demands of the job. I had the ill luck of sometimes employing people more interested in the perks of their position than with the demands of their jobs. They took advantage of the company's resources for personal benefit. They abused their offices. And, on a few occasions, employees were downright quarrelsome and antagonistic. Their capacity for drama would have been better suited for Nollywood, the Nigerian film industry. I was not attentive enough to redress the situation in good time.

(3) Nepotism and cronyism spell disaster. I've said again and again here that it's not a good idea to employ family or entertain requests for political favours, because you're compromising the quality and integrity of your workforce and your company. Family members rarely grow the business or serve its interests faithfully. And because blood is thicker than water, we tend to overlook their excesses and evaluate their performance through rose-tinted glasses. For example, if the rules say you can't bring children to the office, and your sibling does, this opens the door to others following suit. And if they're fond of coming in late, and rushing off before the close of business, law and order breaks down. It's all bad for business.

Similarly, my association with people in power led to employing those they sent to me, and many of these referrals were unqualified. You meet this high-ranking official, and he gives you three people to hire. Depending on the circumstances and the politics involved, you may have to employ them, whether there's space or not. The company loses focus when saddled with staff you don't need, or people whose experience and skills are a mismatch. The idle hands begin to disturb the diligent ones, preventing the latter from doing their job.

Luckily, I got a second chance to start from scratch, and learned from—and committed to not repeating—my mistakes. I weighed all the issues that led to the collapse of Zenon and addressed them methodically and factually, without sentiment.

MY PATH TO REINVENTION IN SEVEN STEPS

First, I had to concentrate on my reinvention agenda. Here are the steps I took when I held a 21% stake in AP PLC (held as collateral by Zenith Bank for some of their loans to me) and three properties: my Abuja house, Ikoyi home and Victoria Island office:

Step 1: I repurchased the AP shares from the banks. The ₦52 billion worth of stock they underwrote were sold to me to increase my stake in AP. Because the share price had dropped ridiculously low, due to the company's negative image and some bankers' underhanded manipulation, I repurchased them from Access Bank, FCMB, GTBank, UBA and Zenith at an adjusted mark-to-market price—that is, valuing them by the most recent price—of ₦300 million.

Step 2: I relinquished my executive position and told my sister to leave hers as well, to allow more tech-savvy and forward-looking young men and women independent reign. I explained to my sibling that I would find something else for her to do.

Step 3: There were indications that Afribank, the offer's registrar, had criminally manipulated the public offering. They were accused by the Securities and Exchange Commission of forging documents relating to the deal. Afribank's[12] 20% share was confiscated and sold to existing shareholders. I also acquired those.

Step 4: I bought more shares from dividends disbursed from real estate sales. AP sold two of its high-end properties in Ikoyi to pay dividends. I used the profits to acquire more shares.

Step 5: I described earlier how I'd decided not to be the MD of the rebranded company, and redeployed Akin Akinfemiwa from my London office to take over as CEO. This improved our image, but we now needed more money to trade and bounce back. To this end, I approached Segun Agbaje, my good friend at GTBank, who listened as I worked through the changes that would bring the company back to profitability. And, as mentioned, I asked him to nominate a CFO, who would ensure prudent deployment of monies and keep proper accounts. Segun offered us a new line of credit and nominated the finance head, which gave us a fresh lifeline.

Step 6: I searched for a new company name that aligned with my initials, F. O. That way, I figured, my personal reputation would be on the line, and the bank would look at the company in a different light, as would the public. We played with names like First Oil, Fossil Oil and Fort Oil.

My daughter Tolani suggested Forte Oil, but we discovered that someone had already registered it. I instructed my lawyers to pay the man ₦20 million for the rights, despite his never actually having used the name. I also changed my image to fit the rebranding philosophy. And my new beard and glasses signalled that there was something new and exciting in the offing. With rebranding finalized in December 2010, we went to work.

Step 7: I put together a diverse and experienced board that was committed to following best practices. As I've described, we needed proven directors from different backgrounds to build confidence in Forte Oil, allowing it to rebuild and grow again. Those professionals, who I introduced to you in Lesson Twelve, gave us the maturity, gravitas and air of legitimacy we needed. Along with stricter corporate governance procedures, they helped us become one of the most compliant listed companies, and always the first to submit financial reports when they were due.

HOW TO KNOW WHEN TO QUIT

Knowing when to stop your relentless push forward is a different matter altogether. When it's the right time, you can either cut your losses and/or cash out on the upswing for maximum return on investment. Whichever the case, it is a tough decision to make and execute. Wisdom and caution are required.

Knowing when to quit can come with deciding you've had enough of a venture, and no longer feel ready to take further risks, which is what I finally did with Forte Oil in June of 2019.

That decision to sell came after I'd asked myself these five questions:

- How old am I?
- What are my primary goals?
- How many of these goals have I achieved?
- What are my expenses?
- What gives me happiness?

After working through these questions, I concluded that my happiness was the most important factor. I realized that charitable giving gives me enormous joy. So, I calculated how much I would be willing to give. I also considered that it was possible to lose everything, and I'd have to start back at square one at the age of 56. For months on end, I weighed all the factors and crawled through all the figures, in quiet contemplation.

After some time, as I stared at the figures and looked to the future, I also asked myself:

- How much do I get in dividends in a year?
- If I cashed out and placed my money in deposits, how much interest would I receive?
- Would my income from the interest support my desired lifestyle?
- What's the future of my sector?

My conclusion was that if I found a buyer at my estimated sale price, cashed out, placed the money in deposits and got interest that I could live on, then I would sell. This would achieve the goals and answer the questions on my list, and I would be spared the headache of further business challenges and an uncertain future. Once I knew I could get what I wanted, I buried my ego. But it was a difficult decision, because Nigerians aren't favourably disposed towards the idea of selling their businesses. That has always been a white man's thing.

When people heard that I was selling Forte Oil, many were shocked. My friends pressed me for an explanation. Some wanted all the details, so they could try and replicate what I was doing. A few were quick to point out that selling a public limited company requires the strictest possible adherence to the rules and procedures laid out by the regulators. In the end, passing the test of the Securities and Exchange Commission demonstrated to all exactly how well my company rated on the corporate governance scale.

My assumption had been that selling the company would take just a few months. It ultimately took 16 months to conclude the sale of 75% of the shares. I give kudos to Akin Akinfemiwa, the CEO, for his unrelenting effort and endeavour on this journey. It was another journey—one that taught me patience and precision all over again.

In the beginning, Total Oil PLC showed up hoping to be the sole bidder. Vitol SA/Helios Partners also expressed interest, as did Carlyle Energy, NIPCO, Eterna PLC and the Ignite Investment arm of Prudent Energy & Services. There was even a Spanish company in the running. Instead of rushing the process, we decided to go through a standard vetting procedure. It was only Ignite Investment that moved beyond just showing interest. And then the game was on.

When we started the negotiations, I invited Standard Chartered Bank of Dubai to represent me, and Prudent Energy's Abdulwasiu Sowami recruited the Standard Bank of South Africa. I had never seen such thoroughness. It was a rigorous process that was at times quite stressful. We had to hold an extraordinary general meeting to seek shareholder approval. There was no back door, and every step was transparent.

The process of selling Forte Oil opened my eyes even further, and I learned many business lessons from the meetings and negotiations. It was a tiresome but ennobling experience that I wouldn't trade for anything. Quitting Forte Oil taught me two important things:

(1) Everything worth doing must be done well. There was no way we could have fast-forwarded the process, because the procedures all had timelines. Speed was sacrificed for precision, for the sake of thoroughness.

(2) Everything you do well takes longer than projected. Anything that requires fastidious precision takes more time, but satisfaction is guaranteed. A process I thought would be concluded in a few months took almost a year and a half, with no break.

TAKEAWAYS

Reinvention is an often overlooked but powerful tool in the arsenal of a talented entrepreneur, but it takes experience to master. Remember this: Don't be complacent. Routine is the enemy of growth, for both you and the consumer

- Reinvention can give a failing business a new lease of life
- It can reignite the thrill of challenge and the fire of passion, within you and your team
- Don't forget that running a business that isn't properly structured never works out, and neither does nepotism
- Allow yourself to reflect on whether it is a good idea to quit, if you feel such an urge

LESSON SIXTEEN

WEATHER THE STORM WISELY AND BRAVELY

The first storm I had to see out at Zenon was purely political. It was no secret that I was close to top military figures in the days of General Sani Abacha, Nigeria's Head of State from 1993-1998. The late Major General Patrick Aziza—the man who headed the military tribunal that sentenced Chief Olusegun Obasanjo to death in 1995 over allegations of plotting a coup—was my very close friend. He was Minister of Communications under Abacha, who died suddenly on 8 June 1998. General Abdulsalami Abubakar replaced Abacha and released Obasanjo from prison. Obasanjo was then elected civilian president and sworn into office on 29 May 1999.

And that marked the start of my problems.

Zenon was just beginning to climb the diesel ladder when Obasanjo took office. Those who felt threatened by our company's rise went and whispered in his ear. They alleged that it was military officials, presumably his enemies, who owned the company. Aziza was a friend, and Obasanjo hadn't forgiven him for the role he played in the latter's trial. After struggling to get diesel supply directly from NNPC—the sole importer at the time—I woke up one day in 2002 to the news that the state entity had to stop allocating to me. Others, who did not own any facilities, were now getting the allocations. I had to buy from them. This injustice gravely limited my profit margin.

The late Dr Rilwanu Lukman—a former minister of petroleum, and at the time an adviser to the new president on petroleum and energy matters, who doubled as the head of NNPC—did not want to see me or hear about Zenon. It seemed that I was like a plague to be avoided, and for no good reason. They locked the door firmly against us. I needed to sort out this problem, and fast.

I called all the people I knew but was kept out in the cold. It seemed that I was down for the count. It was a silly lie that military people owned Zenon; I started and ran this business by myself. How my detractors succeeded in deceiving Obasanjo was beyond me.

After an especially fruitless lobbying trip to Abuja in 2002, I came back to Lagos, gathered the staff together and gave them the bad news: I was going to shut down Zenon. No business can survive persecution from state officials in a developing economy. I felt that we weren't going to be able to thrive without being allowed access to NNPC for product. Although they had liberalized the market, this was only on paper, as the pricing mechanism favoured only the NNPC. Any other importer would run into a brick wall and go bankrupt.

At the time I contemplated calling it quits, Zenon had about 200 employees. I was going to render scores of people jobless, not because I wanted to, but because I was the victim of deceit. Despite announcing to them that we were shutting down, after fruitlessly chasing NNPC for allocation for six months, I eventually changed my mind. Maybe I was just bluffing. Perhaps I was just upset. One way or the other, it led to a bold move.

I was reviewing the sequence of events one day and came to the conclusion that I needed to personally reach out to Obasanjo and explain the situation. I would plead with him to ask NNPC to review its position on Zenon. The task was not going to be easy, but like everything in my life's journey, it would surely be a valuable learning experience.

Here is how I survived political obstacles, management crises and instability, myriad storms and calamities:

(1) Pinpoint the source of the storm and implement an action plan. Maybe I had contributed to my problem without knowing it. I remember that before the 1999 presidential election, I brokered a meeting that might have exposed me politically and given fuel to lies about the founding and ownership of my company. I'd told Aziza, who was then Minister of Commerce and Tourism and a member of the Provisional Ruling Council, the highest decision-making body at the time, to make peace with Obasanjo, because it was obvious that he was the president-in-waiting. My intention was for Aziza to secure safe passage for himself, because of the role he'd played in jailing Obasanjo in 1995. If Obasanjo became president, Aziza would be in trouble, I reasoned.

"You need to meet with Obasanjo before he becomes president," I prodded him, saying I would join him in the sit-down. He took this seriously, even though he'd been saying Obasanjo would never be president. He told the Chief of Army Staff, who was against holding the meeting, Obasanjo will never be President.

I secured an appointment with Obasanjo. It was Stephen Olakunle Bakare, a chief of the Ijebu Kingdom and a successful businessman, who was very close to Obasanjo, who made it happen. His building on Awolowo Way in Ikeja served as the headquarters of Obasanjo's campaign team. He said we would meet Obasanjo on the ninth floor of the Hilton Hotel in Abuja. We were to ask for 'Mr Ojo,' a codename that would open the door for us. Aziza and I went there and Obasanjo received us.

I only took Aziza to Obasanjo for reconciliation, and the meeting was supposed to be between the two of them, so I made to leave as soon as we exchanged greetings. But Obasanjo commanded me to stay.

"You have to witness the meeting," Obasanjo said. "You are his friend."

Without wasting time, Obasanjo turned to Aziza and asked pointedly, "Who gave you the judgment you read as Chairman of the Special Military Tribunal?"

That was the judgment that found Obasanjo guilty of being an 'accessory after the fact' in the alleged coup plot, which brought about his death sentence. They commuted the sentence to life imprisonment after international pressure on Abacha. Major General Shehu Musa Yar'Adua, Obasanjo's second-in-command when he was head of state in the old military regime, was sentenced to death as well. Although they also commuted Yar'Adua's sentence to life, he died in prison in 1997, under mysterious circumstances. Other alleged conspirators received reduced sentences after Abacha succumbed to pressure.

Aziza, who was the face of the coup trial, did not look ruffled by Obasanjo's blunt question. "I take full responsibility, General," he said.

"You bloody fool!" Obasanjo thundered. He stood up, as if ready for a fistfight. "I asked who gave you the judgment to read. Who wrote that judgment for you?"

The room was tense. My heart was racing at full speed, and I didn't know what would happen next. I kept asking myself, "Do you still think this was a good idea? Are you sure you won't regret bringing Aziza here?"

The general impression—or the prevalent belief among the public—was that the tribunal had initially come to a verdict of 'not guilty,' but Abacha was desperate to get rid of Obasanjo and other accused people. This was why Obasanjo kept asking who was behind the judgment. There were rumours that a different judgment had been faxed to the Aziza panel 'from above,' but that the tribunal had disregarded the verdict and condemned Obasanjo to death.

Still unruffled by Obasanjo's mien, Aziza responded, "Sir, I take full responsibility."

"OK!" Obasanjo said, throwing his arms in the air. He then seemed to calm down. "When I become president, I'll find out." That was ominous: *when* I become president. Not *if*.

A few moments passed and Obasanjo became agitated again, firing off another question. "How about the navy guy? Why did you jail him? Why did you jail that innocent guy?"

They had accused the Navy Director of Legal Services, Commander Lawrence Fabiyi, of sneaking out sensitive documents about the trial to the human rights community, which led to the global outcry against the judgments. They jailed him for life. Obasanjo went on and on, clearly livid.

Then, in a dramatic turn, he said, "No problem. You've come to apologize. You people should go and bring money for my campaign. The election is just six weeks away."

This meeting brought down the tension, but I didn't end up making a contribution to his campaign. Aziza told me privately that he was not going to donate either.

"Obasanjo will not be President," he said confidently. "Obasanjo will win," I countered.

Of course, Aziza was wrong. On 27 February 1999, Obasanjo, the candidate of the People's Democratic Party (PDP), defeated Chief Olu Falae of the All People's Party and Alliance for Democracy alliance, to win the Nigerian presidential election. Did Obasanjo know that I hadn't donated to his campaign, after he'd explicitly directed me to?

(2) Know there will always be a way out. You should adapt, be patient and, if it comes down to that, await divine intervention. There is always a way out, a window to manoeuvre.

Now that Obasanjo was in the saddle, my competitors were telling him that Zenon belonged to the military. As far as lies go, it was an easy one for him to believe. After all, Aziza was my friend, and I had brought him to the Hilton to apologize. One of the first things Obasanjo did was to retire all military officers who had held political appointments in their careers. This exercise was an attempt to re-professionalize the armed forces. Aziza was affected, along with an entire generation of officers.

It appeared that Zenon was going to be retired from the diesel business as well. With NNPC refusing to give me any product, and the business starting to struggle, I knew the way to survive was to bypass the state monopoly, look for those who had allocations and buy off them. Fortunately, I had an impressive network of consumers, which was expanding. The lucky guys had the allocations, and I had the demand. I was doing volume at tiny margins, but that was better than nothing; it was preferable to shutting down altogether. One company was getting 10,000 tonnes, which it sold to me. Soon there were several cases like that. The profit was still appreciable. Anybody who bought from NNPC at ₦11.40 per litre would add ₦4 and sell to me. It became ₦15.40. It was left to me to add my margin and earn from the large scale of my ready market.

One significant advantage was that I had the cash, which was the most important thing for those selling to me. It was a cash game. People practically queued up in front of my office, gingerly hawking their allocations. It was like the stock exchange, like a clearing house for diesel. You would collect your allocation, bring it to me, and I'd pay cash and distribute to my growing network of consumers, which included most of the big factories across Lagos. Even politicians who landed NNPC allocations were selling to me. I was the man with the cash, which is always appreciated in such an economy. I survived the political storm through adaptation, patience and, I'm convinced, the aforementioned divine intervention.

(3) Don't accommodate fraudsters or saboteurs. Just don't do it, no matter the temptation or public perception. Another major storm that swamped Zenon was the management crisis—or, to put it more academically, our 'organizational instability.' I can choose to be hard on myself by saying I was hiring and firing CEOs at will, but it was not without good reason. For instance, if your chief executive is colluding with thieves, do you look the other way, so you won't be perceived as a boss who's quick to fire people? Unfortunately, the low CEO retention rate meant we could not achieve the stability we needed to create a robust and trustworthy institution. It was also giving us reputational challenges. The word around town was that we changed leadership weekly, at the drop of a hat.

When we built the depot, I always warned the staff that I didn't want to hear about anybody collecting a single penny from anybody. I knew the implications. We dealt in a product that was vulnerable to scarcity, and employees would be tempted to leverage their power for personal gain. A business would lose integrity very quickly if it allowed this to happen. Imagine my horror when several customers informed me that they'd paid bribes at the depot before their trucks were loaded. One of them said the staff demanded that he grease their palms with ₦2 per litre. I was livid. I called my CEO and told him what I had heard. "I want you to go to the depot and keep an eye on it," I directed him.

Because it was evident that I couldn't trust people in my own company, I also called a second individual and asked him to keep an eye on transactions at the depot. I was later told that when the CEO got there, he summoned the manager and told him, "So, this is what you people do here? You collect ₦2 per litre before loading? Where's *my* share? How much is my cut from the ₦2?"

The depot manager, who was probably not part of the racket, and whom I trusted, told me everything the CEO had said to him. I, of course, sacked this crook immediately. There was no way I was going to keep such a two-faced lowlife on board.

In hindsight, I should have waited longer before firing him. That way, I would have been able to identify all the perpetrators. I would have gained deeper insight into the shady business, but I had no patience with such blatant corruption. I couldn't wait another day. I can't remember how much we paid him as his severance package, but he was well compensated. I took over his responsibilities until I found another CEO.

For some reason that I can't fully explain, I have a soft spot for religious people. I am no fanatic, but I believe genuinely religious people hold incredibly high moral standards. I was born into a Catholic family and was baptized in the Catholic Church. I was confirmed as a catholic in 1974 by the Archbishop of Lagos, His Grace Anthony Olubunmi Okojie. In my mind, they're upright and selfless individuals. I decided to appoint a pastor as the next CEO. He had actually been in the oil industry for a while, but it didn't take me long to realize he was not interested in the business. He was more enamoured of power. I fired him after just four months. He was not involved in any scams, as far as I know, but he spent more time fighting for a raise than doing his job. He did not understand the business and had no focus.

The next CEO I tried was an expatriate, a British Citizen, who had some experience in the industry, and I thought he would be a conservative executive, driven by established ethics. I felt I could trust him with the business, but I was mistaken. One day, he came to me with an unbelievable proposal.

"Boss," he said, "you know we can make some money?"

"How?" I asked, thinking he had some legitimate value to add to the business.

"You know, they're stealing crude oil. We can start buying it. We will buy only when the ships have sailed out of Nigeria's waters. We'll be getting the product at a cheaper rate."

I thought I had misheard, or that perhaps he was joking, but he sounded dead serious.

I shouted, "Are you crazy? Buy stolen oil?"

He left my office crestfallen. I was shocked. I immediately contacted one of my allies and asked him to keep an eye on the CEO. I wanted to know more. I had fired a CEO before because he was demanding his share of bribes, and I later thought that was a bit hasty. As I said, I could have gathered information on other offenders by letting him stay on longer. This time, I chose to be more patient. A friend of mine became close to him and was feeding me valuable information.

I later found out from my informants that the CEO had already held meetings with some of the criminals and was going to get involved with a ship's worth of stolen crude. I sacked him immediately, directing him to vacate his company-rented flat. He'd worked with Zenon for a year.

After him, I brought in a born-again Christian. When I was growing up, we had much respect for evangelicals, even though I was born into the Catholic Church. What he did was unpardonable, and only added to the management crisis I was to endure. Savannah Fisheries was the biggest fishing company in Nigeria, and along with Julius Berger it consumed the most diesel. We had tried to court their marketing manager, a Sri Lankan, with enticements that he always rejected. We bought him a TV set, but he decided to give it to the company, and they placed it in the staff room. I was so impressed with his ethics that I approached him with an offer to work for me. He declined the opportunity.

A while later, he called me up one day while I was on a trip to the UK. He said he was sorry to inform me that my new CEO had just told him they shouldn't be buying diesel from Zenon. My chief executive had actually told him that he had another company that could sell to them at a better price. I fired the CEO over the phone, without an investigation. The man at Savannah Fisheries had proved himself honest and trustworthy, and I knew I could take his word as fact.

With this latest CEO gone, I had to start searching for yet another. The instability was getting to me. Candidates would begin wondering how much time they'd spend on the job. This frequent turnover was not good for management, much less for the company. But was I going to keep an executive who was brazenly working against the interests of the company?

I thought I needed a new approach—to groom somebody from the inside and promote them into the position. The first homegrown talent I tried to cultivate was a disaster. I found myself settling quarrels she seemed to find herself in the middle of every day. She was even using company vehicles for personal social events. Her successor did not fare any better. I guess they didn't have enough experience to handle the job, even though I'd thought it did not make sense to be recruiting CEOs from outside.

Suffice it to say the management crisis continued until the business collapsed.

(4) Sometimes, when it rains, it pours. I have had crises in all my businesses, but Zenon's stood out for their sheer brutality, frequency and timing. This was the company that launched me into prominence, and it was where I learned the toughest lessons of business. It was like being in the centre of a cyclone. We actually called it 'the storm house.' We weathered it all, until we were laid low by *the perfect storm*.

As I described earlier, this was a double whammy: the 2008 crude oil price crash and the devaluation of the naira in 2009, which forced me into the arms of 'saviour bank' AMCON.

How did I go from a positive balance into the red in the blink of an eye? It is in the arithmetic. I had loans in dollars, and the interest was in dollars. I took the loans at ₦117/US$1, but now had to pay back at ₦165/US$1 following the devaluation of the naira. As covered in Lesson Three, there was also the differential between what I'd bought shiploads of diesel for and how dramatically the price plunged before I could sell a drop.

All told I lost more than US$1,317,000,000 which was ₦220 billion through the devaluation of the naira, plunge in oil from US$147 to US$34 and the stock market crash.

It was devastating, like a terrible nightmare, but a nightmare would have been better: day would break, and I would wake up. There was no waking up from this. One moment, I was the darling of the banks, who did everything in the world to court me, do business with me, give me loans, take deposits from me. They would send bewitching ladies to make their offers more convincing, and now I was waking up to the sight of hefty, barrel-chested men standing menacingly in front of my gate, waiting for the moment I'd step out of my compound.

For the competitors who had been at the receiving end of my ruthless winning streak, it was time to gloat, even though the crises had not spared them. Yet, seeing blood on my forehead gave them some excitement. For those who couldn't stand my guts, it was 'good riddance to bad rubbish.' I've been told that they would often speak with derision about how I owned a yacht and had ordered a private jet. I could hear their words dripping with envy and malice.

In fact, I was to blame, despite the economic crash helping our demise along. It was all down to deeper causes—a series of mistakes and poor decisions on my part. I believe the journey to the abyss started when the crude oil price rose to US$147 a barrel in July of 2008. That was the highest price ever. As I recounted earlier, I had product worth about US$500 million on the high seas, on its way to Nigeria. I fancied myself a brilliant businessman, about to make a lot of money. But it would not come to pass.

If I had had a solid management structure, I would have received better professional advice and taken more informed decisions on the cargo. For instance, before I'd purchased boatloads of diesel, management could have said, "If oil prices collapse, what next? At what price will we sell? We can't buy at US$147 and sell at US$146!" That would have made me see things from another angle.

They would have advised me—those astute advisers *that I didn't have*—to bring in the banks and hedge, so I would have been better protected. If the price fell, I wouldn't have borne the brunt all alone. Before making the final buying decision, I had asked my CEO for her opinion. "Prices won't come down," she confidently said, setting the stage for the disaster. "Let's bid."

(5) It's wise to know how to let go. I believe that the death of Zenon led to the rebirth of Femi Otedola. I needed to get out of debt as quickly as possible, so I could try to rebuild my life. I had debts of about US$1.2 billion. That was no child's play. I had to be strategic, wise, brave and swift in making the moves that would let me exit this suffocating debt storm. It was a new experience, and there was no handbook to turn to, no manual to study. The way I handled it would make or break me. I was either buried or about to rise from the dead.

The decisions I faced were painful but necessary. The banks wanted me to restructure the debts, but I declined, instead opting to repay the loans. They got a reputable firm to value my assets. I had a property portfolio of about 150 flats in Lagos, Port Harcourt and Abuja, as well as land and storage tank farms. I gave it all up. I'd been the largest investor in the banking sector. I gave up my shares.

I described earlier being the largest individual shareholder in Africa Finance Corporation, and holding huge stakes in Mobil, Texaco and Visafone. I relinquished it all to clear my debts.

It was like seeing something precious you've built collapsing in on you. You see the thing coming down—something you created, felt strongly about and had your whole life wrapped up in—and you can do nothing at all to stop it. It was not a case of humiliation. Bankruptcy is worse than humiliation. Bankruptcy is the elder brother of shame.

One of the worst days for me was when Aigboje Aig-Imoukhuede, then Managing Director of Access Bank PLC, came to my office with his deputy, Herbert Wigwe.

Very matter-of-factly, I was told, "Mr Otedola, you have to shed weight."

I wondered what they were talking about. I was not overweight. Even if I were, a banker would never have told me to go on a diet. It took me a moment before I realized they weren't talking about my body.

Still, I asked, "What do you mean?"

Wigwe replied, "You have to sell your assets, now."

When the going was good, Access Bank did everything to court me, practically begging to do business with me. I had been reluctant, but I eventually gave in. Over time, I thought we had become friends, but it was now apparent that I was just another customer to them. Friendship went out of the window in a flash. That was one of the harsh realities of life I had to deal with in that moment.

I owed Access Bank ₦25 billion. I owed many other banks too: Zenith Bank, ₦75 billion; GTB, ₦38 billion; UBA, ₦33 billion; FCMB, ₦26 billion; Intercontinental Bank, ₦14 billion; Union Bank, ₦5 billion; Bank PHB, ₦6 billion. They understood what had just happened, with the oil price collapse and the devaluation of the naira, and many sympathized with me. But not Access Bank.

"So, what property do you want?" I asked. I hoped my voice didn't betray the grief that I felt rising inside me.

They asked for the property on Bourdillon Road, in Ikoyi. I gave them the papers. They asked for the development in Abuja—in Maitama, opposite the Redeemed Christian Church of God, that featured 52 flats, two maisonettes and eight townhouses—and I gave them those documents, too.

(6) Even the darkest cloud has a silver lining. In all, my bank debts amounted to about ₦220 billion. The banks got a haircut of ₦80 billion. AMCON bought everything for ₦140 billion from the banks. At the time, I had ordered my first private jet, but I never took delivery of it. Instead, I handed the papers over to AMCON as part of the settlement. It was a Bombardier Aviation Global 5000—a large-cabin, longrange business jet—which sold for US$65 million. It was still being built for me, and AMCON downgraded it during configuration to the Global 605 model, costing US$33 million. AMCON took delivery in 2012, and the plane is now part of the Nigerian presidential fleet.

Many advised me against giving up my assets to pay off my debts. Even Mustafa Chike-Obi, the MD of AMCON, couldn't believe it. He thought restructuring was a better option. My staff were all against it too. Jim Ovia, then Zenith MD, didn't want to take my bad loans to AMCON because Zenith Bank had the bulk of my assets. I forced him to do so.

Everybody thought I was crazy. The consensus was that in Nigeria, people in business could just 'owe and damn it.' Why give up your precious assets when you can rough it through, they thought. Why not restructure and push the payments forward? With the political connections I had, it's conceivable that I could have asked AMCON to keep its nose out of my business. But I didn't ply that route. I saw things as a businessman. Debt is like a chain around your neck; it does not give you room to breathe.

(7) Hold your head high and keep your word, no matter what. Doors will not open for you if you don't maintain your good name. This was a concept my father drove home to me, and it played on and on in my mind during the crisis. I could not survive in business without the banks. Doors would be closed in my face if I didn't keep my word, which is what my loans implied: a promise to pay them back. That was why it wasn't difficult for me to go to AMCON. Trust your instincts. At the end of the day, it all falls on you, no matter what advice you get from people.

I've said it repeatedly here and I'll say it again: giving up my assets to settle my debts was one of the best decisions I ever made. I would have still been in trouble today if I hadn't boldly given up my assets, consequences be damned.

I fondly remember how the Governor of the Central Bank, Mallam Sanusi Lamido Sanusi, helped put an end to my troubles. I had written to him, stating that against all banking ethics, my nonperforming loans were not being disclosed by the banks and provisioning was not made. In essence, the banks were not disclosing their exposure to risk because they were afraid that the Asset Management Company would declare them losses and take them over. He convened a meeting with all Nigerian bank MDs and told them that the value of the non-performing loans in their portfolios was so huge that it could cause systemic failure if they were called in. He said it was obvious that AMCON should intervene. The banks were reluctant to surrender the loans to AMCON, knowing they'd take a beating.

Sanusi's intervention turned out to be a blessing for me in the long run. As noted, word around town was that I'd been reckless, had a yacht, and so forth. Nobody seemed to consider how I had toiled day and night to build Zenon. The company was not an overnight success; it had been a long and challenging journey.

(8) Learn your lessons, never repeat mistakes. After settling with AMCON in 2012, I still had 21% equity in AP. I also held three physical properties: the office at Walter Carrington Crescent, my house in Ikoyi and the other one in Abuja. I wasn't exactly starting again with nothing, but when you've been pushed into bankruptcy and surrendered more than ₦140 billion in assets, it felt like it.

AP had mounted a public offer in 2008, which was underwritten by the banks. All the banks bought shares. We raised ₦52 billion. Adverse developments in the market later affected the share price. From the offering price of ₦250 per share in 2008, it crashed to ₦5 in 2010. People were disposing of their shares to cut their losses.

I went to the banks and asked them to sell their AP shares to me. They had written off the stocks mark-to-market—that is, valuing them by the most recent price. As described earlier, the banks started selling to me, mostly at a very low ₦5 per unit. UBA was reluctant, but eventually sold. GTB, FCMB and Access Bank all sold as well.

That was my second break in business. These shares that were worth ₦52 billion in 2008 cost me less than ₦300 million to buy in 2010. The banks lost money, but that was not my problem. They'd taken a risk, and it just didn't go their way. When things were rosy, they made money. After I'd acquired the banks' shares, my stake in AP went up to 40%.

Meanwhile, when AP made its public offering in 2008, the banks paid ₦52 billion into the company's account. But there was skulduggery afoot. I recounted earlier how a bank involved in the deal had criminally manipulated the public offering, and the Securities and Exchange Commission confiscated their 20% stake. The regulators put the shares on offer, and I acquired that 20%. AP sold two of its properties in Ikoyi and we paid dividends from the proceeds. I collected my dividends and bought more shares.

I've also described how I did not do any due diligence when I bought AP in 2007. I just paid ₦17 billion to take over the company. I was purchasing a strategic legacy asset in the downstream sector and saw that as having higher value than anything else. Once I got in and saw all the problems, I had to do a public offering to write off a legacy debt load; that was why we raised the ₦52 billion.

(9) Take things one step at a time. After I'd settled the AMCON issues in 2012, I made moves to break from the past. The company had to move forward, so I decided to step down from the day-to-day running of the business and I also let my entire executive team go. I've noted that, at my request, Segun Agbaje of GTBank nominated our CFO. That individual was Julius Omodayo-Owotuga. I interviewed him and was impressed. And, as I've said, I recruited Akin from the London office of my company Fineshade. After that, I left them to it. That was much better for me, the company and everyone involved.

Gradually, we started getting it right. But there was a reckoning coming. In my quiet moments, I knew I wanted a business that was not dependent on the government. As I've explained here, we all knew the day was coming when diesel would be nudged aside by reliable electric power, and it would become virtually irrelevant, just as kerosene had become when most Nigerians switched to gas for cooking.

(10)Enlist exceptional people and trust their judgment. At the new Forte Oil, we were cautious about everything, especially when it came to borrowing money. The only new thing we did was to go into the power-generation space.

With a competent board and professional management at Forte, it was enough that I was the man with the money and the ideas.

TAKEAWAYS

When you run a business by yourself, emotions are at play. But at a sizeable, serious company, the entrepreneur has to detach once things have stabilized. It's a bit like being an airline pilot. He has to get the craft off the runway, reach cruising altitude and level off before he can consider turning on the autopilot. You also have to realize that knowledge evolves. Let the younger generation—tuned in to the world of today, with their bright ideas and fresh perspectives—take the business to the next level.

If you want to get the job done well, banish all sentimentality, and the misguided sense that it's all about you. Moreover:

- Crises arise in different shapes and forms. Some are self-inflicted; others originate in places beyond your control
- In those moments, once word of your troubles is out, you see people's true colours
- The way you handle these challenges will make or break your business
- Look inward; be patient; find the silver lining
- Through it all, be brave

LESSON SEVENTEEN

HARNESS AND DEPLOY SOFT SKILLS

There are skills, and then there are *skills.* As an entrepreneur, you are putting human capital and material resources together to achieve results. You're focused on technical skills, which are central to achieving your goals. You are looking for experts in finance, management, engineering, law, marketing and other fields. This is specialized expertise, obtained in the classroom and honed by training and practice, including real-world management experience.

An entrepreneur doesn't have to possess these skills. A little knowledge of the basics in a particular industry is important, but the entrepreneur isn't likely to roll up his or her sleeves and operate the machine, even when he has the requisite technical skills.

An entrepreneur needs more than just technical skills to succeed. For instance, let's say a valued employee was responsible for a deal that lost the company millions. Does that warrant dismissal? Do you issue a stern rebuke, but give them one more chance? Do you pretend nothing happened? Do you comfort and reassure the employee? Knowing how to handle tricky situations that require more than technocratic or practical knowledge is an essential soft skill.

How do you recruit the right hands for your enterprise? How do you build and bond with your team? How do you motivate them to deliver the goods? How do you pass your ideas along with clarity and precision? How do you resolve problems and conflicts? How do you adapt to changes in your environment and market? How do you manage stress? How do you delegate duties for effective management?

An entrepreneur needs soft skills in superabundance to navigate these situations. These attributes aren't easily taught or learned in the classroom, although some business schools are beginning to cover them in their curricula. These are the invaluable interpersonal skills, traits and behaviours you bring to various situations and circumstances. They include social and people skills you have to harness and deploy to get the best out of your team. They're also critical in establishing and working through relationships with suppliers, partners and customers.

The place to start is a baseline of self-awareness—know yourself by identifying your strengths and acknowledging your weaknesses.

In his book, *The Virgin Way*, British billionaire Sir Richard Branson says that in his early years as an entrepreneur, he felt the need to know himself. That way, he could hire his 'weaknesses,' providing the company with what was missing because he himself didn't bring it to the table. He calls this focus on self-awareness in his early days the biggest contribution to his success.

I must confess that my self-awareness came a bit late in the game. My weaknesses had been hidden by my early success, but they eventually showed up. And they proved devastating. I only discovered a fundamental truth about myself—that I am an entrepreneur and not a manager—after the collapse of Zenon. Today, after a long and often difficult journey of self-discovery, I am in a position to discuss the soft skills that are essential for an entrepreneur, and how I put them to use to the benefit of my ventures. Here are some thoughts on that:

(1) Cultivate personal relationships with key team members. As I've pointed out in several parts of this book, I did not find it hard to recruit top managers from big companies, despite the apparent fact that I was not running a world-class organizational structure. Prospective employees knew what they were signing up for, and despite people trying to dissuade them, they still decided to team up with me after just one or two discussions.

Many told me later that they liked the fact that I took time to establish a personal relationship with them. That is the advantage of intimacy: you get to win people's trust and build a bond, and things can begin to flow from there. An example is Akin, who has turned out to be my best chief executive. As I've described, he was at Oando PLC, doing well. But after we spoke on the phone twice, and had a few exploratory meetings, he was ready to resign so he could come to work with me. And he did.

This is how it happened. I had an acquaintance at Oando who visited me at some point in 2005. She suggested that I speak with someone, dialled a number, and handed me the phone. It was Akin. We exchanged pleasantries, and I told him I'd call him when I got back to Lagos. I didn't end up calling for a year or so. I connected with him one day while trying to reach Dimeji Edwards, the head of Oando Trading. In 2012, he would go on to become the Managing Director of Hyde Energy Ltd, a position he's held since then. I used to call Dimeji every day. He was trading for Oando while I was the chief trader for Zenon. We were dealing with the world's biggest oil traders—Trafigura,[13] Vitol[14] and the like. Anyway, on this day Dimeji was not at his desk, and it was Akin who picked up the phone.

"Good day," I told him. "Can I speak to Dimeji?"

"Dimeji's not at his desk," Akin responded.

"Do you know where he's gone to?"

"I'm sorry, I don't. Is there anything I can help you with?"

"Tell him to call me. My name is Femi Otedola."

Before I hung up, I asked who was at the other end. "Akin Akinfemiwa," he replied. I remembered the name. I asked him where he had been over the last year, and what was new in his life. We exchanged numbers after some chitchat about the market and promised to speak again soon.

The call was the hand of fate at work, for two reasons. One, I cannot remember another time I called Dimeji, and he wasn't at his desk. And two, Akin normally worked in Oando's London office, as a senior derivatives and products trader, and only came to Lagos every four weeks. But there he was, answering Dimeji's phone in Lagos when I called. Akin regularly refers to that episode as 'the call of destiny.'

The following week, I called Akin again, as promised. Soon, our calls became more frequent, and in May of 2006, I invited him to my house in Ikoyi. When we finally met face-to-face, I got right to the point. "Resign," I urged him. "Come and work for me at Fineshade Energy." He accepted immediately but told me he needed time to disengage from Oando. When Akin went to inform his superiors, Wale Tinubu and Mofe Boyo, they were incredulous.

They lectured him on what was wrong with my company. "You want to go and work for that boy who sacks his CEOs all the time?" Nonetheless, Akin said he was making the move. They offered to double his salary, but he remained adamant. He also informed me that people were saying all sorts of things about me personally—that I wasn't a good employer, that I was erratic and that I fired people at will. But he kept an open mind and left our meeting sold on the opportunity.

When he first joined us, I was getting Akin involved in things one would normally think weren't his responsibility. I'd call and ask him personal questions, seek his opinion on things I was working on, and so on. This two-way communication was a new experience for him. He had worked with many bosses, both Nigerian and European, and never had anything beyond stiff, formal relationships with them.

A good relationship is not built overnight; it takes time. We got along well, and he became one of my most trusted hands and confidants.

A year after he joined, I called Akin one day at his Fineshade office in London. "I'm giving you a 1% ownership stake in the company and making you a director," I announced.

He couldn't believe it. But in my opinion, he had more than earned it.

I also have an excellent relationship with Chris Adeyemi, my lawyer, consultant and confidant, whom I've mentioned here repeatedly. He had handled some immigration consultancy for my family after an acquaintance put my wife in touch with him. He had a law firm in London called Agape Solicitors. Nana went to his office to discuss the issues, Chris helped sort things out, and Nana said she wanted to introduce us. That was in 2004. I spoke to him on the phone from Nigeria and commended his work, and we struck up a relationship from there. I also introduced him to my father, and anytime dad went to England, Chris tended to his legal and travel needs.

We met for the first time in person at my north London house, on The Bishops Avenue. I wanted to sell that property and another nearby, which I discussed with him. On his way out, I said, "Look at the second house there, Chris. Why don't you buy it yourself?"

He looked at me and said, "Sorry? Buy it?"

I replied, "Why not? People buy these houses, right? Don't say you can't."

He'd later tell me that had said a lot to him about me. He said it created a lasting impression. We became friends and he helped set up the Fineshade office in London, handling the lease, interior décor, registration, hiring, legal contracts and virtually everything else.

It was difficult for a Nigerian to do business in England at that time. It was not straightforward, but Chris served as company secretary, keeping everything moving smoothly along. We held offshore meetings in Monaco twice a year, and he organized all of it.

In 2005, Chris's father became very ill. His dad recently retired after a long and accomplished career as an electrical engineer, which ended with his position as Chief Electrical Engineer at Aso Rock Villa, the president's official residence in Abuja. Chris flew in from London to be with him and advised me that it was bad. I was on the phone with him for 45 minutes, consoling him and offering to fly his father abroad for treatment. I was ready to foot the bill.

He replied that nothing could be done, and by the time he'd gotten back from Nigeria to his house in the London suburb of Mill Hill, he received a call to say that his dad had died. It was devastating news, but it clearly meant the world to Chris that I'd stood by him, and it deepened our friendship. I encouraged him to move back to Nigeria, and he did so in 2009. We'd been having a good year or two, and Chris had been instrumental in all of it. He understands me; he knows what I like and what I don't; he gets how I operate. We work well together.

In March 2008, my dad went to England. As he and Chris were chatting, my father told him, "Femi is going to make you a director in AP, but don't tell him I told you."

About a week later, I phoned Chris with the offer. I asked, "What do you think?" He jumped at it, not letting on that my father had tipped him off.

As a commercial lawyer, he said, he liked creating new businesses or turning companies around. He joined AP in the summer of 2008 and stayed until we sold Forte in 2019. He ended up being the longest-serving director in AP and Forte, putting in 11 years.

Establishing healthy personal relationships with key members of your team is a way of telling them that you value them beyond their formal duties at the company. Every employee wants to feel appreciated and wanted, and you can get that extra mile from them when you go the extra mile with them.

(2) Take big decisions, no matter how tough. One soft skill that seems out of sync with building personal relationships is taking tough decisions that may affect your employees negatively. You find that you've established a good rapport with your team, but now, push comes to shove, and you have to take action that's likely to cause them pain. So, how do you handle that? I experienced this a few times. There's no foolproof template for dealing with situations that require swallowing hard and pulling the trigger. Sometimes it took me a long time between knowing what I had to do and actually doing it. I'll share three examples of that with you.

Hitting the brakes on my UK trading company, Fineshade Energy, wasn't easy. At the time, it was making good money, so this decision was not just tough, it was inexplicable to the staff. Why would I do this now, when we were on the upswing, and not back when the company had been making a loss? Regardless, I knew what I was doing, never looked back and never regretted it.

When Akin first joined us, and I made him head of trading at Fineshade, the company had been making a loss for two straight months. I took a gamble on him because we were losing money, I knew I was being lied to by the staff, and I needed help making things right. And so, I chose an experimental approach to evaluate this 33-year-old man in action and see how it would go. We already had a GM and a CFO, so he wasn't even the leader of the trading team. Nonetheless, he was soon setting up trade finance lines for the company. The progress he was making was promising, much more so than with what anyone else was doing. When he had been Senior Derivatives Officer at Oando, he'd built a strong contact network over the years. For example, he was in touch with the team at PNB Paribas, which meant he could fast-track the registration process. He also confessed to a few of his trading counterparts that he didn't have a formal line of credit and convinced them to sell the products to him on credit.

He declared to me the first day he traded that Fineshade would make US$1 million. I was taken aback. I asked him, "Are you sure?" He said we could do it. We had been trading at a loss, and when Akin had said he wanted to trade, the GM and CFO were not receptive. But I believed in him, and wanted to go through with the experiment, threatening to fire my senior executives if they resisted. It was not a pleasant thing to say to people who'd worked with me for years, and with whom I'd struck a bond, but there comes a time when you have to draw the line.

After reading them the riot act, I called Akin and asked if he was sure of what he was doing. He said he would actually make us US$1.2 million; the million-dollar target had been a conservative, lowball estimate. "If it's anything less than a million," he added, "don't ever trust me again." Frankly, I figured that if he made just half a million, I'd be pleased. We were coming from a position of loss, for goodness' sake. I just wanted to be sure he realized what he was promising, because I was wary of the grumbling from my managers.

It wasn't long until US$1.2 million hit our account. He'd made it! That was it. From there on out, I just told Akin, "Let's go!" That was how we started trading big time, with Fineshade becoming one of the most successful trading companies of its size in London. We only had half a dozen employees, but quickly started recruiting people in Lagos, getting them involved in the operation.

Once we'd made a bundle trading, I gave Akin the 1% ownership stake I mentioned earlier, and made him a director, in addition to head trader. When we wound down the company, I gave him 1% of the cash.

Fineshade revolved around just the two of us, but Zenon was having serious issues, and I asked Akin to come back to Nigeria and deal with the crisis. His stint in London had shown me his capabilities, and I liked the sound of the advice he was giving me on Zenon.

Akin wanted to coach someone to take over Fineshade's trading from him and volunteered to oversee the transition. But my previous experience with new hires wasn't pleasant, and I didn't want to go through that again. Instead, as Zenon demanded our attention, I followed my instincts and shut down Fineshade, so we could concentrate our energies on the Nigerian businesses.

Indeed, the danger was that both companies could go down in the end, with the unhealthy weighing down the healthy. But it was essential to keep Zenon going until we found a solution, and Fineshade kept it alive for that purpose. With Zenon's debts then sorted and restructured, I moved Akin to the rebranding of AP, so we could start a new life altogether. I was already discussing AP with him behind the scenes, because that was, at the time, my last, best hope of staging a comeback. Changing the name to Forte Oil was easy, but changing the people and processes was difficult.

One day in 2011, Akin asked to see me. I was in Abuja. I suggested he wait until I returned to Lagos, but he said it was a pressing matter. He insisted that my core team needed to see me in person. I couldn't imagine what would make that necessary but agreed to them flying down.

And so, Akin, Chris and Olumide Onakoya, my restructuring consultant, came to Abuja. They came to tell me some hard truths—that Forte was going to run aground if I didn't make fundamental changes. What they told me next shook me to my bones: It was imperative that I replace the executive management team.

"You have to fire all your executive management if you want the company to grow," Akin said.

Fire the executive management team?"

"Yes, sir," he replied.

"All of them?"

"Yes, sir," he repeated.

The trio laid out all the problems, one by one. They reminded me that Fineshade had been sacrificed to restructure Zenon, which was now also gone, and I only had Forte left. If drastic action wasn't taken, right now, Forte would go down too.

But the entire executive team to go? I was silent for a long time. At the end of the discussion, they left. They could not read my mood. Akin would later tell me that he thought he had lost his job that day.

After sleeping on it, I spoke with Akin again.

"So you came to tell me to make a decision that will effectively mean I let go of all our top execs? Well, I have heard you," I told him.

Later in the day, I picked the phone, and made several calls to the executives at Forte Oil, first to those that I was closest to. I told them that we were restructuring, and how it would affect them. I had to do it. We had to chart a new course. I needed to rebound, and Forte was the key to my renaissance. I then did the same with the others who would be affected.

It's important to note that Akin had an excellent relationship with several members of the executive. And so, it was clear to me that his sole motive was to advance my cause. He didn't want me to have the same problems I'd had in Zenon. He had been through thick and thin with me and knew where it hurt the most. The truth was that, as it stood, the executive team didn't have the leadership abilities to pull through. AP was inherited from the government by Sadiq Petroleum, and they hadn't changed the structure. After I bought the company, the staff continued going through the motions, along the same rigid, bureaucratic lines, with incompetence and zero operational efficiency, buoyed up by the money I had pumped in.

The executive team didn't have the will or capacity to make changes, which was precisely what the new team, led by Akin, did when they came on board. They acted without fear, expecting nothing from anybody in return.

Some in the company were hostile to them, but they were undeterred. In 2011, a year before the new team took over, we'd reported a loss of ₦20 billion before taxes. In 2013, a year after they joined, we posted a profit of ₦1.003 billion. And from there on, we started making more and more profit, and began paying dividends. By the third year, we had replaced our underperforming board altogether.

It seemed that my decision making had been fruitful. I wouldn't say I was entirely sure of what I was doing, or that it had been effortless, but I never looked back once I gave my word. It all turned out well.

(3) Identify talent and put it to good use. This is where leadership really matters. I rely on my instincts, but much more than that, I believe I can sense people's talents and match them with the appropriate tasks. I believe there is a gift in every human being. Each of us may have different gifts, but nobody is 'useless.' In a business sense, at least, problems arise when the wrong duties are assigned to the wrong people.

If a manager doesn't have what it takes to identify, nurture and make appropriate use of talent, everybody will end up frustrated. You will put somebody to work on things that are above or below their capabilities, and you'll be disappointed. They will either not be able to do it properly or be completely unmotivated because it's too easy for them. If you trust people with the wrong assignments, you'll end up frustrated because they won't deliver.

As I have noted, when I'm conversing with a potential employee, I'm sizing them up. I gain as much insight into their mindset, disposition, work ethic and attitudes as I can. When I begin to give them things to handle, I can judge what they are or aren't good at. This is an important soft skill for an entrepreneur. I am all about giving out assignments to those who can, and will, accomplish them.

One tough task I handled unilaterally was to change the rebranded AP's Board of Directors. I had let executive management go, which proved to be helpful, but the board also needed turning around. I took my time in identifying those who would make a difference. This required wisdom and maturity and knowing when to strike. It's possible to do the right thing at the wrong time, and that can be counterproductive.

I'm also prepared to play the long game, when necessary, because I have a long-term vision. I look ten years down the line and ask myself where we will be, what the market will look like and what the competition will be doing. I am no sprinter; I'm a marathoner.

I began making and fine-tuning my plans for the AP board, and it went on to become one of the most respected on the Nigerian Stock Exchange.

Because we had people with experience, integrity, technical knowhow, soft skills—you name it—everything we needed was there.

We had people who could talk frankly to me instead of just trying to massage my ego. From my experience, there is nothing as good as having an independent board, because management knows they're going to be evaluated objectively, and not even the chairman can intervene. And so, employees strive to be on top of their game, continually stepping up and sharpening their skills. It works like magic.

(4) Flexibility can be a lifesaver. When I was neck-deep in debt, and needed to do something to survive, I was on the receiving end of all kinds of suggestions. The bankers were particularly vocal, wanting to enslave me for life. As I've outlined in some detail, my total debt was ₦220 billion US$1,317,000,000 and the banks took about N140 billion (US$838 million).

But how were we going to raise ₦140 billion (US$838 million)? The bankers had tried to take Forte Oil from me, but I resisted. In 2012, I called AMCON and requested a meeting, to find a way forward. I said earlier that I was unwilling to pursue the obvious 'Nigerian' option of using political connections to keep the creditors at bay. That would only bring a momentary respite, as the real problems would remain unsolved. AMCON obliged, and we began a long process of meeting with all the banks, who were pressing hard on where all the monies had gone.

First, we had to prove where the funds were, showing that we hadn't squandered them. We could credibly explain where the assets were. As I was preparing for the AMCON meeting, in the second quarter of 2012,

I decided that Akin was the right person to take along, even though I'd already moved him to Forte Oil. The conventional approach was to arrive with a panoply of lawyers and financial experts, but I wasn't going there. I needed to remain flexible.

When Akin, Philip Akinola and I arrived at the government agency's offices in Ikoyi, AMCON executives—Mustafa Chike-Obi, Hewitt Benson, Abbas Mohammed Jega and Folake Dosunmu—were waiting for us. I took time to walk through exactly how Zenon had run into trouble. I explained how we'd paid top dollar for cargo, and crude oil prices crashed before we had a chance to sell the diesel. I described how the dollar debts went up as a result of the devaluation of the naira. I told them how pretty much anything that could go wrong went wrong for us—it was a textbook example of Murphy's Law.

After my narrative, they asked us just one question: "So, how do you want to clear the debt?" I wasn't expecting this, and I drew a blank. Ordinarily, I would have taken my fate into my hands and made a commitment there and then, but I was off-balance and not sure where to go. I pivoted and told them that Akin would answer that question for us. It was completely impromptu; I had not prepared Akin for this and had no clue what he would say next.

He said something astonishing. "Here's what we're going to do," he calmly told the AMCON officials. "You are going to take all our assets and do a valuation. And when everything has been assigned a value and tallied up, you'll tell us what is left of the debt."

I was shocked, but I didn't show it. He hadn't consulted me. He just made a commitment on my behalf to relinquish all our assets. He hadn't hesitated, laying it all on the line. It made sense, though. There was no cash, so we had to do an asset-swap deal.

"AMCON is long term, and you can take the assets in because they'll appreciate," he went on. "You can sell or rent, and some of the properties are operational, like the tank farms. One key thing is that we will exclude some strategic assets from the deal—for example, Zenon shares in Forte.'

He went on to tell them, without my knowing what was coming, that if I had to give up everything, including my house, I would do so. But, he insisted, we wouldn't part with the shares, because that was the only way we could make a living in future.

From there, everything went by in a blur. Soon, we were out of the meeting and sitting in my car. I hadn't said a word to Akin about what had just transpired.

He spoke first. "Sir, what do you think about what I said?"

"It's an alarming proposal," I replied. "I'll give up all my properties, just like that?"

"Yes. If we keep the AP shares, we can make money. Property is nowhere near as important."

I wasn't happy, but knew the circumstances called for a healthy dose of pragmatism. I slept on it and agreed on the property swap, with some caveats.

I called Akin the following day. "My house in Lagos, my house in Abuja, my office in Lagos and the Forte shares stay—everything else can go," I said. He seemed surprised, perhaps expecting me to push back. I'd just said we could give everything up, no problem.

"We'll just start over again," I told him.

"Thank you," he replied. "That will make my life much easier."

We got into intense negotiations with AMCON over valuation and the payback model, and we pulled through. It was the second quarter of 2012, and we didn't get out from under the agency's shadow until the end of that year.

One of the lessons I learned through that ordeal was that it's good to be daring, in everything you do. I went into our engagement with the government liquidators with humility. I was flexible enough to consider parting with virtually everything I had, and the proposal sailed through. Most people wouldn't have done it. Some entrepreneurs are still stuck with AMCON, a decade later. They're slaves to their debt. I, on the other hand, am now completely free.

If you can be flexible and humble, you'll realize there's nothing you cannot part with, except your life itself. Even if it seemingly meant everything to you, at the end of the day, you could give it up. There's nothing too precious to part with to save your life. You hold onto your honour until death, but you can part with everything else.

TAKEAWAYS

An entrepreneur may not necessarily possess the technical skills needed to run a business longer term, but soft skills are critical in building and sustaining enterprises. You'll find that they come into play in so many different situations and circumstances. You're always dealing with people, after all. Here are my thoughts on that:

- Interpersonal skills can make or break a company. Go the extra mile to build quality relationships, with employees, clients and suppliers. It can make a world of difference
- Decision making is an indispensable soft skill. Some situations require a firm hand. Don't be unduly emotional or indecisive
- You need to manage talent. Identify your team's merits and shortcomings, and assign people the right tasks, at the right time, for optimal results
- Be humble and flexible when difficulties arise; it will help you get things back on track. Don't be stubborn. Instead, be courageous, be different, and dare to do the unexpected

LESSON EIGHTEEN

FORGIVE THOSE WHO HURT YOU

As long as the Earth exists and human beings dwell on it, there will be aggression. There will be hate. There will be deceit. People who are jealous and envious of you will badmouth and attempt to destroy you. Yet, it is a mistake to live your life focused on these negatives. An entrepreneur must learn to forgive and move on. It is in his or her self-interest.

In 1973, one of Nigeria's greatest musicians, the Juju legend Chief Commander Ebenezer Obey, released a deeply philosophical record titled 'The Man, The Boy and The Donkey.' As the name implies, this adaptation of one of *Aesop's Fables* is the story of a man who is on a journey with his son and a donkey.

As they set out, he sits on the horse and his son walks by their side. People criticize him for not giving priority to the boy, so he puts him on the horse and starts walking next to them. Seeing this, people call him a stupid old man, for not taking advantage of the horse, as the elder. He then decides to mount the horse together with his son. People call them merciless for trying to kill the poor creature with their weight. The man despairs as he tries to find a way to please everybody. He and his son dismount, now walking behind the steed. And, of course, people start calling them fools for not riding the horse. That's when Obey, in his song, concludes that there's really nothing you can do to please others.

To lose your focus in life, all you need to do is pay attention to the restless mob—listen to their negative words, breathe them in, internalize their hostility, let them kill your spirit. You're guaranteed to lose confidence in yourself and your abilities. You will never be able to take a single step forward because you'll be afraid of being criticized. The haters will have a field day. You will open yourself to being discouraged and depressed.

If, on the other hand, you want to grow as an entrepreneur, you have to learn to ignore the haters. Face it, everybody has their doubters. It doesn't matter where you are in life. There will always be people who dislike you, badmouth you and try to pull you down.

When they came for me, especially in the early days of Zenon's outrageous success, my strategy was to throw their brickbats back at them, firing off in-your-face retorts. I did not lack self-confidence, so I didn't give them a square inch in my mind on which to build their nests. I tossed their negativity back to them in full force. I am very strong-willed, and do what I want to, regardless of what people say. I simply don't care about the gossip and slander. And I've taught my children to be the same way.

Don't listen to detractors and don't dwell on the distractions they throw up. If you like what I'm up to, great. If you don't, that's your choice. I just evaluate what I need to do and go ahead with it. It's my life.

Here is some of the hatefulness I experienced, and what I did to protect myself and get ahead:

(1) Most of the time, lies deserve no response. One vile rumour that was peddled about me was that Zenon was sabotaging the power sector in Nigeria, so we could remain in the diesel business. That made no sense. Nigeria began to experience power generation and delivery problems in the 1970s, when I was still cutting fingernails in my parents' living room. These problems got progressively worse as our country's population kept growing, but we failed to build capacity to keep up. We went through various governments, both civilian and military, for decades, and the power situation kept getting worse. Although I only started selling diesel in 1999, there were those who inexplicably wanted to hold me responsible for Nigeria's age-old power problems. It seems the haters can sell this kind of nonsense to the gullible, even when it's so foolish and illogical. I don't have to defend myself against such nonsense, and I let it roll off my back.

I used to say that Nigeria's unaddressed problems created business opportunities that any entrepreneur could tap into, but to hold the entrepreneur responsible for these issues is ridiculous. They could peddle similar theories about those selling generators, candles, lamps, torches, inverters and solar panels! They could argue that these people too would be out of business if Nigeria enjoyed stable electricity, and had to protect their interests, and were therefore responsible for the poor state of the power sector. Right, it's the candlemakers' fault! That would be like blaming lawyers for instigating crimes so they can keep earning a living. After all, I was also buying diesel to power my own home and business. It was not fun for me, even though I was dubbed the 'King of Diesel.'

(2) If the attacks are damaging, state your case publicly. There are situations in which taking the facts to the public can help. When President Obasanjo deregulated diesel in 2004, Zenon took an unassailable lead in the market. My opponents' reaction was to tell the president that we'd turned the market upside down. The economy was about to be brought down because there was no diesel, and Obasanjo was mad at me because he'd sought and received assurances from us that NNPC's exit from diesel importation wouldn't affect supply. My critics then fanned the flames by telling him there was no diesel in the country, that trucks couldn't move and that industries were shutting down.

The President of Nigeria called me at 2 am, shouting through the phone. "You're a stupid boy! God will punish you! You persuaded me to deregulate diesel, and now there's no diesel in the country!" He was livid.

I flew to Abuja the following day, despite my well-placed fear of flying within Nigeria. As soon as Obasanjo saw me, he flew into a rage again. "What kind of rubbish is this? What kind of nonsense is this?" He was right in my face, screaming at the top of his lungs.

I allowed him to cool down, and when he stopped talking, I tried to explain the situation. "Baba, they're lying to you. It's all lies. I have six ships waiting to discharge big supplies of diesel."

I told him there was diesel all over the country and showed him letters of credit for all the cargoes. I was even paying demurrage, charges for being unable to unload ships at the originally scheduled time. I told the president that I was the victim of competitors' backbiting.

"Let's see what they come up with next," I added. "You'll see that it's me who's telling you the truth."

To address the disinformation head on, I told him I would start advertising the availability and price of diesel on the front page of the newspapers, addressing any concerns about fair and consistent pricing.

I knew it was people in NNPC—the state monopoly, in their now-teetering positions of power, who were against deregulation—who'd been telling him these lies. They wanted to continue to import, and rake in the subsidy money.

Obasanjo was a determined and robust president. Jealous people did not easily sway him. Once he made up his mind that someone was trustworthy and genuine, as he seemed to do about me that day, he stopped listening to the naysayers.

Rather than ignoring all this negativity, as was my normal style, I went on the offensive. I called Nduka Obaigbena, the publisher of *ThisDay* newspapers, and offered to buy the first seven pages. Nduka was shocked.

"What for? What do you want to put there?"

I said I wanted to advertise Zenon, from the front page through to page seven. I can't remember how much I paid, but I was the first advertiser to take over the front pages of Nigerian newspapers. I did it to send a message to my enemies that they were never going to destroy my confidence or take me down. And the message was sent, loud and clear.

I went on to do this for quite some time. The first page carried the Zenon logo, an image of a ship adorned page two, and our messaging continued to page five. Then, page six featured a roster of all my customers, who also happened to include my competitors. The list spilled over onto page seven.

As they were all buying from me and seemed happy enough to take delivery of my product, I used their logos in the advert. Total asked me to remove their logo, and I declined. "Go and buy diesel somewhere else if you don't want to be on the list," I told them. I even instructed my people to refund an order Total had placed and did the same with Oando when they objected. Later, when I purchased my last ship, I decided to christen her *Zenon Conquest*. I had conquered them all! Let the haters go and eat grass.

(3) Adversaries are part of life. Rich or poor, you cannot escape them. The haters were quite happy when Zenon ran into problems. They gloated. But they didn't know that I would survive the wreckage and go on to much greater things.

They underestimated the power of self-belief. I rose from the ashes of Zenon stronger and better, with a fine new life. That does not mean all the doubters and critics have disappeared. I still have enemies out there. Only dead people don't have adversaries. If your heart is still beating—whether you have money or don't, are successful or not, are on top or at the bottom—you'll have your detractors. Don't be discouraged by them. Just continue to believe in yourself and keep following your instincts.

At any rate, my family name, Otedola, set us up as a target for haters. In Yoruba, 'ote' means shaming or reproach, and 'ola' means wealth. So, together it literally means taking disapproval and transforming it into wealth. Stated another way, it can be read as 'conspiracy turns to fortune.'

Indeed, after all these years in business, I sincerely believe that any time there is a conspiracy against me, big money is around the corner. I'm actually not entirely happy when I'm not being targeted. I encourage the trouble caused by my foes. I taunt and provoke them. You can't accuse me of running away from a fight. I say, "Bring it on!"

(4) Haters love associating with success. There's no need to be too sensitive. If you do your work and aim high, you will be successful to one degree or another. And once you're successful, those who'd taken shots at you will want to associate with you. "He's my friend," they'll say. "I know him." Success is the solution to all this negativity. When I started in the diesel business, I was the butt of jokes. "Can you believe Femi, a former governor's son, is now selling diesel?" That was whispered behind my back. They didn't know what lay ahead. Some feel a need to laugh at you when you do the unusual. Don't let this deter you from doing the extraordinary. You must follow your instincts and your dreams. What others think shouldn't bother you. When you make up your mind and know you want to do something, keep at it. A strong person will not allow others to dissuade them.

On the other hand, keep in mind that there's value in the negative talk of detractors, and their attempts at discouragement. As long as you continue to believe in yourself, their ugly words can push you to aim higher. There was a time my daughter, DJ Cuppy, would cry to me, broken-hearted about what people were saying about her on social media. Their hostility could have broken the faint-hearted. The trolling was toxic, and initially difficult for her to handle. I took her aside and explained, "It's good for you. You need more of it!"

Take that to heart. You can turn lemons into lemonade. You can choose to look at things in a way that will make you stronger, keep you on your toes and encourage you to press ahead, so that even the antagonists will have no choice but to congratulate you for a job well done.

Using their hate to feel motivated means this behaviour can have more advantages than disadvantages. That is our strategy.

The best way to deal with haters is just to continue to be successful. Frank Sinatra once said, "The best revenge is massive success." George Herbert, the 17th century English poet, put it another way: "Living well is the best revenge." These dictums are essential for the entrepreneur. That is the way we deal with enemies. Your foes might simply be acting this way out of jealousy but know that when you make a success of life, you effectively throw their mud back at them without physically confronting them. Let the animosity inspire you to shoot for success.

(5) Don't seek revenge or be driven by malice. It is difficult to be successful if you're malicious. That's why I always say you should forgive those who hurt you. I've been hurt many times in the course of doing business, but I forgive my foes. It is the right thing to do. Sometimes people will argue that offending people is a valuable business tactic, and if you don't attack others, they will destroy you. That is taking things too far.

I look at it in a different way: nobody can compete with God. You cannot compete with destiny. If God has destined someone for greatness, you can't stop it. People may act like the devil, but karma awaits them. There is a spiritual dimension to forgiveness. You are always on top of your game if you forgive. If you forgive, God will continue to bless you. That is the way nature designed life. You sow, you reap. If you plant forgiveness, you will reap mercy.

When you think about it, how many people can you fight at the same time? I embrace the words of the ancient Chinese warrior-philosopher Sun Tzu: keep your friends close and your enemies closer.

TAKEAWAYS

Whatever bad things people do to me, I never forget the good they've also done. I remember how positively they have impacted my life. Take these thoughts to heart:

- Almost everyone has haters—those who envy and deride. Success, no matter how modest, attracts malice
- You must rise above ill will and keep your eye on your goals. Use their malice as motivation to achieve your purpose
- Be forgiving because envy and hatred can consume and derail you
- Use truth and openness to counter fabrications and lies

LESSON NINETEEN

ENGAGE WITH POLITICAL AUTHORITIES

In a developing country where democracy is struggling to gain a foothold, and the policy environment is heavily dependent on the whims of political actors, it is practically impossible to play big without engaging with the decision makers.

In an earlier section of this book, I described the experience of my father and his investment with a very close family friend.

In the early eighties, this founder of Debo Industries Limited and Adebowale Electrical Industries Limited came up with the brilliant idea of manufacturing fluorescent lamps and light bulbs in Nigeria, after the Federal Government announced the ban on the lighting's importation. It was a move designed to catalyse Nigerian entrepreneurs. Chief Adebowale got his friends, my father included, to invest in a venture that ultimately fell victim to the unreliability of the government's policy. It seems that licences were granted to several Indian companies with operations in Nigeria to start importing fluorescent bulbs and fixtures. My father lost his ₦2 million investment, which at the time was equivalent to US$2 million.

The lesson was that one's business cannot exist in a politics-free vacuum. If you think you can do big business in a way that's insulated from politics in a developing nation, you're making a huge mistake. Government offices will become a graveyard for your applications and documentation. You will invest billions, only for the government to come up with a policy that can ruin you in seconds. They will tell you to pursue homegrown opportunities in fluorescent lighting, while issuing permits under the table that allow foreign competitors to come in and steal the march.

If you do engage with political authorities, you can benefit from the association in these and other ways:

(1) You can push a case for policy. If Adebowale had been visible in the corridors of power, he could have pushed for the government to stick with its protectionist policy. He took the government at its word, landed badly, and suffered, as did investors like my dad. I don't think we should be debating the role of political engagement in high-level entrepreneurship in Nigeria. Rather, we should talk about the nature, and logical extent, of this involvement, and the principles that should guide it. There ought to be some sense of fair play and consideration for the Nigerian people, particularly in certain sectors.

Some businesses do not need to engage with the political authorities. Small companies certainly don't. If you have a medium-sized company that feeds off big firms, there's nothing you can do to influence high-level policy, although you might have to lobby and fight over state and local-level regulations. However, there are also some sensitive industries that cannot do without government interference, including telecoms, banking, oil and electrical power. It's true that when your business grows into a big enterprise, making billions, you have to court the government, no matter the sector.

(2) Service political affiliations. Government is like an owl that's watching you, but you probably don't know it. Once your business is sizeable, they look for a way to come at you from different angles. If you are in a country like mine, you will soon see politicians making demands. They want you to finance their campaigns. They want you to attend their parties—birthdays, weddings and funerals. You'll be made to feel insecure unless you factor their interests into whatever you are doing. Yes, it depends on your line of work, but you cannot escape it. If you're big enough, the demands will come from the very top. This can be frustrating, especially if you are sweating to make your money. If you choose not to play, it can even be dangerous.

(3) Benefits from the corridors of power do not come on a silver platter. I've talked about how some have tried to downplay all my achievements in business as something handed to me, because of my closeness to certain people in power. You'd think all I ever did to succeed was make phone calls or attend dinner parties. People have made insinuations that I'm a beneficiary of crony capitalism, exerting undue influence on the government. It is a debate I usually prefer to avoid, because in most cases it's based on bad faith arguments, with accusers misrepresenting the facts in order to feed their narrative. This platform—this book—is my opportunity to offer some insight into my relationship with the political class.

Insinuations about Zenon intensified in 2003, when I donated to the campaign of President Obasanjo, who was seeking a second term. Ever since, everything I achieved has been perceived as me reaping the reward for my donation, or due to my closeness to Obasanjo.

I would certainly be lying if I said there's no benefit in engaging with political figures. I did benefit, but not in a way that came on a silver platter. I did not receive anything I didn't work for. I just had the advantage of access to those in power, to argue for what I felt was fair and right. It would be suicide to sit at home, fold my arms and expect my business to magically flourish in a developing democracy, amid fiercely competing interests. Think of it as fighting a rear-guard action to protect what had already been built.

(4) Be bold when you play the game. I have shared in a previous chapter how the authorities at one time blocked Zenon from getting diesel allocation directly from the NNPC monopoly, simply because of political considerations. It was outrageous to see people who didn't own a single tanker being given diesel while Zenon, with its depots, had to scavenge. There was a time in 2002 when I was deeply frustrated and wanted to pack it all in.

It soon became apparent that if I were to survive in Nigeria, I had to build bridges with those in power. I had to play the game. My initial efforts didn't yield much fruit. I was never at the presidential palace between 1999 and 2002, but with my business facing sudden death, I had to do something out of the ordinary.

I became friends with Colonel Chris Jemitola, the aide-de-camp to the president. I told him about my challenges and asked him to help.

He advised me to meet Obasanjo myself. And so, I went to Aso Rock Villa, the Nigerian White House, in September 2003. As I was waiting in the anteroom, I noticed that the president would spend on average just two minutes—five minutes maximum—with each of his visitors. In no time, he would walk them to the door and bid them goodbye. But I had a lot of issues to discuss with him. When I went in, Obasanjo didn't even sit down or invite me to do so.

"Yes, yes," he said, clearly eager to dismiss me.

"Baba, I've been supporting your party. There was no letter to even thank me for all the donations."

"OK," he replied dismissively, "we will send you a letter."

A letter of thanks was not my problem, and he knew it. My business was under threat, and this was my opportunity to engage with the leader of the country, in a desperate bid for relief. I wasn't going to ask for special treatment, but request that the embargo on Zenon be lifted. I thought I'd supported the party enough to have an opportunity to do business unhindered. It did not appear so.

I decided to fight back with a psychological approach.

"Baba," I said, trying to show as much respect as I could muster. "What have I done to deserve this punishment from you?"

His face was blank, and he was already shooing me off to the door. What could he have heard about me?

This was our second one-on-one meeting. The first had been six weeks before the 1999 presidential election, when I took Major General Aziza to him to apologize for his role in sentencing Obasanjo to death over allegations of a coup plot. That day, when I'd gone to leave them alone to talk, the president had insisted I stay. Now, he didn't want to be in the same room as me.

As I walked towards the door, I turned back, looked him straight in the eye and said, "Do you know General Murtala Muhammed died so you could lead? God took him out for you. God took Abiola out, took Shehu Musa Yar'Adua out, took Abacha out. All for you."

"What?!" He sat down, no longer in a hurry to dismiss me. I had gotten his attention, and he decided to hear me out. I cleared my throat, as if I had a message from God to deliver and began to talk slowly and deliberately. I decided to take full advantage of this meeting and make him understand that it was divine favour that was guiding his life. "If Murtala were in a bullet-proof car, Dimka would not have killed him," I stated. "If Murtala lived in the Dodan military barracks,[15] Dimka would not have killed him. And you would not have become our president."

General Muhammed became head of state in July 1975, after the overthrow of General Yakubu Gowon in a coup led by mid-level officers. Obasanjo became his second-in-command, as Chief of Staff, Supreme Headquarters. On 13 February 1976, Muhammed was on his way to the office from his private residence—rather than Dodan barracks, his official residence. He was in a black Mercedes-Benz that was not equipped with bulletproof panels.

He was shot dead in the abortive coup led by Lt Colonel Buka Suka Dimka. Obasanjo succeeded him as head of state by default, and Dimka was publicly executed a few months after the failed coup.

As for how divine favour led to Obasanjo's second stint as president, there was an annulment of the election results. Chief Abiola had won the 1993 presidential election, but that was reversed by the government of General Ibrahim Babangida[16] who suddenly left power on 26 August of that year. That paved the way for General Sani Abacha to become president in November. Shortly after, Abacha detained Abiola for trying to reclaim the mandate, and also jailed Obasanjo and Yar'Adua, who'd been Obasanjo's deputy from 1976 to 1979.

Yar'Adua died in jail in 1997. Abacha died in office in 1998. Abiola died in detention in 1998. Obasanjo came out alive in June of 1998 and became the first elected president of the current democratic order in 1999.

Linking Obasanjo's good fortune to the misfortune of others was my way of saying he should be thankful for his unique place in Nigeria's history.

I continued, "I remember when my father was governor. General Babangida sent my father to you because you were disturbing his government with the critical interviews you were giving. He said that you should keep quiet and let him run his government. You asked my father to tell them to get out of there. Then, Abacha came in and couldn't stomach your public criticism. They set you up in a phantom coup. But look at what God did. He took Abiola out, took Abacha out. If any of these men had been alive, you wouldn't be president."

He appeared fascinated by this, and replied, "Yeah."

President Obasanjo was going to give me only a minute, but I was ultimately there for an hour and forty minutes. The aide-de-camp kept coming in every ten minutes to see what was going on. He looked surprised that I was deep in conversation with the president, despite the short time he gave to everybody else. That day, Obasanjo and I became close.

(5) When you find an eager ear, do your best to please. In late 2005, Obasanjo invited me to have breakfast with him in Ota, in central Nigeria, where he had farms. He was very warm, friendly and jovial that time around. As we were eating, he would take yam from his plate and put it on mine. Same with some fried eggs. I was wowed. He'd won my heart.

"Femi," he said, "you know what I like about you?"

"What?"

"You have what everybody wants: money. I need you to kick-start the completion of the Ecumenical Centre in Abuja. I can't use government money."

He explained how he was on his way to the airport when he saw the abandoned church. He'd pledged to complete the interdenominational centre—also called the National Christian Centre—without government funds. It had been conceived as a national monument, similar to Abuja's National Mosque, but was abandoned because of a lack of funding.

"No problem," I replied. "How much will it take to complete the project?"

"₦300 million," he responded. "But you should just contribute a small donation, to get things moving.'

"No, Baba. I'll do it all—anything for God."

We were having our breakfast on a Wednesday, and I committed to deliver the money on Friday. I called the accountant to cut a bank draft. I went to Obasanjo's office in Abuja and handed him the cheque.

"Baba, here's the draft."

"No, I can't take it just like that," he said. "We need a witness. I need to make this public."

I told him I didn't want the publicity, but he said he wanted other billionaires to see what I had done, so that they too would donate. And so, I presented the draft in front of an NTA network television news crew.

As I got closer to Obasanjo and the influential policymakers, I saw a bigger picture. The government had no business importing diesel and selling at a loss in the first place. It was a scarce commodity, and this was driving up the price. Obasanjo was determined to deregulate the downstream sector of the oil industry, and I decided to press him to go ahead with it, starting with diesel. Petrol was very sensitive. Most Nigerians relied on it, and the unions would resist the slightest increase in price. The general public was not interested in the diesel market, though.

With that in mind, I scheduled a meeting with the president and discussed the deregulation question.

"Baba," I asked, "since you want to deregulate, why don't you start with diesel?"

Every year, NNPC was losing ₦400-800 billion subsidizing the fuel. They bought the product at ₦45 and sold to distributors at ₦18. The distributors then sold at ₦60 a litre instead of the mandated retail price, which was much lower. It made no economic sense, but many were profiting enormously from this import scheme and didn't want Obasanjo to touch it.

After listening to my analysis, he replied, "That makes sense."

He picked up the phone and said, "Get me Kupolokun."

Funso Kupolokun was the Managing Director of NNPC. Obasanjo couldn't reach him immediately, but he soon returned the call and they discussed the diesel issue, going into how much the government was wasting on the subsidy, and the inefficiency in the market. They agreed that it made sense to deregulate so the private sector could relieve NNPC of the burden and make diesel more available.

The day after the conversation, I went to see Kupolokun. He was worried about diesel availability if NNPC were to stop importing.

He felt there might be gaps or even shortages. I assured him that the distributors could meet the demand. And that was assurance enough, apparently, as he proceeded to inform his team that in four weeks, NNPC would stop importing diesel.

That was how diesel was deregulated in Nigeria, and how the market opened up. The private sector flourished. Of course, Zenon, with its built-up capacity, was ready to tap into the opportunity. Because of our established clientele and built-out infrastructure, we became an even bigger player after the deregulation. We had invested heavily in tank farms and haulage.

Nonetheless, when people retell this story, you would think the government gave free diesel to Zenon and stopped others from coming into the market. That's so far from the truth. I did play a crucial role in deregulation, but by doing so I saved the country trillions of naira in taxpayers' money that was wasted on subsidies. My involvement was limited to asking the president to look at what a mess the old way had made of things. There was nothing underhand about it.

(6) Stand up for yourself and your interests. I'd also like to provide more details about one of the rumours I mentioned earlier. Of all their schemes and intrigues, the most hurtful thing my enemies did after deregulation was lie to Obasanjo that there was no diesel in the country.

He had sought and received assurances that distributors could handle importation themselves, so he was right to feel aggrieved if we had failed to deliver.

"You are a stupid boy!" he said, after hearing from my detractors. "Why did you advise me to deregulate? Where are you?"

I was in Lagos. He asked to see me immediately. I flew to Abuja and headed straight to the presidential villa. Diesel deregulation was supposed to help him sell his other deregulation plans, and here he was being told that things had gone completely haywire.

Fortunately, I had evidence that there was adequate diesel supply in the country. I made my case, and he saw through the lies.

Dr Ngozi Okonjo-Iweala, the economist who would go on to become Nigerian Minister of Finance, saw me on a British Airways flight after I'd started advertising diesel prices in newspapers, and she was full of praise. She said that the country was opening up, and that free and open competition was finally being encouraged.

As I have said, because of my business ventures, I couldn't afford to be distant from governmental authorities. If I hadn't been close to Obasanjo, I would have fallen victim to the vile rumour-mongers. I probably wouldn't have had a say in the matter, and he could have reversed the deregulation and put NNPC back in the dubious subsidy business. My business would have died. And, more importantly, the nation would have suffered.

Years later, NNPC reintroduced the importation of diesel, and nobody could compete with it. It was like things had gone back to the bad old days.

(7) Sometimes, the liars will win. Let me tell you about my experience with President Umaru Musa Yar'Adua, who succeeded Obasanjo in 2007. I was close to him, as one of the funders of his election campaign. I donated ₦1 billion towards the People's Democratic Party Secretariat. After that, I was courted by all and promised the world. After Yar'Adua's inauguration, I was with him one evening when he made complimentary remarks about my business.

"You're a fine businessman," he said. "I've always observed you from afar. I also want you to help my government. What can you do?"

I thought about kerosene, which was used as household fuel by mostly low-income earners. Yar'Adua was someone who cared a lot about the masses. I told him I was worried that ordinary Nigerians had no opportunity to buy kerosene at reasonable prices. The distributors were buying from NNPC at ₦30 a litre, and the official selling rate was ₦50. However, everyday people had to pay double that because of scarcity.

NNPC was not importing enough, and distributors were not selling at the official price.

"Mr President, I will flood the stations with kerosene and the price will come down," I told him.

I decided to begin offering ₦50/litre kerosene and asked him to come and announce it. He agreed. The following day, I was ready and waiting at my AP station in Abuja. Senate President David Mark informed me that he had just left the president at the villa, and Yar'Adua was on his way.

Ten minutes later, Colonel Mustapha Onoyiveta, the presidential aide-de-camp, called to say that Yar'Adua was not coming. Instead, he sent Henry Odein Ajumogobia, the Minister of State for Petroleum and future Minister of Foreign Affairs. I was taken aback. We had already issued word that the president would announce the ₦50 kerosene initiative. I knew that someone had discouraged him from coming, but we moved on with the programme. After the event, I came to learn that certain jealous people told the president that kerosene fumes at the petrol station would affect his health if he attended. That's how jealousy works. But you will always get to where you are destined to be, regardless of the twists and turns. I was called to come and see him afterwards, and he apologized for not coming to the event.

(8) Don't believe everything you hear. Those who say the government made me what I am are stretching the facts. Some think I should be eternally grateful to Goodluck Jonathan because AMCON helped me get out of debt. Sure, but I hope they know that I relinquished virtually everything I owned. To this day, AMCON staff ask their recalcitrant debtors, "Can't you be more like Mr Otedola?" They use me to market their brand, encouraging debtors to give up their assets too.

I understand that some did not know that I'd forfeited those assets. They thought I just paraded into AMCON and they forgave my debts. They thought Jonathan directed AMCON to write it all off and buy me a bottle of champagne to celebrate. As I've detailed here, the debt was ₦220 billion and AMCON bought it for ₦140 billion, after much evaluation and negotiation.

I gave up everything and started anew. No debt was written off.

(9) Political engagement works both ways. On 23 November 2009, President Yar'Adua was flown to Saudi Arabia, due to a medical emergency. Because he did not officially write to the National Assembly, formally transferring power to Vice President Jonathan, there was a sudden power vacuum that threw the government into disarray.

Many vital decisions could not be made as Jonathan declined to perform these presidential functions. He said his lawyers had advised him that carrying out official presidential duties without due authorization was an impeachable offence. Nigeria was, in a very real sense, hanging by a thread.

Worried by the tension and uncertainty, I decided to do something myself. In early February 2010, the businesswoman, Hajia Bola Shagaya, and I went to the city of Minna, in Niger State, to join General Ibrahim Babangida in mourning the death of his wife, Maryam, who'd passed away at age 61. At his hilltop residence, we talked about a wide range of issues, but I said I needed to discuss a particularly urgent matter. He took me to his study, where the two of us were alone. I confessed that I was becoming increasingly agitated over the state of the nation.

"Your excellency," I said, "how can we get out of this logjam? The political heat is too much."

Calm and resolute, he replied. "Femi, advise your friend that when he gets to the Council Chambers next week for the Federal Executive Council meeting, he should go and sit on Yar'Adua's chair." He was referring to Vice President Jonathan and the leadership crisis. I found this fascinating and assured him I would pass the message along. I travelled back to Abuja that evening and went straight to a dinner with Dr Jonathan, where I wasted no time in delivering General Babangida's message.

Jonathan nodded and asked me: "What do you think?"

"Your excellency," I said, "go and sit on that chair." He looked at me for some time and said that he'd think about it.

The following week, on Tuesday 9 February, the National Assembly adopted the famous 'Doctrine of Necessity' to make Dr Jonathan the Acting President, pending the return of Yar'Adua from his medical leave. Behind-the-scenes moves by prominent Nigerians preceded this decision. The legislative resolution was unprecedented, but the nation had been so tense, and the fault lines so stoked, that an unusual solution was needed to address the situation.

With Jonathan now legally empowered to act as Nigeria's President, there remained the critical optics: would he visibly stand in for Yar'Adua, with confidence and an air of authority? Or would he attempt to maintain a subdued demeanour? The Federal Executive Council was meeting on the following day.

At that session, as Jonathan entered the council chambers, the protocol officer pulled out the VP's chair for him, but the acting president marched past it. He proceeded to the seat reserved for the president and sat down. That was the moment he took power in earnest. Through that act, he sent a strong signal to the nation that he was now in charge.

Later that day, Jonathan reshuffled the cabinet. He redeployed Chief Michael Aondoakaa, the Attorney General of the Federation and Justice Minister, who had been a central figure in the bid to stop Jonathan from taking the reins of power. Prince Adetokunbo Kayode, until then the Minister of Labour, replaced Aondoakaa, who was shuffled aside to 'special duties.' By 16 March, the acting president had dissolved the cabinet and a new one was sworn in on 6 April.

President Yar'Adua, who had been quietly ferried back into Abuja earlier, passed away on 5 May.

While many will certainly insist that political engagement by entrepreneurs is a one-sided proposition—in the sense that only the entrepreneur surely benefits—the reality is that it works both ways.

I tapped my political connections to help resolve a crisis that almost set the country on fire. This was one of several instances where I used my access to political heavyweights to contribute to nation-building and socio-economic development. Entrepreneurs need to appreciate the fact that their country's peace and stability means peace and stability for their businesses too. We need a steady, safe and well-functioning country, first and foremost.

(10) Be Careful of Shady Players in the Corridors of Power. To be clear, I am advocating that big-time entrepreneurs should not isolate themselves from the corridors of power in a country where politics, policy and commerce mix. They need to be right there, sitting at the table, making sure that shady players, sycophants and poor decisions do not injure their business interests. I did everything I could to protect my business from political vendettas and destructive policies. But this does not mean that they did not happen. In 2010, being the chairman of African Petroleum Plc and also the CEO of Zenon Oil and Gas Ltd, I realised that companies in Nigeria were claiming money for subsidy on petroleum products they never imported. When I saw how much was being stolen, I went to the then President, Dr Goodluck Jonathan. I told him my observations. Several days later he told me that he had consulted with the Minister of Petroleum who assured him that what I had alleged was not happening.

I was frustrated by this response, so I reached out to Senator Bukola Saraki, the senator from Kwara State, who raised the issue on the floor of the senate. This caused enough concern that the lower chamber, the Federal House of Representatives, eventually set up the panel to investigate the issue. By 2012, the fuel subsidy scam crashed into the public consciousness following the subsidy protests of that year, and the government could no longer pretend the subsidy fraud was not an issue.

The lesson here is that you, as a businessperson who is engaging with the leaders of your country, must give them your honest updates. It is lonely at the top and the risk from having only a few sources of feedback on their policies and blindspots can escalate easily into big mistakes. Even when your advice is not initially received well, honesty always pays.

If you want to climb the ranks, you must learn how to play the game. The danger of not courting government in a country like Nigeria is that your business could collapse completely, as Chief Adebowale's did back in the 1980s.

It's easy for my critics to guess at how Zenon came to be, suggest how easy things had been for me, how my father's name opened doors, and how my closeness to politicians made me rich. Talk is cheap. What they don't know is that nothing fell into my lap. I went through sleepless nights. I survived treachery and backbiting. I was financially ruined. I battled blackmail. I strove hard to continue to believe in myself. I had good and bad times and relied on my instincts and self-belief in working through it all.

I lived through it and outlived the haters. I learned bitter lessons, and I learned forgiveness along the way, knowing well that nobody can tamper with my own destiny.

Cultivating the political class does not have to be solely in your own favour. You can contribute to national peace and progress by leveraging your connections, and bringing your entrepreneurial abilities to bear, to negotiate and convince.

TAKEAWAYS

There are valuable lessons in my experience with all these, and I hope they'll help readers navigate the corridors of power with confidence. Here are some things to keep in mind:

- Sometimes, you cannot help but get caught up in politics, especially in developing countries like Nigeria
- When you do, it makes sense to push fair but useful policy changes, as I did with deregulation
- Not everything will go your way when speaking to politicians, but many will reward honesty, boldness and conviction
- Political engagement works both ways, and everyone benefits from peace and prosperity

LESSON TWENTY

INDISCIPLINE WILL RUIN YOUR BUSINESS

Why do Nigerian businesses fail? Why do so many entrepreneurs fail? There are probably a million and one reasons.

Academic enquiry into the issue can positively influence policy and shape entrepreneurial behaviour. There will be discussions around the policy environment, the structure of the economy, the infrastructural challenges and access to affordable capital. These studies can also examine managerial competence, as well as corporate governance concerns—particularly accountability, transparency and processes. We must address all this and more if Nigerians are to thrive in business and go global.

However, in this chapter I'm more interested in honing in on what entrepreneurs can do on a personal level. Let's scrutinize what destroys businesspeople, rather than what ruins companies in general. How do entrepreneurs undermine their businesses with their own hands? Why do they fail, and take their companies down with them? There are factors that are beyond our control, but others are well within our ability to manage.

I'm primarily thinking about lack of personal discipline. I think we're long overdue for a frank, open discussion about how a discipline deficiency impacts the profitability of a business. There's precious little talk about how these harmful habits end up pulling down companies, and even impacting our country's health and wellbeing.

Here are my thoughts:

(1) Let me give you an example of spending projected profit. Say I have a business, I've done all my calculations, and I have a good sense of how much money it's going to bring in. Let's talk about diesel, for instance. My cost is ₦20 per litre. The market price for retail customers is ₦70, and I'm going to import and sell 300 million litres. This means my profit margin is ₦50 per litre, and if we do the maths, the projected profit is ₦15 billion. However, as happened to me, it's possible that by the time the shipment arrives, the market price has dropped. So, if based on my profit projections I'd already taken ₦15 billion from my company and bought a private jet, and that ₦15 billion never materialized, I would have spent money that I simply didn't have. And thus, my company begins to tailspin into debt and disaster.

I would strictly advise entrepreneurs not to spend projected revenue. After three months of Zenon, I recruited salespeople and bought them new cars. I did all that from the capital outlay, not from projected income. If you do not take care of the kobo, you will not be able to take care of the naira. If you are faithful in little, you are faithful in much.

I have plenty of examples of Nigerians who spent their firms' projected revenue. Unfortunately, it's quite common in my country. There is no respect for the concept of delayed gratification.

Before you start spending the money on yourself, you must ensure that you have no debt. The reverse is the case in Nigeria. People are indebted and they still spend the money on themselves. They're busy financing their ego.

(2) Spending all your money is not a good idea. I've developed a well-tested formula to encourage financial discipline when starting out. Since the entrepreneur earns dividends rather than a salary, I'd recommend that in the beginning, they save or reinvest the first 80% of their earnings. That should be the starting point.

For both peace of mind and solid results, I prefer a strict sense of financial discipline. Prioritize savings, compulsively—it's a good addiction. If you do not cultivate that savings habit, you are dead. You'll be gone in no time. You have no future if you cannot save money. If you save 80%, you can then spend 20% on your wants—wristwatches, clothes, shoes, yachts and planes, whatever. If you make ₦10 billion, you save or invest/reinvest ₦8 billion.

You're then free to spend ₦2 billion. Face it, that's still a lot of money to blow. How much will you spend on hotels and vacations? A struggling entrepreneur who's just starting out should not blow anything. Save the capital so you don't have to go borrowing money. He who goes a-borrowing goes a-sorrowing, as my father drilled into me. Why would you have a business in debt and be blowing money? Why would you deposit the money in a savings account and collect interest of 10%, when your company borrows at 20% and you're the sole guarantor for the loan? It doesn't make sense. You can only start talking about having control over 100% of your money when your business is not in debt.

Nigeria is full of entrepreneurs who can acquire the trappings of affluence on credit because they don't need to pay up front. If you want to buy a jet today, you only need a 30% down payment. Anything you want to buy, once you have 30% equity, they will give it to you. They hold onto the title, and if you don't pay up, they take it back. They foreclose on it. You'll find that many Nigerian entrepreneurs have adopted this as a lifestyle. Easy come, easy go. Here today, gone tomorrow.

If you want to do big business, you have to make many sacrifices. You must deny yourself many things until your company reaches that level where you've saved enough to spend on nonessential luxuries. For younger people just starting out, savings and reinvestment must be 100%. You should wear the same suit until you finish paying back the banks. OK, maybe two suits—one for the office and a better one for meetings with the bankers.

(3) Philandering kills enterprise. Apart from the scourge of spending projected income, philandering can quickly ruin a business. My father always said this to me. Look at the older generation of Nigerian entrepreneurs, so many of whom saw their companies go extinct. Many were philanderers, cheating and juggling mistresses and living secret—or not-so-secret—double lives. Infidelity is a big distraction and a destroyer.

It may look like fun, but it opens the door to circumstances that will eventually pull you down. For starters, you can't focus on your business because your emotions and attention are elsewhere. That's a big minus for someone who wants to build an empire. Certainly, running around and cheating is not the only thing that ruins business—there are of course many who were not philanderers, whose companies still collapsed. However, we all know that anything done in excess is ruinous.

Philandering is a job on its own and will consume all your time as you lose control of yourself. It costs a lot of money. What's more, in the Nigerian context, these affairs can become very dangerous. You may end up having numerous children with different partners. That headache alone can be the end of you. I have only four children, and I have to treat them all in a fair and equal way, which is not easy. If I had 20 or 30 kids from different women, the headache of managing them all would kill me. And there is nothing you can do about it; they are your children and need your attention.

(4) Distractions of any type are never to your advantage. So, how do you ward off women and men who are more likely to throw themselves at you when you have money and power? For one thing, always bear in mind that you are exposing yourself to danger. Your competitors may even send someone to flirt with you, hoping to distract or pull you down. Banks can send women to set you up if they have issues with you. In fact, it's happened to me. As alluded to earlier, one bank I owed money to sent a woman wearing a wire to tape me. They were trying to obtain incriminating recordings that could be played in court. Basically, they wanted to ensure that I didn't claim not to owe them money. And, of course, you make yourself vulnerable to blackmail.

If you're married, devote more time to your spouse and children. The headache of keeping a retinue of lovers is enormous. You are already managing your business and home life, which should be enough stress. Imagine that you have a crucial meeting. If you got caught up in an argument with your partner the previous night, you're already badly set up for the meeting. That is bad luck in itself. Your mind will be elsewhere, and you won't be at the top of your game. You won't rest well, and you won't be able to perform.

I know many in my generation whose businesses have been damaged by affairs. Sometimes, when you are in the adultery game, your ego takes control—the more lovers in your life, the more you feed your ego. You begin to do things that make no sense. You're pulled into unnecessary spending as you try to impress your paramours. You fly them around on private jets, purchase outrageously priced handbags, go to dinner, ask them to bring friends along. You transfer money to your lovers' accounts. Many people in Abuja do not work; they depend on the largesse of adulterers. That is their preoccupation and their occupation. The older generation didn't spend as much on paramours. They took them on car rides, and that was it.

I ward off such temptations by programming my mind to see the whole thing as pretty much the same old story. Philandering will affect your business. It affects your decision making within the company. There are those who, when it's time to promote, promote the ones who smile at them. They approve the promotion without even looking into performance and evaluations. Underperforming employees can feel comfortable just coasting along at work because you're sleeping with them. Naturally, this will encourage wider indiscipline in the office. There is no way such a thing would not affect your business. Those who view sleeping with others as a conquest cannot really have any control. They will eventually obsess over this and lose themselves in the process.

(5) Substance abuse will ruin you faster than your enemies. Lavishly spending unearned income and philandering can torpedo your chances of success, but so can drug abuse and excessive consumption of alcohol. I see them as similar threats, because these two vices have a similar impact on your personal life.

Drugs and alcohol alter your state of mind, impact your physical health, and affect your ability to take control of your life. It's not that you won't make money—you may even be motivated to make more to feed and sustain these bad habits—but the quality of your life will be substandard. You will also be the subject of rumours, as word of your behaviour inevitably spreads. Your supporters will think less of you and your rivals will use it against you. Your bankers and partners will begin dealing with you with caution and cynicism. They won't find you worthy of their trust, and they would be right not to.

Every person I've come across who abuses drugs has been unsuccessful. You cannot consider them role models; they don't make anything out of their lives. People who are hooked on cocaine and heroin completely lose it. Yes, there are those who have overcome such terrible addictions, but so many more crash and burn. That's the quickest route to destruction, far worse than philandering. All bad behaviours are toxic, but drug and alcohol addiction are downright deadly.

Apart from the health implications that come with drug abuse, decisions taken under the influence of alcohol can be ruinous. You are not in control of your mental faculties. I should note that I'm referring to the real alcoholic here, not the social drinker who gets tipsy once in a while. An alcoholic will drink in the office, gulping it down as it blurs his vision and taints his decisions. Alcoholics are not that rare in business, but I've never seen a successful entrepreneur who's hooked on booze. Some things just do not go together, and that's the case with business and alcohol. If you can't be abstinent through sheer personal discipline and willpower, you should seek professional help for your problem.

(6) Gambling is a vicious enemy. Closely related to the other vices we've been talking about is gambling. Gamblers cannot succeed in business. Even when they seem to, the success will be short-lived. They'll eventually gamble their fortune away. It's a nasty habit, one that's bound to lose you everything. It will rob you of your income, your savings, your assets. You collect your dividends, gamble, and the money disappears, but you keep on assuming you'll win big the next time.

Gambling takes a toll on you slowly; you can sit at a card table and gamble for days on end. It's so time-consuming and addictive that it robs you of time to focus on your business. What's more, those who gamble never have money to take care of themselves or their families. They even sell their businesses, literally gambling everything away. Any entrepreneur who wants to build an enduring empire will avoid gambling altogether.

With deliberate self-discipline and the help of God, one can overcome such ruinous habits. My father made sure to warn me to avoid gambling, philandering, drugs and alcohol. I'm doing the same with you. Stay on the straight and narrow if you want to succeed in business and in life.

TAKEAWAYS

- A fool and his money are soon parted
- Don't spend money you don't yet have, such as your projected profits. They are just an estimate, not something you own
- To survive the first few years after setting up your firm, save 80% of your earnings
- Steer clear of philandering, drugs, alcohol and gambling
- Self-discipline is imperative

SECTION FIVE

REDISCOVERY

EXPERIENCE IS THE BEST TEACHER,
AND MATURITY BRINGS WISDOM,
SO 'EASY DOES IT'

LESSON TWENTY-ONE

MY TYPICAL DAY AND WEEKEND

My schedule has always changed, depending on the business at hand. Over the years—from Impact Press to Centre Force, Zenon, AP, Forte Oil and now Geregu Power—my workday has evolved. What used to be an intense, activity-filled, almost 24-hour marathon workday is now a more leisurely itinerary. I have free time to reflect on past experiences and plan for the future, using the lessons I have learned.

Back in 1981, when my father was starting his printing operation, the workload was heavy. We were setting up the new company, managing our lean resources and scouting for customers to bring in enough income to pay salaries and offset our loan. As I have described, I was driver, personal assistant, office assistant, labourer, cashier, account clerk, storekeeper, estimator, procurement officer and salesman. To save money, my dad held off on employing extra hands at first, so we worked longer hours. We even slept at the press some nights during those first weeks.

As the business got on a better footing, we would leave home at 7 am and retire at 7 in the evening. The 12-hour routine went on for years, until I moved into the sales consultant role in 1987. This lasted until 1991. I then had enough free time to play and party. At this time, I also published the fan magazine of musician Shina Peters, which had me attending a lot of the Juju star's concerts and after-parties. Since performances usually lasted all night, from dusk to dawn, I became a night owl.

The Centre Force days were different. Between 1994 and 1998, I relaxed my schedule. The loan business followed a word-of-mouth testimonial model and did not require a 9-to-5 workday. It was my sleep-late period.

Zenon was a different thing entirely. I've described my routine of days at the office and nights at the depot, subsisting on just a few hours of sleep at night. The weekends were different: I caught up on sleep and avoided parties, although I still logged in a few hours of work. For instance, I've described how Sundays saw me head from church to the depot for a while.

It was an exciting time. I was young and full of energy. Once I realized what colossal opportunities the diesel market held, a passion to succeed propelled me. I never fell ill, despite the punishment my body endured. When I bought into African Petroleum PLC in 2007, my schedule became even more complicated. I was managing two companies, as the CEO of Zenon and Executive Chairman of AP. I started work at AP at 8 am, on Broad Street, Lagos Island, leaving at 1 in the afternoon for Zenon, on Victoria Island, where I toiled until 7 in the evening.

When I appointed Akin and the board in 2010, relinquishing executive powers, the pace of my day slowed considerably. I still went to the office every morning, but had a much more relaxed routine, usually leaving by 3 pm.

Forte Oil didn't make for much of a change to my work routine, but as Executive Chairman of Geregu, things scaled back dramatically for me.

These days, once the weekend is here, I wake up around 9 am, say my little prayer and go to the gym. I have a late breakfast, and on Saturdays meet my friend Aliko Dangote at around 2 pm. We catch up, have lunch, and if there are no weekend engagements to attend, we'll have dinner together, on my boat or at his house or mine. We might hang out together until 11 pm or so.

We repeat the same routine on Sundays. During the week, we make an effort to meet up every other day.

What can budding entrepreneurs learn from how I organize my day? Here are a few tips:

(1) Plan ahead. I mentioned earlier that I plan my schedule three months ahead, so I know where I'll be and what I will be doing on any given day. My meetings are lined up for the quarter, each with its timing and agenda written out in advance. I even include the social activities of friends and family in my programme, so I can stay abreast of what everybody's up to. Once I have a new appointment, I forward the details to my secretary. She arranges the meetings and my engagements on a spreadsheet, which she emails to me. There used to be a time when I took every day as it came, working through things as they cropped up. Not any more. I have the most tightly structured schedule of anyone I know.

(2) Set goals for yourself and for your business. Another useful habit I've developed, and live my life by, is goal setting. I set quarterly goals. Because I've planned the quarter, hour by hour, I tailor my quarterly goals to fit my schedule.

For entrepreneurial goals, I meet regularly with my team, and we brainstorm. We have long-, medium-and short-term goals. There are targets for the next three, six and 12 months. We even have a 10-year plan, and I regularly update and check the targets and milestones to see how well we're doing.

Granted, it's difficult for younger people starting in business to have clear-cut goals to methodically pursue. I certainly didn't have concrete goals at the start of my entrepreneurial journey. My mission was to provide for my family—to put a roof over our heads, provide three meals a day, keep us all well-clothed, pick good schools and try to enjoy life, even if only modestly so. Back then, it was never extravagant, but we lived well.

At Centre Force and Zenon, I did not have goals in the sense that I do today. These firms started like every young person's dream of having their own business, without knowing the level their endeavours would reach. It is usually when you become modestly successful, when the necessities of life are no longer a struggle, that you realize you can aim higher and achieve more.

You cannot make ambitious plans when you're struggling. That would be like a footballer setting out to say he is going to play in the most expensive Premier League club when he is not even in the top club of his local league. It's not impossible, but he needs to get to a level to be seen and scouted first. You play from club to club and are then offered better deals. Once you're good enough, after enjoying better deals with more and more successful clubs, aiming for the top Premier League club can be an achievable goal.

(3) Don't sweat the feasibility study. You don't need a comprehensive feasibility study to start your business. As described earlier, I didn't have one done when I set up Centre Force or Zenon. I just founded the companies when I saw the opportunities. As a young, aspiring entrepreneur, you just need to get started and do what you have to do. No matter how detailed and seemingly fail-safe your plans, preparations and projections are, you can never know whether the business will be successful.

One of the fallacies around entrepreneurship is that people think they have to write a comprehensive business plan and follow it to a T in order to kick things off and move forward. That's just not feasible. Conduct your business conscientiously, give the public the best product you can, at the right price, provide outstanding customer service, and pray for the best. Do you think the boys who play football barefoot in places like Mushin or Ajegunle,[17] the working-class suburbs of Lagos, and end up becoming stars, consciously set out to reach those heights? They do what they do, and take their journey one step at a time, while adapting and readjusting along the way. It is the same for most professions and vocations.

(4) Choose a sleeping pattern that aligns with your goals. I no longer wake up at a particular time. I'm not the morning person I once was, who only slept a couple of hours before dashing out of the door. I did that when I was young and adrenalin fuelled. I had to do what my business required, whatever it took, to make a go of it. Different enterprises demand different schedules and sleeping patterns.

Nowadays, being in my sixties, I may wake up at 11 am or so on weekdays, depending on how late I went to bed the night before. I try to get a minimum of seven to eight hours of sleep. Sleep makes me happy, and I can indulge in it like this because I don't have any debt. I could not have slept comfortably when the business was just taking off, or at the height of the calamity that kicked me bloody, between 2009 and 2012.

Free from debt, I can sleep soundly. The fact that I am in control of my time now brings me peace and happiness. There is this excitement I cannot explain, akin to spiritual fulfilment. If you owe money, the bank can tell you that they want to see you at 8 am, and you have to be there. Another bank will call and direct you to come in at 9, and you don't have a choice but to race from one terribly stressful encounter to another. And then there will be another, and another. When you owe money, your time is never really yours. Today, I am under no pressure to live a life of appointments or engagements and can get the sleep I need and want.

(5) Take care of your body. I exercise every day and follow a strict diet. After my morning prayers, I put in an hour on the treadmill, walking at a brisk pace. It's not overly strenuous; I don't lift weights or engage in backbreaking workout routines. I listen to music as I exercise and aim to burn 700 calories.

As discussed earlier I eat a balanced diet. I talked earlier about how I used to eat three times a day but eat just two meals now. As one grows older, you do not need as much food. I follow a painstakingly organized diet, which I started in 2016, when I turned 54, as discussed here earlier. I eat protein, vegetables and fruits daily. I am alcohol-free and drink coffee sparingly.

Finally, as part of my morning routine, I read through a series of websites. I spend time with *Nairametrics*, *CNBC*, *TheCable*, *Premium Times*, and monitor the Nigerian Stock Market. They help me keep abreast of financial developments, breaking news and the state of the world.

TAKEAWAYS

My typical days and weekends have evolved over the years. Now, in semi-retirement, in my 60s, I'm taking things at a more relaxed pace.

I've shared my typical schedule and routine, and the stability and comfort they bring me at this stage in my life. I'd advise you to try and adopt the same general approach:

- Take care of your body and mind
- If you're just starting out, don't obsess over feasibility studies and business plans, but do try to plan well ahead
- Set short-and long-term goals for yourself and your business, and adjust them as needed

LESSON TWENTY-TWO

BE A CHEERFUL GIVER

My shoulders dropped, and I was red with shame. As the eminent trio left, I was enveloped by gloom, and tears trickled down my cheeks. That meeting in my Ikoyi house, sometime in 2009, brought home the depth of my desolation.

With me were Sir Steve Omojafor, the advertising guru and co-founder of Rosabel Advertising Ltd, Chief Molade Okoya-Thomas, the Lagos power broker who is one of the prime movers at the manufacturing conglomerate CFAO, and Chief Sena Anthony, the oil and gas legal consultant who was just about to retire after 30 years of service with NNPC.

I was not quite sure what their agenda was when they came to meet with me, but they got straight to the point: "We need your financial support to start the Augustine University in Ilara-Epe."

They planned to establish the school in Odoragunsin, where my father had allocated land to the Catholic Church decades ago but not much had been done with it. Unfortunately, I could not help, either then or in the foreseeable future. I could not even help myself. I was in a financial mess of unimaginable magnitude.

"Gentlemen and madam, I am not in a position to help because I have a debt of ₦220 billion around my neck," I told them. At the time, my debt was not public knowledge. I laid it on the line but did not want to be pitied. That was not my style.

When they departed, I went to my room and cried. I was weeping because they had come with what I saw as an appeal from God. And I resolved that at some point, if and when I was able, I ought to help with the development of Augustine University. I beseeched God: "Please, give me another break. If you do, I am going to build this school." It was a vow that came from the depths of my soul.

It was a startling revelation for my visitors, because apart from the banks we owed and a select few insiders, my desperate position was still a secret. I wanted to keep a lid on it, in hope of convincing my creditors to give me one more chance to work through rebuilding my business and future. Sadly, the press was already on the story.

Just about a week after the meeting with that eminent trio, the *Next* newspaper broke the story of my misfortune. Its eye-catching headline, "Femi Otedola's sinking empire and his floating £12 million yacht," upended my world. Adorning the front-page story was a picture of my yacht, with a subheading: "The sharks smell blood, and they are circling."

As soon as *Next* broke the story, others feasted on it. One of the banks I was indebted to gleefully gave interviews to every paper and broadcast outlet. They stripped me bare, splashing my picture on their front pages with morbid delight. The news blared from TVs and radios. They even dragged my wife and children into the fray because they were directors at Zenon. We all suffered. Today, we can appreciate the lessons learned and count our blessings, but back then it was a horror story playing out on prime-time television. I'm sure my detractors watched with delight, over popcorn and cold drinks.

Much later, when I moved on to better times, my mother, Lady Doja, discussed supporting the school with me. Shortly after we'd buried my father, in May of 2014, she suggested that we give Augustine University ₦500 million from his estate. But there was no consensus in the family, and we deferred the contribution.

Months later, I told her: "Don't worry, Mum. I'll do it."

After consultation with the authorities, I agreed to fund the engineering school complex to the tune of ₦2 billion. I provided the first tranche in 2017. They received sign-off from the archbishop and the University of Lagos, which provided the designs and technical advice, and things moved forward. Slowly but surely, as more donations are made, the university buildings are now popping up one after another. So far I have handed over the first phase of the engineering block I completed at the cost of ₦670 million. The second phase is now progressing which I named after my mother Lady Doja Otedola. It is called The Lady Doja Otedola Engineering Block.

Giving cheerfully to help the less privileged—making the world a better place for us all—has long been a priority in my life. As Paul the Apostle states in his Second Letter to the Corinthians, "Each one must give as he has decided in his heart, not reluctantly or under compulsion, for God loves a cheerful giver."[18]

Here are my thoughts and convictions on giving:

(1) Anyone and everyone can give. Giving is in my DNA. My mum gives readily—it's in her nature, and she passed on the spirit of charity to me. I learned generosity from her, and it's also a habit of some of my siblings. When people come around, she invariably takes care of them, making sure no one goes hungry. She is a blessing to everyone who comes in contact with her. I help her with her finances, so I'm privy to some of her generous gestures, including building houses for her staff. One of them got a ₦70 million home. Her commitment to the church and the community is exemplary, and her largesse incredible.

My father, too, was kindness and generosity personified. His magnanimity is remembered far and wide. He started a large scholarship scheme for indigent students, which I later began supporting. He too had been the recipient of a scholarship, which allowed him to study in the UK. He touched many lives, long before he became the second civilian governor of Lagos State, and he continued to do so afterwards. My elder brother followed our parents' lead and would give you the shirt off his back. He'll hand you the keys to his car and walk home.

As long as I can remember, sharing and giving have given me pleasure. When I was in primary school, I willingly shared my lunchbox goodies with classmates, and they eagerly looked forward to partaking in the scotch eggs and sandwiches. With my mum's catering position, you can imagine the effort she put into packaging the family's food. In high school, I readily handed others my dinner.

This giving spirit became more pronounced as I matured and started earning a salary or commission. I gave a little to help others pay school fees or their rent, or to offset medical bills. I'd quietly hand out ₦2,000 here, ₦5,000 there. Over the years, as I amassed more resources, I stepped up my charitable giving.

(2) Giving warms the heart. Philanthropy gives me an inner joy. It brings me a sense of happiness I find difficult to describe. The beneficiaries are genuinely grateful and joyous, and their euphoria is infectious. Anyone who isn't in the habit of helping others should give it a try, and experience just how gratifying it can be.

Big-hearted magnates who take the time to give back to the community fascinate me. I read about the ways of wealthy philanthropists, follow them keenly and seek them out personally. When I was in high school, I used to walk to Executive House on Oil Mill Street, the monument erected by Sir Mobolaji Bank Anthony, the 20th century's leading light in philanthropy in our country. I'd stand in front of the building, size it up and calculate in my young mind how much it had cost—an arm and a leg, I concluded. I would stare at it, stupefied.

Sir Mobolaji's donations of a ward to the National Orthopaedic Hospital in Igbobi, and of Ayinke House, the Institute of Maternal and Child Health in Ikeja's General Hospital, literally save lives. They've made all the difference in the world to so many, with arms and limbs repaired, and babies delivered in safety. I greatly admire the giving spirit of this businessman, who was fond of pairing sharp hats with well-cut suits. He was a true entrepreneur, starting out as a palm oil merchant, becoming a big importer of clocks, watches and fountain pens, and moving on to interests in major construction, insurance, oil, automobiles, plywood and food concerns.

Also notable is the philanthropy of my old landlord. From encouraging entrepreneurs to inspiring the innovators and leaders of tomorrow, Chief Bode Akindele, who ran the Modandola Group, which operates in manufacturing, real estate, shipping and agriculture, brought joy and hope to thousands of people. The colossal medical facility he made possible, which is visible to anyone travelling on the Lagos-Ibadan expressway, is testament to his commitment to humanity. Named after his mother, Alhaja Rabiatu Adedigba, the centre was formally inaugurated by President Obasanjo in May of 2003, in Orisumbare Village.

His philanthropic organization, the Bode Akindele Foundation, was established in 1985. It empowers more than a thousand people a year in entrepreneurial, innovation and leadership collaborations with Good Worker Ministries International, the University of Ibadan, and Federal University of Technology in Akure. Its charitable arm, the Bode Akindele Yield Initiative, promotes entrepreneurship, innovation, leadership and development for Nigerian youth.

Those whose lives are made better by such programmes will always remember who helped them arrive at their new circumstances. Their cheerful expressions are worth far more than any competition trophy. Every time I remember the readiness of Chief Wahab Iyanda Folawiyo, my friend Tunde's dad, to assist those who worked on behalf of worthy causes, I appreciate the pull of philanthropy even more. In addition to building mosques, the man lovingly known as Baba Adini lavished his wealth on many other projects that helped in our nation's progress.

Once, I was on a University of Lagos fundraising committee where Yemi Onabowale, the elder brother of the owner of Reddington Hospital, served as chairman. The politician Lanre Tejuoso represented the students. We had recruited Chief Folawiyo as one of the donors, and he gave the school a cheque for ₦500,000 (around US$22,727 at the time). Giving was in his genes, and he never made excuses to avoid parting with his hard-earned money, even if it was for something he didn't benefit from directly. To him, the good cause alone was justification enough. As it should be.

(3) Those who are better off have a responsibility to help others. It is the responsibility of the blessed to make life less burdensome for the afflicted and disadvantaged. When one has been the recipient of enormous, good luck—especially if he has amassed resources he couldn't conceivably exhaust in several lifetimes—it rests on him to give a helping hand to the troubled. Humankind is a brotherhood, and good ethics dictate that we help each other.

Microsoft's Bill Gates—who with his former wife founded the Bill and Melinda Gates Foundation in 2000, with the slogan 'All lives have equal value'—once personally encouraged me to commit to The Giving Pledge. Introduced in 2010 by Gates and billionaire philanthropist Warren Buffett, the campaign encourages the world's wealthiest to contribute considerable funds to philanthropic causes. The 200-plus signatories, who hail from 20 countries, have pledged more than US$500 billion in total.

It's wonderful to see giants of entrepreneurship commit their time, money and effort to helping those in need, just as I've dedicated myself to giving back to my local and national communities.

There are many who change the lives of the disadvantaged by helping people cope with their circumstances. The Gates Foundation focuses on improving health, wellbeing and access to food, and on eliminating extreme poverty in developing countries, among other causes. Its mission in the US is to provide the underprivileged with opportunities to succeed in school and in life. In Nigeria, the foundation has been involved in eradicating polio, improving family health and healthcare systems, increasing access to financial services, boosting agricultural productivity and, in collaboration with the Dangote Foundation, addressing malnutrition and broader childhood nutrition issues.

In Africa, the Dangote Foundation is a leader in supporting worthwhile causes. It has contributed more than US$100 million in the last four years to its fight against polio, in partnership with the Gates Foundation. Incorporated in 1994, the Dangote Foundation has a staff of more than 50, dedicated to 'adding value to people's lives across Africa by facilitating health, education and empowerment initiatives.' It partners with GBC Health, the UN Economic Commission for Africa, ONE, Chi Health, the Global Alliance for Improved Nutrition, the African Development Bank and others.

Easily sub-Saharan Africa's largest private foundation, it has contributed ₦1 billion to Nigerian universities; ₦500 million for the development of a Bayero University business school; ₦100 million for the proposed Otuoke University in Bayelsa State; ₦230 million to Kogi State women in the form of micro-grants; ₦50 million in relief to Jos's community leaders following rioting in that city; and US$2 million to the World Food Programme during flooding in Pakistan.

(4) Spreading your wealth improves the world. Those who can give have an opportunity to make the world more beautiful and bearable for us all. I remember when CNN founder Ted Turner donated US$1 billion to the UN in 1997. The unprecedented move involved allotments of US$100 million that were disbursed each year for a decade. This was so inspiring that I got a premonition that I'd do something similar one day.

Turner explained that the money was going to be put to use in programmes geared towards, "...refugees, cleaning up landmines, peacekeeping, UNICEF for the children, for diseases, and we're going to have a committee that will work with a committee of the UN." As the funds were being disbursed, Turner's net worth had climbed to US$3.2 billion. "I'm no poorer than I was nine months ago, and the world is much better off," he said of the philanthropic pledge.

Such humanitarian donations have always helped the causes that give mankind a better chance of living in a fairer and more just world. From war, famine, hunger and floods to diseases that require urgent attention, money provided by donors big and small ameliorates suffering and the consequences of conflict. The sick, hungry, displaced, wounded and dying can be helped immensely by donations to various official bodies and non-governmental organizations.

(5) Nothing compares to the spiritual pleasure of giving. Helping others is a spiritual act. The prayers, kind thoughts and warm wishes that the beneficiaries send in return contribute to a virtuous circle. I have witnessed intense emotions—from tears and tight embraces to lengthy prayers of intercession and benediction, carefully written letters of gratitude and messages of appreciation—and the feeling is incredible. Those who wish me well with sincerity send up prayers for blessings, protection and guidance. Such prayers find God's favour.

Imagine the gratitude of those who receive scholarships, who otherwise would have been poor and working in low-level jobs, but instead go on to a quality education and then lead better lives because of it. They send gratitude to their benefactors, as do their families and those who enjoy the benefits of their new circumstances. Just one scholarship, a kind gesture to a single person who becomes a breadwinner, can help improve the standard of living of many.

(6) Philanthropy teaches contentment. 'How Much Land Does a Man Need?' I'm mesmerized by the short story with that title, by Russian novelist Leo Tolstoy. Published in 1886, it is the story of a man who wants as much land as he can possibly grab. He makes a deal with the Bashkirs, an ethnic mountain tribe, that for a thousand roubles he will receive all the land he can set foot on in a single day, from sunrise to sunset, as long as he has returned to the starting point by that evening. Sure enough, his greed leads him so far away that he can't possibly make it back to his origination point by dusk. He starts running, harder and harder, and although he manages to reach the starting point as the sun dips beneath the horizon, he drops dead of exhaustion. He gets buried in a commoner's grave that's six feet long, from his head to his heels, which in the end amounted to all the land he'd ever have.

The moral of the story really resonates with me. That's all the land we need in the end—we'll all be buried in a grave whose length scarcely exceeds our height. And so, it follows, what's the point—if you don't share it—of amassing enormous wealth that you won't be able to take with you? God has blessed me, I have enjoyed the best things in life, I have the ways and means, and I'm eager to share whatever I can.

Our time on this planet, as part of the community of humankind, is about far more than personal enjoyment. It's about more than all the land one can own. I derive more pleasure from philanthropy than from personal satisfaction or comfort.

I have spent ₦640 million on scholarships for indigenous students via the Sir Michael Otedola Scholarship Scheme. It was launched by my father in 1987 and received a ₦200 million boost from me when I stepped in. We re-christened the programme in its present name in 2005. The ₦100 million I gave to the Lagos State government in 2007, for the Otedola College of Primary Education in Epe, was independent of this scheme. I try to keep my contributions varied, spreading them out in order to benefit as many as possible.

I find such interventions infinitely more meaningful than personal indulgence.

(7) With charity, you can give others better chances. Being able to give people a better chance to survive and blossom is an incomparable feeling. Sometimes, the difference between living and dying is a few thousand naira. So many times, I have been moved and galvanized by appeals to save lives. One of my first major public gestures was the ₦7 million I gave to a young man with kidney problems. When I read about him in *Punch* newspaper, I just reached out to his family and handed them a cheque. Unfortunately, the beneficiary died four days later. Only God gives life, but people like us—doctors and health workers, philanthropists and those of every stripe who care for their fellow human beings—can put our resources to good use. We become instruments of God in helping to extend and improve the lives of those in need.

WHY I DONATED ₦5 BILLION TO THE SAVE THE CHILDREN FUND

For years, I had considered ways to scale up my philanthropic efforts via a foundation that would allow me to transform lives and circumstances in a more methodical manner. I had already made significant donations. I talked earlier about helping with completion of the National Ecumenical Centre in Abuja. There was also ₦100 million to Lagos State College of Primary Education; ₦100 million for the Ilorin Central Mosque in Kwara State; ₦100 million to the University of Port Harcourt in Rivers State; and ₦2 billion to Augustine University in Epe. I also provided medical assistance for the football great Christian Chukwu; former ace goalkeeper Peter Fregene; reggae superstar Majek Fashek; the legendary actors Sadiq Daba and Victor Olaokun; and various others.

Yet, I wanted a more official platform for my charity-minded ventures, through which to channel my philanthropic giving. I made plans to establish my foundation as a full-fledged organization. However, when I considered the logistics of setting up an office, recruiting a CEO and staff, and planning for growth to achieve our objectives, it became apparent that it would take too long and siphon away resources that could more directly help those in need.

A non exhaustive list of donations that I have made to charities, organisations and individuals for charitable, religious, educational, medical and humanitarian purposes over the years include the following – I have outlined the summary in chronological order:

i. ₦200m (US $1.4m) to Sir Michael Otedola Scholarship Awards for indigenous students (2004 to 2008)

ii. ₦300m ($2.5m) to Construction of National Ecumenical Centre, Abuja (2005)

iii. ₦25m ($178,571.00) for Construction of Abuja Central Mosque (2006)

iv. Over ₦75m ($535,714.28) to Ilorin Central Mosque (2007)

v. ₦100m ($574,712.64) to Michael Otedola College of Primary Education (now Sir Michael Otedola University of Education (2009)

vi. ₦50m ($26,408.00) to Christ the King Catholic Church (2010)

vii. ₦100m ($543,478.26) to University of Port Harcourt (2011)

viii. Over ₦30m ($57,471.00) for the construction of Our Lady of Perpetual Help, Victoria Island (2017)

ix. ₦100m ($255,141.00) to Lagos State Security Trust Fund (2017-2019)

x. Over ₦30m ($57,471.00) for the Renovation of Holy Cross Cathedral, Lagos Island (2018)

xi. ₦5b ($14m) to Save the Children Fund (2019)
xii. ₦391m ($1m) for the Establishment of African Centre New York (2019)
xiii. Over ₦65.6m ($130,000.00) for medical treatment of Victor Olaotan (2019)
xiv. ₦19.5m ($50,000.00) Medical treatment for Christian Chukwu (2019)
xv. ₦20m ($39,682.00) Medical treatment for Peter Fregene (2020)
xvi. Over ₦10m ($17,695.00) for medical treatment of Sadiq Daba
xvii. Over ₦17m ($29,929.57) for medical treatment of Prof Daramola (2021)
xviii. Over ₦15m ($26,408.45) for medical treatment of Mr. Kayode Ajala (2021)
xix. ₦7.5m ($8,695.00) Medical treatment of Charles Bassey (2021)
xx. Over £5,500.00 for medical treatment of Majek Fashek in London (2021)
xxi. ₦2b ($2.1m) to Construction of Faculty of Engineering, St Augustine University, Ilara-Epe (2023)
xxii. ₦1b ($1.1m) to Renewed Hope Initiative (2023)
xxiii. ₦1bn ($1.2m) for scholarship donations to all students of Augustine University, Ilara-Epe, Lagos State for the 2023/2024 academic year i.e. ₦1m each to the 750 students in the University (2023), ₦140m for the furnishing of the recently completed engineering faculty building and ₦110m for the installation of street lights around the campus and a new standby generating set
xxiv. ₦22m ($19,130.43) per year for student scholarships for large number of students from nursery to university education
xxv. ₦1bn ($1.2m) to the Lagos State Security Trust Fund (3rd donation)

I considered supporting the Dangote Foundation in the same way Warren Buffett supports charities like the Gates Foundation.

My daughter, DJ Cuppy, started the Cuppy Foundation, which concentrates its efforts on child protection and education for girls with disabilities. Her foundation partnered with other well-established charities, including Save the Children, Global Citizen, the Dangote Foundation, Angel for Life, and Kreative Arts Foundation for Youths.

As I strategized my charitable path forward, two events unfolded that helped me choose my next steps. The first was my July 2019 meeting with Princess Anne, the daughter of the United Kingdom's Queen Elizabeth and patron of Save the Children. That was at the invitation of DJ Cuppy, who serves as one of the organization's ambassadors. Our interaction opened my eyes to the activities of this 100-year charity, which was started by two sisters, Eglantyne Jebb and Dorothy Buxton, in 1919. My daughter and the princess educated me on the history, objectives and worldwide good works of this wonderful group. It is the second-biggest charity for children in the world, after UNICEF, and struck me as being even more focused and results oriented. By the time my family and I attended the Patron's Centenary Dinner at Buckingham Palace in October of 2019, I'd made up my mind that I would support the cause in a big way.

The second event that helped reel me in was DJ Cuppy's visit to a displaced persons camp in Maiduguri, Nigeria, in August 2019, under the aegis of Save the Children Foundation. Her call for urgent intervention in a region devastated by the Boko Haram[19] insurgency touched me. "I was able to observe and learn about childhoods that come to an early end, because of ill health, malnutrition, exclusion from education, child marriage, early pregnancy, and violent death," she has written of the experience. "The Humanitarian Needs Overview estimates that 2.2 million school-aged children and teachers in north-eastern Nigeria need immediate emergency support. My vision is to save every child I can."

I initially thought of giving Save the Children ₦2.5 billion, but after reviewing my income and cash flow, I decided to double my donation to ₦5 billion.

When that became known, one of my daughters was overwhelmed by the amount. "Papa," she said, "you're giving away our inheritance." Once the dust settled, and my family came to understand that this was my calling, they were thrilled. We hosted the Cuppy Gold Gala at the

Transcorp Hilton in Abuja on 10 November 2019, and my daughter Tolani presented the ₦5 billion donation.

My dream is to do more. I know I will, God willing.

It is the responsibility of us all, no matter our position or how deep our pockets, to be grateful for things big and small, and to show others love and tolerance, sympathy and empathy.

TAKEAWAYS

To be a cheerful giver, you need to give away your widow's mite—that Biblical offering that represents most of what you have, even when you're poor—for the sake of improving the life of your neighbour, who might not have as much. This unifies humanity. To that end:

- You don't need to have parents and siblings who give back in order to do so yourself. You can learn kindness and empathy, and develop the spirit of giving cheerfully, no matter your condition
- The wealth of positive emotions you experience when you help others is beneficial to your health and wellbeing, and the recipients of your goodwill will pray for you
- Those spared calamities have the responsibility to assist those so impacted
- We ought to give the disadvantaged fair opportunities, including access to education, healthcare, food and shelter. Cheerful givers can make this possible
- Philanthropy echoes the virtue of contentment. I'll say it again: you can't take it with you

LESSON TWENTY-THREE

APPRECIATE THE GOD FACTOR

Nobody gave my father a chance of winning in 1991 when I broached the possibility of him running for governor of Lagos. Even he thought it nonsensical. He thought I was delirious and asked if I'd lost control of my mental faculties. He was too gentlemanly for politics and was understandably irritated when I pushed the idea.

"What's your son drinking?" he asked my mum after I'd first proposed it. I had shared my big dream for him after the political parties had zoned the seat to Epe, our constituency. After all, a handful of his colleagues in the western region, from back when he worked as editor of *Western Nigeria Illustrated* and at the Western Nigeria Broadcasting Service, had ventured into politics. They included Alhaji Lateef Kayode Jakande and Chief Olabisi Onabanjo, journalists who went on to become governors of Lagos State and Ogun State, respectively.

My father was not that easily convinced, and others seemed to share in his scepticism. As the weeks wore on and I brought the idea up again, doing my best to spin things positively, he still wouldn't warm up to it. "You cannot compete with destiny," I'd say, telling him he was meant to become governor.

Finally, after a couple of months, he called me to say that he'd thought long and hard about it, and he agreed to run. He campaigned on the slogan, 'That Lagos May Excel.' He won, was sworn in, and served as governor for a total of 685 days.

Destiny plays a significant role in how events play out in our lives. Despite our struggles, trials and travails, our fighting tooth and nail to outshine and outsmart others, providence eventually rules supreme. But you also have to watch and pray, do your bit decently and unobtrusively, never tearing down others or abandoning your dreams, and never resorting to crooked ways. The God factor, destiny and fate at play, is everything. I learned valuable lessons from my father's miraculous victory, and life's many twists and turns, as I'll touch on below:

(1) Don't hold grudges against those who dismiss your dream. The part played—or not played—by family, friends and associates during my father's run for the governorship showed how God alone decides whom he blesses. Many did not support or contribute to his campaign, despite their closeness to the gentleman. When those who ignored his ambition were the first callers to our house after his astonishing victory, it dawned on me that God decides whom he blesses.

My dad's road to winning the election was a long, arduous and exhausting process, with more than its share of intrigue. Only the hand of God gave us supremacy. If victory relied solely on strategic thinking and political advantage, we wouldn't have stood a chance. Apart from not being in the most popular party among south-westerners and progressives, he had to compete with his childhood friend and estranged business partner. My father's erstwhile associate, who is now deceased, and whose name I will not mention out of a sense of decorum and respect, ran against him. He threw in with the progressives and counted on the support of former governor Lateef Jakande.

That wasn't all. In an attempt to get my father disqualified, his opponent submitted a petition to the State Security Services listing all sorts of fabricated allegations against him. Dad's subsequent interrogation was tormenting. His antagonist-in-chief was the same guy who'd fleeced him out of his investment in a joint business they'd once established. What's more, the man succeeded in appropriating my father's land on Akin Adesola Street, Victoria Island, for himself and confiscated our family house on Tokunbo Street, Lagos Island. He had always seemed to feel that my father's success guaranteed his own failure. In his twisted logic, he needed to see my father fail in order to succeed himself, and in his jealous paranoia he responded in the most underhanded ways.

This man died soon after writing up that petition. And right away, drama consumed the Social Democratic Party (SDP).[20] Jakande—who had supported Prof Femi Agbalajobi against Chief Dapo Sarumi in the SDP primaries—was shocked when the electoral body, led by Prof Humphrey Nwosu, disqualified them both, and the party picked Dr Yomi Edu as its candidate. As a result, Jakande withdrew his support for his party and told his supporters to vote for the National Republican Convention (NRC),[21] which fielded my father.

Even though he was uninterested in politics at first, my dad rose to the challenge, campaigned like a champ and beat Chief Oluremi Adiukwu in the NRC primaries. Before reaching the midway mark, he'd expended all his savings, some ₦33 million, on the campaign. But fierce SDP infighting worked in his favour, and he won the election. The hand of God was clearly at play.

(2) Your heritage can be your guide. Your heritage tells a riveting story about who you are and gives you a clear picture of your path. You are born into a particular family for a reason. You carry along attributes that characterize this family, and the history of your forebears has much to do with your future. There are no accidents of birth. My great-great grandfather enjoyed acclaim and success, towering over his peers in Odoragunsin, near Epe. His good fortune made him numerous enemies, especially at the tail end of the slave trade, and he was ambushed by African profiteers involved in this inhumane enterprise.

Captured, beaten and chained, he was manacled to other victims, set to be ferried to the coastal town of Badagry and shipped to the west. He was so frail, sick and weak that he was abandoned and left for dead. Some of those who'd been abducted alongside him were sent to a life of slavery in the Americas. He made a full recovery, found his way back to his town and triumphantly led his people.

From that point onward, he became known as Otedola. As alluded to earlier, the term means that your enemies' machinations have translated into good fortune for you. That name, which was how everyone now addressed him, served my ancestors well, with plots against us always seeming to work in our favour. I acknowledge the role that slanderers and backbiters have played in my life. Our surname is a testament to the handiwork of evil plotters whose conspiracies benefit us in the end, turning their schemes into public acclaim for us.

(3) Pray for what you want. As I've said, when I wake up in the morning, before I do anything else, I pray silently for about five minutes. I am *aji b'Olorun s'oro*, someone who talks to God as soon as he rises. Even at the start of a new day, there is something to be thankful for. I could have passed away in my sleep. There are people we talked to, or shared dinner and exchanged banter with, who then went to bed at night and never saw the break of dawn. For every day I miraculously make it, I thank God for his goodness and mercies.

I was born a Catholic and attended church without fail from a young age, continuing to do so all through secondary school, spending much time in the school chapel. I wanted to be a priest when I was younger. It's difficult to attend church regularly in Nigeria now because of sectarian violence, but I do what I can for the faith. I pray with my family when I am around them. I remain a spiritual person. I have started reading my Bible again. I never fail to offer prayers of thanksgiving, and I plead with God for good health until old age.

(4) Everything happens for a reason. There are no accidents or coincidences. Nothing is by chance.

I remember visiting British Petroleum in 1975, when I was in Form 1 at Methodist Boys' High School. It couldn't have been a coincidence that I also accompanied my father, who was with Mobil then, when he went to see the Managing Director of BP Nigeria on some business matter. They handed me a bottle of Coca-Cola and biscuits to enjoy while they had their meeting. I bought the company in 2007.

At the time, my dad worked for Mobil Downstream. The Federal

Government owned 40%, while 60% was in private hands. Executives enjoyed high-flying lifestyles, with houses on Victoria Island. My father, his boss, Ogbeni Oja Bayo Kuku, as well as Chief Bade Ojora, Godwin Adokpaye and hundreds of others moved in these well-to-do circles.

The wooden walls and décor of BP's offices brought back a flood of memories when I returned there 32 years later, as the new owner of the business. I was overwhelmed by the feeling that there'd been a reason I had gone to BP in 1975. It wasn't a coincidence. That is how life and divine providence works.

(5) Watch those you choose to be close to. Before I attempt to get close to the people I meet, I try to figure out whether they're coming into my life for good or evil. Have they been sent by God or by the devil? The people who enter your life make it better or worse; to aid in your victories or usher in your downfall. But God usually intervenes. If the devil brings headaches, God gives you an analgesic. Look at how my father's one-time best friend turned out to be his adversary, ready to sacrifice him on the altar of ambition.

I, too, have had my fair share of tormentors. A close friend who was fond of championing 'sure-fire moneymaking ideas' comes to mind. Any deal he proposed always ended up as a loss for me. Not once did any of his schemes turn out to be profitable. I began to grasp that our association was harmful to my wallet, and my wellbeing, when I noticed that he seemed to be unhappy whenever fortune smiled on me. There was veiled jealousy there, which I'd ignored for years. Any time I told him about my plans, he was quick to shoot them down. He was always emphasizing hurdles and obstacles, real or imagined, as reasons why my schemes could never get off the ground.

A long while back, I had just bought a Datsun sports car, and I offered him a ride. We cruised around Lagos with the roof down, as I basked in the pleasure of my purchase. But a few minutes into our expedition, on Eric Moore Close in the Surulere district, another car crashed into my new ride, and I was overcome by sadness. As I reflected afterwards, memories of a series of misfortunes tied to my association with the guy flooded back. After that, I started avoiding this friend, making sure I kept him at a distance.

There are people like that in our lives. Since childhood, I have always been careful about who I mingle with. I said earlier in the book that I'm essentially a loner at heart, but I think I'm warm and sociable. I don't go seeking friendships and choose acquaintances cautiously. This had consciously become a thing for me since the plot to impeach my father, just months into his tenure as governor. A friend of mine, who was scheduled to be best man at my wedding in 1992, was one of the masterminds. He schemed and plotted with my father's enemies and threw our friendship to the dogs just as we planned my nuptials, with matching suits, shirts, ties and shoes. On my wedding day, I was accompanied by no best man.

With some practice, we can detect those who don't like us, have an axe to grind, are secretly jealous, and will in one way or another bring us sorrow. Be vigilant in sorting through fakery and pretence to see who's genuine and who isn't.

(6) Events play out to show you your path. To fix my eyes on my studies, my parents shipped me away to high school, thinking that being away from Lagos, in the care of strict guardians in a boarding school environment, would be helpful. It did nothing to improve my academic performance. I was finished with formal schooling, and I've shared with you what followed—my life as an entrepreneur, through thick and thin.

It took the very hand of God, and many twists and turns, to show me the course I needed to pursue.

(7) Affirm your desires at every opportunity. Some people have taken to calling me 'the prophet,' for my apparent ability to see into the future. Time and again, I've accurately predicted how things will play out. When I was small, I was called 'Joseph the dreamer,' after a Biblical story. I suppose it's all a reflection of my spiritual nature. Whenever so moved, I'm fond of making pronouncements. And I have always been a positive person, constantly hoping for the best, believing that I will succeed against all odds. I seek to turn predicaments into triumphs, always looking on the brighter side.

In 1980, our neighbourhood was hit by a power outage that lasted some time. I needed to iron my clothes, so I arranged them in a bed sheet, rolled and tied them all in a bundle and headed for my friend Bube's[22] house nearby. His father, Chief M. E. R. Okorodudu, was once High Commissioner of Nigeria to the United Kingdom, and also the first dead body I would see as a kid, during his lying-in-state in 1975. We watched him and we shook him, thinking he was asleep. "Daddy, wake up!" we shouted, until we were chased away.

I ironed my clothes at Bube's, and as I returned with the bundle of clothes on my head, my parents were waiting in front of the house. "*Femi, nibo l'oti nbo? Ki lo gbe sori?*" my father asked. Femi, where did you go? What's in the bundle on your head? "*Owo!*" I replied mischievously. Money!

My mum and dad laughed heartily. You see, I had always dreamt of being successful. I talked earlier about how wealthy people fascinated me, and I obsessively kept tabs on men of means. Reading their inspiring tales fired my imagination. It made me believe it was feasible for me to replicate their feats and become a man of wealth and stature. And, as I've said, I would eventually go on to actually meet many of them. Again, there was foreshadowing of what would come to pass. Alhaji Aliko Dangote, whose Rolls-Royce was an object of enchantment for me in 1981, is my best friend today. I have been lucky enough to hobnob with some of the billionaires I grew up studying.

(8) Listen to your inner voice. Pay attention to your instincts and your gut feeling. Your inner voice is one of the ways God speaks to you, constantly nudging you towards the steps you should take. When you're reflective, taking time away from the everyday drudgery and noise, you sharpen your instincts and sense what is of benefit to you. We have always been admonished that 'heaven helps those who help themselves.' Well, those who help themselves listen to their inner voice and do as it directs.

As I cowered with shame following the events of 2008-2009, it was a banker—someone I'd counted among the facilitators of my misfortune—who first raised my hopes. "Femi, you are going to bounce back," said Jim Ovia, the founder and MD of Zenith Bank.

What was this man saying? How in the world could I possibly bounce back? I'd had my ups and downs with Jim, as described earlier in this book. I wondered, staring at him with barely restrained anger, if he realized how deeply I had fallen?

I was unsure whether he was convinced of it, or just consoling me, or perhaps trying to get me to hand over ownership of the Walter Carrington office. But whenever I sat alone, following the calamity, his words hung in the air. Today, I am convinced that was the voice of God speaking to me through Jim. His encouragement echoed in my ears for months. They influenced my decision to face all the troubles head-on and resolve the issues in favour of my creditors. I also drew strength from the words of my father, who told me to always keep my word, to let it be my bond.

My inner voice became loud and clear. It led me in the right direction, persuading me to ignore the advice of those who were trying to convince me to coast along, postponing the day of reckoning.

I have come to realize that we are where we are for a purpose, for a more beautiful future. God wants you to succeed, but events that test and torment you are usually just around the corner.

Your courage and positive outlook during these trials and tribulations, as well as the way you respond to the misfortunes, lay new foundations for blessings that come your way.

TAKEAWAYS

One of the examples I offer to prove the control over of our lives by a higher power is the fact that we cannot remember our first birthday. It is such a pertinent example of how little say we have in our fate and destiny. But what we can do is discern the path chosen for us.

More than any event, my father becoming Governor of Lagos—as well as hundreds of incidents that colluded to set me on my life's trajectory—are signs that God controls everything.

Without God, we labour in vain.

To end, I offer these thoughts:

- Appreciate the guiding hand of the Almighty, as he ensures the occurrence of events that clearly show the path forward
- Being thankful and offering prayers of thanksgiving each day makes us eligible for more favours, protection and guidance
- It is important to avoid those who believe that our downfall means their success. Don't repay their evil; leave justice to God
- Our family history foreshadows our future. Learn the stories of your ancestors and put the lessons that defined them to good use
- Affirm what you want in your future. Echo your dreams as much as you can, and let the universe hear you loud and clear. Pursue interests that resonate with your objectives
- Your life is not an accident; the events that pepper your course aren't coincidences. Everything in life is for a reason
- Your inner voice is a tool for your guidance and promotion. Pay attention to your instincts and gut feelings

BEFORE YOU GO

You can count on the fingers of one hand those who'd voiced fears that a pandemic could ravage the world, killing some 6.6 million people and plunging humanity into chaos. But the world has been in turmoil since late 2019, when the COVID-19 virus emerged in Wuhan, China, before creeping into Thailand, Japan, South Korea and beyond. The World Health Organization declared a pandemic in March 2020 and the world went into lockdown.

Few had imagined that a respiratory disease could change the way mankind lives and conducts business in the 21st century. I certainly hadn't. Over the years, I had randomly thought about God exerting his power one day, to show us he exists. But how would he do that? I never knew.

This pandemic was beyond imagination, but it gave me ample time to ponder the existential challenges of staying alive and contributing all I could to finding a solution to this clear and present danger.

I joined the efforts in my country to build isolation and treatment centres and ease the effects of the disease. I'm a member of the Coalition Against COVID-19 (CACOVID), led by the former Governor of the Central Bank of Nigeria, Godwin Emefiele. I also expanded my charitable activities.

Fortunately, the pandemic did not ravage my business or directly strike my family. My major enterprise has, since 2013, been Geregu Power. The power generation facilities in Nigeria's Kogi State operated relatively smoothly. Although we experienced delays in payment for the services we delivered, we got by. The most important thing was to stay afloat; we could tally our losses later.

As I've described here, since 2010 I have held a supervisory role in my business, meaning I don't have to be physically present at the office.

Before the coronavirus crisis assumed alarming proportions, I went to London for an urgent appointment on 29 January 2020. I was still there when the lockdown went into effect in late March. There was ample notice that a quarantine order was imminent, so many chose where they wanted to be. I stayed in London for many reasons. Of course, these days one can oversee their business from anywhere, as long as the phones and internet are functional. Throughout the first lockdown in the UK, I was in constant touch with the team at Geregu, through Zoom, WhatsApp and phone calls.

The pandemic affected our income, but not disastrously so. We didn't lay off a single employee and we paid salaries as scheduled. It was the same for my domestic staff, at my residences in Lagos, Abuja, Monte Carlo and London. My personal staff in Nigeria even got a COVID-19 hardship bonus of one month's salary.

I followed with trepidation the devastation the pandemic wreaked on businesses, with millions of workers furloughed or laid off, thousands of companies closing, the pressure of loans with rising interest, and the threat of food shortages. It was a difficult time.

Many once boisterous and extroverted people struggled with mental health issues exacerbated by the pandemic. They found it hard to handle being restricted to one place or being told what to do whenever they stepped out.

I also struggled because I enjoy travelling. However, my introverted nature helped me in this challenging time. I'm used to being by myself, enjoying my own company.

Meanwhile, the isolation made me reflect more about life, about how finite it is. It taught me not to leave until tomorrow what I can do today. That's one lesson I learned from the lockdown; if you have a dream or want to do something for someone, attend to it immediately. Don't wait. You never know what tomorrow will bring.

Another thing that became apparent was that history repeats itself. We'd all but forgotten the Spanish Flu pandemic of 1918–1920, which claimed as many as 50 million lives worldwide. Europeans brought smallpox to the New World in the early 1500s, and it killed an estimated 25–55 million indigenous Americans over the next century. That pales in comparison to the Black Death, the great plague that killed more than a third of the population of Europe—possibly as many as 200 million people—in the mid-1300s.

Everything in life is cyclical. I tell my children that there will always be a global financial crisis around the corner, and encourage them to cultivate the habit of saving, and not spend what they haven't earned.

What I missed most through the pandemic was my freedom. I hated not being able to move around the world; enjoy eating in restaurants with family, friends and associates; gather together for holidays. And when I say that I am of course painfully aware that it's nothing compared to the death and misery the disease sowed.

Everybody managed, taking the effects of COVID-19 in their stride, acknowledging that it was God's doing. It was beyond us. And don't forget that the pandemic continues to evolve as we speak. People continue to contract the disease, become ill and die. We witnessed its grim progress until the worst of it blew over. As it was adequately studied, we gained a better understanding of how this all came about, and how we can protect ourselves from—and hopefully prevent—a repeat performance.

In the meantime, we are all hoping for an end to this dreadful virus. And as we wait for that day, the best we can do is think, analyse and improve ourselves.

And so, having said all that—and shared my life story with you, through all its ups and downs—here are my last few bits of accumulated wisdom, to help you on your way to becoming an entrepreneurial success.

THREE BUSINESS PRINCIPLES I ADOPTED WITHOUT KNOWING THEIR ORIGIN

My objectives were clear and well thought-out as I matured in life. As the years rolled by, and I met with more and more successes, I tweaked and refined my goals.

At first, like everybody, I was out to provide for the basic needs of my family and myself. Later, I wanted to improve our lifestyle. Eventually, my objective was to grow a much bigger business.

Along the way, I came to recognize the importance of working harder and smarter and concentrating on the essential elements that advanced my dreams. I devoted my energy to those factors I believed would carry me closer to my targets.

Yet, while writing this book, I realized that these personal goals were based on certain principles that had been propounded by great business minds, and social and behavioural scientists. It was self-affirming to see that success comes with practising such time-tested principles, even when I knew nothing about their origin.

Here are three business and lifestyle precepts that defined my life when I didn't know the theories behind them, and my suggestions on how to deal with them:

(1) Watch out for decision fatigue. Continually having to decide about things we do every day tires us out and can lead to errors, in addition to wasting time we could have spent on more important things.

Social psychologists such as Roy Baumeister have for decades researched and catalogued how ultra-successful people handle the many choices they have to make.

They've found that these high achievers limit the number of decisions they make by not worrying about those associated with mundane repetitive activities, such as choosing what clothes to wear. The term decision fatigue was coined by Baumeister, who linked it to so-called 'ego depletion.' This is the diminishing willpower and self-control that comes with excessive deliberation over ongoing, unrelated tasks. That is, the more decisions you make over a given period, the lower the quality of the output will be.

When I wore only white as my business gear, I hadn't heard of this concept. I told you of my dream, where my grandfather instructed me to wear white to pave the way for greatness. Despite criticism from family and friends, I stuck with my white two-piece ensembles.

I told everyone to see this as a uniform; my office uniform not unlike those worn by soldiers, who didn't need to worry about what to wear every day. Like Steve Jobs, Mark Zuckerberg and Albert Einstein. One could have worse role models.

(2) The 80/20 rule is incredibly useful. I have always believed that I had to be laser-focused to achieve my objectives. Whatever is important to me, whatever I crave and desire, I concentrate my energies there and pursue it. I separate trivial pursuits from worthwhile endeavours and map out the path to success. In my businesses and in my life, I have learned to spend all my energy and resources on those things that truly give me joy and fulfilment.

I am at home with the Pareto Principle, which is also known as 'the law of the vital few' or 'the principle of factor sparsity.' The American engineer Joseph Moses Juran expanded upon and popularized the work of economist-philosopher Vilfredo Pareto, who had first espoused the so-called 80/20 rule in 1896. Pareto pointed out that 20% of the population owned 80% of the land in Italy. Juran went on to posit in the 1950s that 80% of effects come from 20% of the causes. Using sales volume as an example, the rule predicts that 80% of sales will come from 20% of your clients. It suggests that managers should identify this critical 20%, which will be the basis of 80% of their success. Similarly, I mentioned earlier that I believe new entrepreneurs should save 80% of their initial profits, and only spend 20%.

(3) The 10,000-hour rule will help you excel. In his 2008 book, *Outliers: The Story of Success*, pop-sociology author Malcolm Gladwell asserted that it takes 10,000 hours of 'deliberate practice' to master a given field. The formula, originally espoused by psychologist K. Anders Ericsson, suggests that commanding expertise in each area of business, sports, arts or the sciences can be achieved in ten years if one dedicates 20 hours a week to its study and practice. That amounts to less than three hours a day. Gladwell said this daily practice ought to be intense and focused, to eventually produce the desired result.

Critics argue that long hours of practice alone do not guarantee expertise, and that talent must also come into play. Such arguments, I believe, misrepresent Gladwell's work.

Dean Simonton, a psychology professor at the University of California, Davis, offers a more nuanced take. In his books, *Greatness: Who Makes History and Why*, and *Origins of Genius: Darwinian Perspectives on Creativity*, he explains that performing more experiments is what guarantees success. It's the notion that those seen as superstars and geniuses outperform others simply because they churn out more work. Despite producing many flops, for instance, successful recording artists nonetheless have more hits than musicians who produce less output. In Simonton's view, that's because they release an endless string of records, increasing the odds that a certain percentage of them will resonate with the public.

Thomas Edison is an example of this. In 1878, the 31-year-old inventor was a late starter in his field of endeavour, as 23 others around the world had already introduced different sorts of electric light bulbs. But in one year, working day and night, tinkering through more than a thousand experiments with his team—famously grabbing bits of sleep on a cot alongside his lab bench in New Jersey—he created the first long-lasting incandescent lamp.

I experimented with many ideas and attempted to perfect them along the way, putting in long and painful hours. I catalogued them all here earlier: my quest for success included Femco, Centre Force, Zenon Petroleum and Gas, African Petroleum, Forte Oil and Geregu Power, along with all my side ventures, projects and investments. I put in thousands of hours, continually trying and reworking different approaches to improve my game.

Experiment, experiment, experiment. This will without a doubt help you reach ever higher.

I wish you all happiness and success.

“

IN MY LIFE, IN MY JOURNEY, I HAVE TAKEN THE RISK, I’VE DONE THE CHASE, I HAVE ENJOYED THE THRILL, I HAVE ACHIEVED SUCCESS AND RECOGNITION. WHAT NEXT? YOU GIVE IT BACK

”

– FEMI OTEDOLA

KEY AWARDS TO FEMI OTEDOLA 2005-2021

2005	Entrepreneurial Excellence Award by Rotary International District 9110 Nigeria
2006	Meritorious Service Award by LACOPED Alumni Association
2007	Outstanding Alumni Award by Olivet Baptist High School, Oyo
2008	Personality of the Year Award by *ThisDay* Newspaper
2008	Oil and Gas Company of the Year Award by *ThisDay* Newspaper
2008	Outstanding Personality of the Year by *National Standard News* Magazine
2010	National Honour of Commander of the Order of Niger (CON) by The Federal Government of Nigeria
2011	Merit Award by Petroleum and Natural Gas Senior Staff Association of Nigeria (PENGASSAN), Lagos Zone
2012	Recognition and Appreciation Award by Nigerian Chamber of Shipping
2015	Award of Excellence and Pacesetter by Nigerian Professional Working Women
2016	Appreciation Award by The Apapa Club
2018	Philanthropist of the Year by *Sun* Newspaper
2019	Philanthropist of the Decade Award by *ThisDay* Newspaper
2019	Man of The Year Award by SilverBird Group
2019	Personality of the Year Award by *The Vanguard* Newspaper
2019	African Philanthropist of the Year by *African Leadership* Magazine

2019 Appreciation Award by Ijebu Muslim College Old Students Association

2019 Recognition of Lifetime Award by Nigeria Automobile Technicians Association

2019 Award of Excellence by FIDA

2020 Humanitarian Award of the Year by *New Telegraph* Newspaper

2020 Award of Recognition by College of Medicine, University of Lagos

2021 Personality of the Year Award by *Vanguard* Newspaper

NOTES

1. Regent Street Polytechnic, the first polytechnic in England, established in 1838 as the Royal Polytechnic Institution, is now the University of Westminster.
2. Chief Jeremiah Obafemi Awolowo was a Nigerian statesman and politician. He was the first premier of the western region and was leader of the opposition during Nigeria's first republic.
3. Formally termed the Nigerian Enterprises Promotion Decree of 1972, as amended in 1977. It mandated that companies operating in Nigeria had to be substantially owned by Nigerians.
4. Charles Ponzi (1882-1949) was an infamous swindler and con artist who paid returns with new investors' money. He was eventually charged with 86 counts of fraud on August 12, 1920.
5. Local purchase orders. These are commercial documents produced by a customer for a seller for the purchase of goods with the agreed price and quantities.
6. Constructed by Julius Berger, the Third Mainland Bridge is the longest of the three bridges connecting Lagos mainland and the island, and the longest in Africa at the time at 11.8 kilometres. It opened in 1990.
7. Olorogun Oskar Ibru (born on August 11, 1958) is the first son of Olorogun Michael Ibru, the patriarch of the Ibru dynasty.
8. With flight operations between May 1997 and December 2012, Chanchangi Airlines was headquartered in Kaduna. The airline had two planes.
9. The Asset Management Corporation of Nigeria was established in 2010 to revive the financial system. The company buys nonperforming

loan assets of Nigerian banks, blacklists recalcitrant debtors, and fast-tracks debt recovery.

10. The Economic and Financial Crimes Commission.
11. The Ministry of Finance-supported Bank of Industry is the only lender in Nigeria that offers longer-tenored single-digit interest loans to big, medium and small businesses.
12. The bank, founded by French investors in 1959, closed its doors after the Central Bank of Nigeria revoked its licence in 2011 and took over its operations under the "Bridge Bank" mechanism. The operation was subsequently renamed Mainstreet Bank and eventually acquired by Skye Bank. Skye Bank itself subsequently lost its licence and its assets were taken over by a new entity, Polaris Bank, in 2018.
13. Founded in 1993, the multinational trading company Trafigura has its headquarters in Singapore and over 80 offices in 41 countries. It trades in oil and metals, and also has a shipping division.
14. Vitol is a Dutch energy and commodity trading company based in Geneva, Switzerland. Established by Henk Viëtor and Jacques Detiger in 1966, in Rotterdam, they have over 40 offices worldwide.
15. The military barracks was the seat of government from 1966 to 1999, and was located off Awolowo Road in Ikoyi and Obalende (Lagos).
16. General Ibrahim Badamasi Babangida (born on August 17, 1941, in Minna, Niger State) served as Chief of Army Staff from January 1984 to August 1985 and Military President from August 1985 to August 1993. An interesting fact: as a Colonel commanding the armoured corps, Babangida was likely one of the mid-level officers who overthrew Gowon in the coup that brought Murtala, and by default, Obasanjo, to power.
17. Mushin and Ajegunle are working-class suburbs of Lagos.
18. 2 Corinthians 9:7 English Standard Version.
19. Active since 2002, the jihadist terrorist organisation Boko Haram turned violent in 2009. Based in north-eastern Nigeria, it operates in Chad, Niger, northern Cameroon and Mali.

20. The SDP emerged as a centre-left political party after General Ibrahim Babangida (IBB) proscribed the earlier 13 parties. Its manifesto called for improved welfare and social justice. Alhaji Babagana Kingibe (who later became a three-time minister) was its first chairman.
21. The other party in the Third Republic, with Chief Tom Ikimi, an architect, as chairman. It was classified as centre-right.
22. Bube Okorodudu runs Car Link Ltd, one of the foremost vehicle merchants in Nigeria.

AUTHOR'S NOTE

Dear reader, working on *Making It Big: Lessons from a Life in Business* was exciting and immensely gratifying. I wish more successful and wealthy entrepreneurs in Nigeria had penned similar books for my generation.

My main objective with this compilation of business lessons—and thoughts on life—is to save a new generation of entrepreneurs enormous time and resources, by teaching them what I had to learn through experience.

I hope you have learned from my trajectory and feel inspired to follow your calling.

Until next time, keep dreaming!

ABOUT THE AUTHOR

Femi Otedola, iconic Nigerian businessman who has graced the front cover of *Forbes Africa*, is a philanthropist, and former chairman of Forte Oil PLC. He hails from one of Nigeria's prominent families, and is the son of the late Sir Michael Otedola, former governor of Lagos State, and Lady Doja.

His vision transformed Forte Oil PLC into one of the highest performing companies on the Nigerian Stock Exchange, which grew exponentially to become a model of possibilities inherent in Nigeria, winning accolades, and crucially becoming the investment of choice within the Oil and Gas Industry, including the Nigerian Stock Exchange. A business magnate, he founded Zenon Petroleum and Gas Ltd, and is the owner of several other businesses across shipping, real estate and finance.

Recognized for his contributions to the growth of the Nigerian economy, he was awarded the prestigious honour of "Commander of the Order of the Niger (CON)" in May 2010 and is the current Chancellor of Augustine University in Ilara, Epe, Lagos State.

He has held several board memberships from president of the Nigerian Chamber of Shipping; past chairman of Transcorp Hilton Hotel, Abuja; member of the Governing Council of the Nigerian Investment Promotion Council, member of the National Economic Management Team and Honorary International Investors Council under the leadership of Baroness Lynda Chalker.

A philanthropist at heart with strong values, and a keen involvement in educational causes, Femi Otedola continuously demonstrates his passion for his community, Epe, Lagos State, and Nigeria, through generous donations supporting financially disadvantaged students via the Sir Michael Otedola Scholarship Awards Foundation. In November

2019, he donated $14m (USD) to the Save the Children Fund, supporting programmes for destitute children in the north-eastern region of Nigeria. He is the vice-president of Save the Children UK.

A family man, he is married with four children.